Addiction Treatment
Homework Planner
Sixth Edition

Wiley Practice*Planners*® Series

Treatment Planners

The Complete Adult Psychotherapy Treatment Planner, Sixth Edition
The Child Psychotherapy Treatment Planner, Sixth Edition
The Adolescent Psychotherapy Treatment Planner, Sixth Edition
The Addiction Treatment Planner, Sixth Edition
The Continuum of Care Treatment Planner
The Couples Psychotherapy Treatment Planner, with DSM-5 Updates, Second Edition
The Employee Assistance Treatment Planner
The Pastoral Counseling Treatment Planner
The Older Adult Psychotherapy Treatment Planner, with DSM-5 Updates, Second Edition
The Behavioral Medicine Treatment Planner
The Group Therapy Treatment Planner, with DSM-5 Updates, Second Edition
The Gay and Lesbian Psychotherapy Treatment Planner
The Family Therapy Treatment Planner, with DSM-5 Updates, Second Edition
The Severe and Persistent Mental Illness Treatment Planner, with DSM-5 Updates, Second Edition
The Intellectual and Developmental Disability Treatment Planner, with DSM-5 Updates, Second Edition
The Social Work and Human Services Treatment Planner, with DSM-5 Updates
The Crisis Counseling and Traumatic Events Treatments Planner, with DSM-5 Updates, Second Edition
The Personality Disorders Treatment Planner, with DSM-5 Updates, Second Edition
The Rehabilitation Psychology Treatment Planner
The Special Education Treatment Planner
The Juvenile Justice and Residential Care Treatment Planner, with DSM-5 Updates
The School Counseling and School Social Work Treatment Planner, with DSM-5 Updates, Second Edition
The Sexual Abuse Victim and Sexual Offender Treatment Planner, with DSM-5 Updates
The Probation and Parole Treatment Planner, with DSM-5 Updates
The Psychopharmacology Treatment Planner
The Speech-Language Pathology Treatment Planner
The Suicide and Homicide Risk Assessment & Prevention Treatment Planner, with DSM-5 Updates
The College Student Counseling Treatment Planner
The Parenting Skills Treatment Planner, with DSM-5 Updates
The Early Childhood Intervention Treatment Planner
The Co-Occurring Disorders Treatment Planner, with DSM-5 Updates
The Complete Women's Psychotherapy Treatment Planner, with DSM-5 Updates, Fifth Edition
The Veterans and Active Duty Military Psychotherapy Treatment Planner, with DSM-5 Updates

Progress Notes Planners

The Child Psychotherapy Progress Notes Planner, Sixth Edition
The Adolescent Psychotherapy Progress Notes Planner, Sixth Edition
The Adult Psychotherapy Progress Notes Planner, Sixth Edition
The Addiction Progress Notes Planner, Sixth Edition
The Severe and Persistent Mental Illness Progress Notes Planner, Second Edition
The Couples Psychotherapy Progress Notes Planner, Second Edition
The Family Therapy Progress Notes Planner, Second Edition
The Veterans and Active Duty Military Psychotherapy Progress Notes Planner

Homework Planners

Couples Therapy Homework Planner, Second Edition
Family Therapy Homework Planner, Second Edition
Grief Counseling Homework Planner
Group Therapy Homework Planner
School Counseling and School Social Work Homework Planner, Second Edition
Child Therapy Activity and Homework Planner
Addiction Treatment Homework Planner, Sixth Edition
Adolescent Psychotherapy Homework Planner, Sixth Edition
Adult Psychotherapy Homework Planner, Sixth Edition
Child Psychotherapy Homework Planner, Sixth Edition
Parenting Skills Homework Planner
Veterans and Active Duty Military Psychotherapy Homework Planner

Client Education Handout Planners

Adult Client Education Handout Planner
Child and Adolescent Client Education Handout Planner
Couples and Family Client Education Handout Planner

Complete Planners

The Complete Depression Treatment and Homework Planner
The Complete Anxiety Treatment and Homework Planner

Wiley Practice*Planners*®

Addiction Treatment Homework Planner

Sixth Edition

Brenda S. Lenz
James R. Finley

SERIES EDITOR
Arthur E. Jongsma, Jr.

WILEY

Library of Congress Cataloging-in-Publication Data applied for:

Paperback ISBN: 9781119987789
ePDF: 9781119987802
ePub: 9781119987796

Cover Design: Wiley
Cover Image: © Ryan McVay/Getty Images

Set in 11.5/14.5 pts and New Century Schoolbook LT Std by Straive, Chennai, India

SKY10059548_110723

For all those who have found hope that recovery has to offer,
and to those who haven't . . . yet.
—BSL

CONTENTS

ABOUT THE DOWNLOADABLE ASSIGNMENTS

Thank you for choosing the Wiley Practice*Planners*® series. *Addiction Treatment Homework Planner, Sixth Edition's* website includes all the book's exercises in Word format for your convenience.

To access the assignments, please follow these steps:

Step 1 Go to www.wiley.com/go/hwpassignments

Step 2 Enter your email address, the password provided below, and click "submit"

Password: addiction2024

Step 3 Select and download the listed exercises

If you need any assistance, please visit www.support.wiley.com

PRACTICE*PLANNERS*® SERIES PREFACE

Accountability is an important dimension of the practice of psychotherapy. Treatment programs, public agencies, clinics, and practitioners must justify and document their treatment plans to outside review entities in order to be reimbursed for services. The books and software (TheraScribe) in the Practice*Planners*® series are designed to help practitioners fulfill these documentation requirements efficiently and professionally.

The Practice*Planners*® series includes a wide array of treatment planning books including not only the original *Complete Adult Psychotherapy Treatment Planner*, *Child Psychotherapy Treatment Planner*, *Adolescent Psychotherapy Treatment Planner,* and *Addiction Treatment Planner* all now in their sixth editions, but also Treatment Planners targeted to specialty areas of practice, including:

- Addictions
- Behavioral medicine
- Co-occurring disorders
- College students
- Couples therapy
- Crisis counseling
- Early childhood intervention
- Employee assistance
- Family therapy
- Group therapy
- Intellectual and developmental disabilities
- Juvenile justice and residential care
- LGBTQIA+ community
- Older adults
- Parenting skills
- Pastoral counseling
- Personality disorders
- Probation and parole
- Psychopharmacology
- Rehabilitation psychology/neuropsychology
- School counseling and school social work
- Severe and persistent mental illness
- Sexual abuse victims and offenders
- Social work and human services
- Special education
- Speech-language pathology

- Suicide and homicide risk assessment
- Veterans and active military duty
- Women's issues

In addition, there are two branches of companion books that can be used in conjunction with the *Treatment Planners,* or on their own:

- ***Progress Notes Planners*** provide a menu of progress statements that elaborate on the client's symptom presentation and the provider's therapeutic intervention. Each *Progress Notes Planner* statement is directly integrated with the behavioral definitions and therapeutic interventions from its companion *Treatment Planner.*

- ***Homework Planners*** include homework assignments designed around each presenting problem (such as anxiety, depression, chemical dependence, anger management, eating disorders, or panic disorder) that is the focus of a chapter in its corresponding *Treatment Planner.*

The Series also includes the following:

- ***Evidence-Based Psychotherapy Treatment Planning Video Series*** offers 12 sixty-minute programs that provide step-by-step guidance on how to use empirically supported treatments to inform the entire treatment planning process. In a viewer-friendly manner, Drs. Art Jongsma and Tim Bruce discuss the steps involved in integrating evidence-based treatment (EBT) Objectives and Interventions into a treatment plan. The research support for the EBTs is summarized, and selected aspects of the EBTs are demonstrated in role-played counseling scenarios.

A companion Treatment Planning software product is also available:

- ***TheraScribe*®,** the #1 selling treatment planning and clinical recordkeeping software system for mental health professionals, allows the user to import the data from any of the Treatment Planner, Progress Notes Planner, or Homework Planner books into the software's expandable database to simply point and click to create a detailed, organized, individualized, and customizable treatment plan along with optional integrated progress notes and homework assignments. TheraScribe is available by calling 616-776-1745. See TheraScribe.com for more information.

The goal of our series is to provide practitioners with the resources they need in order to provide high-quality care in the era of accountability. To put it simply: We seek to help you spend more time on patients and less time on paperwork.

Arthur E. Jongsma, Jr.
Grand Rapids, Michigan

PREFACE

If you've found your way to this manual, I'm certain you are looking for new ways to engage with your clients, help them, inspire, and motivate them toward recovery. Maybe you're looking for additional ways to address those areas that co-occur or interfere with the work of helping them move themselves toward a path of sustained recovery. There are many paths to recovery from a substance use disorder. Addiction itself is a complex disorder, and the recovery process is as complex. At the heart of both, though, is a person trying to do their best with what they've been given. Any opportunity to work with people should be done with the greatest of care and respect, allowing them to maintain their dignity. Keeping them in treatment and helping them get better matters. Intervention should be individualized to meet their unique needs, respecting diversity in its broadest sense. Certain things work for many people, and the field of addiction treatment and evidence-based intervention continues to evolve to help us hone in on how to help people. My hope as a decade's old practitioner is that you find exercises or resources in this manual that allow you to individualize your care that helps your people. I hope you find something that sticks, something that works, something that reaches and engages people who need your help.

This edition of the *Addiction Homework Planner* is a companion manual to the sixth editions of the *Addiction Treatment Planner* and *Addiction Progress Notes Planner*. This edition continues to emphasize client-centered, assessment-driven, evidence-based treatment in the field of substance use disorder psychotherapy. We continue to emphasize the importance of client motivation and shaped the content of this planner to help people in treatment move ahead in their readiness to work toward positive change. Each exercise was designed to address motivation, meeting people where they are, with some educational content to increase knowledge, awareness, and insight of addiction recovery process and to include a skills component for further instruction in therapy and/or work at home.

All previous exercises and the few additions have been edited to reflect gender-inclusive, recovery affirming language with a strength-based focus where that was possible. Two new sections were added with two new exercises each, Opioid Use Disorder and Panic Disorder, respectively. This aligns with the changes made in the two edited companion manuals.

The exercises can be done within or processed within individual sessions and, where appropriate, for group therapy. The exercises can be completed in various levels of care. Yet a homework planner is ultimately designed for homework between sessions. Homework helps clients keep their therapy and recovery efforts in the forefront of their awareness and makes it easier to bring it into their daily lives; it also allows clients to collect real-time data so therapy can address relevant issues quickly and collaboratively.

I appreciate Wiley & Sons allowing me to revise this most recent edition. I would like to thank James Finley, my coauthor on all previous editions, for the foundational work he did on our earlier editions and the collaborative work we did in addiction treatment many years ago; I am a better clinician because of it. I wish him only the best!

USING THIS BOOK

This revision is a companion to the sixth editions of the *Addiction Treatment Planner and Addiction Progress Notes Planner*. You can use the website to download the assignments on your computer as Microsoft Word documents and print them as they are designed or customize them by rewording items, adding a logo or other art, or however else you choose. For further instructions, please see "About the Downloadable Assignments."

As always, if you have suggestions, especially about which features you find useful or would like to suggest topics to cover in future volumes, please contact us via this publisher. We are always eager for feedback we can use to make this a better resource with each edition. There is no work more important than helping people. Thank you for serving the people with whom you work, and through them, your communities and the world.

ABOUT THE AUTHOR

Brenda S. Lenz, MS, is a licensed professional counselor and certified substance abuse counselor with extensive experience assessing and treating clients with co-occurring issues in a variety of settings. She specializes in prevention, assessment, early intervention, and treatment of substance use disorders in college-aged students. She is a strong advocate for inclusive recovery programming and supportive services for students in recovery on college campuses. She trains on motivational interventions and destigmatizing help-seeking for mental health and substance use concerns. Currently, she has administrative oversight over clinical services and maintains a clinical caseload.

INTRODUCTION

More and more therapists are assigning homework to their clients. Not only have short-term therapy models endorsed this practice, but the benefits are being recognized by many traditional therapists as well.

WHY HOMEWORK?

Assigning homework to psychotherapy clients is beneficial for several reasons. With the advent of managed care, which often requires shorter and fewer treatment sessions, therapists assign between-session homework to help maximize the effectiveness of briefer treatment. Homework is an extension of the treatment process, provides continuity, and allows the client to work between sessions on issues that are the focus of therapy.

Homework can also be a tool for more fully engaging the client in the treatment process. Assignments place more responsibility on the client to resolve presenting problems, counteracting the expectations that some clients may experience that it is the therapist alone who can cure them. For some, it even may bring a sense of self-empowerment. Another added benefit of homework is that these assignments give the client the opportunity to implement and evaluate insights or coping behaviors that have been discussed in therapy sessions. Practice often heightens awareness of various issues. Furthermore, homework increases the expectation for the client to follow through with making changes rather than just talking about change. Exercises require participation, which creates a sense that the client is taking active steps toward change. Homework also allows the client to try new behaviors, bringing these experiences back to the next session for processing. Modifications can then be made to the client's thoughts, feelings, or behaviors as the homework is processed in the therapy session.

Occasionally treatment processes can become vague and abstract. By adding focus and structure, homework assignments can reenergize treatment. Moreover, homework can increase the client's motivation to change as it provides something specific to work on. Additionally, homework increases the involvement of family members and significant others in the client's treatment using assignments that call for their participation. Homework promotes more efficient treatment by encouraging the client to actively develop insights, positive self-talk, and coping behaviors between therapy sessions. Consequently, many clients express increased satisfaction with the treatment process when homework is given. They are empowered by doing something active that facilitates the change process, and it reinforces their sense of control over the problem. These advantages have made the assignment of therapeutic homework increasingly prevalent.

HOW TO USE THIS HOMEWORK PLANNER

Creating homework assignments and developing the printed forms for recording responses is a time-consuming process. This *Addiction Treatment Homework Planner* provides a menu of homework assignments that can easily be photocopied. In addition to the printed format, the assignments in this *Planner* are provided online to allow the therapist to access them on a word processor and print them out as is or easily tailor them to suit the client's individual needs and/or the therapist's style. The assignments are grouped under presenting problems that are typical of those found in an adult population. These presenting problems are cross-referenced to every presenting problem found in *The Addiction Psychotherapy Treatment Planner*, Sixth Edition. Although these assignments were created with a specific presenting problem in mind, don't feel locked in by a single problem-oriented chapter when searching for an appropriate assignment. Included with each exercise is a cross-referenced list of suggested presenting problems for which the assignment may be appropriate and useful called "Additional Problems for Which This Exercise May Be Most Useful." This cross-referenced list can assist you in applying the homework assignments to other situations that may be relevant to your client's particular presenting problem.

A broader cross-referenced list of assignments is found in the appendix "Alternate Assignments for Presenting Problems." Review this appendix to find relevant assignments beyond the two or three exercises found in any specific presenting problem chapter.

For example, under the heading of Conduct Disorder/Delinquency in the appendix, you will find 15 alternative assignments originally created for other presenting problems but relevant and easily adapted for use with a client struggling with conduct disorder issues. In this appendix, every presenting problem is listed with relevant additional assignments from throughout the book. Remember, each assignment is available online and, therefore, can be quickly edited for use with a specific client. This modified assignment can be saved on your computer's hard disk for repeated later use.

The newest edition includes improvements in the *Addiction Treatment Homework Planner*, Sixth Edition, which makes it a valuable therapeutic tool/resource for the practicing clinician.

ABOUT THE ASSIGNMENTS

Therapists introduce the homework assignment with varying degrees of detail and client preparation. Recommendations regarding this preparation and post-exercise discussion are made on the title page of each assignment under the heading "Suggestions for Processing This Exercise with the Client." Clinical judgment must be used to assess the appropriate developmental level and motivation/readiness to make change necessary for a specific assignment, as well as choosing the homework assignments that focus on relevant issues for the client. The title page of each assignment contains a section on "Goals of the Exercise" to guide you in your selection of relevant homework for your client. Remember, all assignments can be modified as necessary for the individual client.

CARRYING OUT THE ASSIGNMENT

It is recommended that you review the entire book to familiarize yourself with the broad nature of the type and focus of the various homework exercises. Select a specific assignment from a chapter titled with your client's presenting problem or from the alternative list in the appendix and then review the list of homework goals. Assigning therapy homework is just a beginning step in the therapy treatment process. Carrying out the assignment requires a follow-up exploration of the impact of the assignment on the client's thoughts, feelings, and behavior. What are the results? Was this assignment useful to the client? Can it be redesigned or altered for better results? Examine and search for new and creative ways to actively engage your client in participating in this homework process.

ADDRESSING ACA TRAITS IN RECOVERY

GOALS OF THE EXERCISE

1. Implement a plan for recovery from addiction that reduces the impact of adult-child-of-an-alcoholic (ACA) traits on sobriety.
2. Increase self-reliance by beginning to meet one's own needs.
3. Reduce the frequency of behaviors that are exclusively designed to please others.
4. Choose partners and friends who are responsible, respectful, and reliable.
5. Overcome fears of abandonment, loss, and neglect.
6. Understand the feelings that resulted from being raised in an addictive environment and increase ability to see similarities to others raised in nonaddictive homes.

ADDITIONAL PROBLEMS FOR WHICH THIS EXERCISE MAY BE USEFUL

- Borderline Traits
- Dependent Traits
- Partner Relational Conflicts
- Sexual Promiscuity

SUGGESTIONS FOR PROCESSING THIS EXERCISE WITH THE CLIENT

The "Addressing ACA Traits in Recovery" activity is for clients with patterns of codependent relationships, enmeshment, boundary issues, and burnout in love, friendship, and workplace relationships. It teaches clients about addictive relationship dynamics, then heightens motivation by focusing on the threat this poses to recovery, ending by directing clients to further exploration of issues of codependency. Follow-up may include discussing the issue with the therapist, group, and sponsor; support group referrals; bibliotherapy, specifically content written by Claudia Black; and videotherapy (e.g., *Rent Two Films and Let's Talk in the Morning* by John W. Hesley and Jan G. Hesley, also published by Wiley).

ADDRESSING ACA TRAITS IN RECOVERY

Adult children of alcoholics, or ACAs, are adults who grew up in families where one or both parents chronically abused alcohol and/or other drugs, suffered from other mental illness, or had other problems that made them unable to meet their children's needs. When those children become adults, they may have feelings and behavior patterns that resemble those of their parents, especially in relationships. This can happen whether they abuse alcohol or other drugs—ACAs often become "addicted" to unhealthy patterns and people in their love, friendship, and work relationships. They are drawn to situations that feel in some ways like their childhood family life and to people who treat them in ways like the ways their parents treated them and others. ACAs often fall into the trap of trying to please, "fix," or "save" others, and their own lives are left in turmoil. Their motives are caring, but their efforts to please or rescue others seldom work. The results cause these ACAs great emotional pain and may put them in dangerous situations or lead to a work-related cycle of starting new jobs with great hope and energy but ending up burning out on those jobs or careers. No one can really control anyone else; other people's troubles are mostly caused by patterns only they can change, so trying to change them leads to one painful disappointment after another. As part of your recovery, this activity will help you learn to recognize and change these patterns, which are also often called *codependency*.

1. There are reasons we're drawn to relationships in which we try harder to solve other people's problems than they do. If we are ACAs, these patterns often echo those we experienced in our families as children. It's as if we're trying to replay the same story and get it to have a happy ending. Have any of the feelings listed here drawn you into painful relationships or situations in love, friendship, and/or workplace situations? *Check* all that apply.

    _____ You felt sure that if you tried hard enough, you could win approval.

    _____ You felt needed.

    _____ It was intense and exciting from the start.

    _____ You felt intensely and magnetically drawn to the other person.

    _____ They made you feel strong, smart, and capable.

    _____ The sex was incredible.

_____ You identified with the hardships they'd suffered.

_____ You felt that you could help them and change their lives.

2.   Here are signs of this kind of relationship. Please *check* off any you've experienced:

_____ Manipulation and mind games take up a lot of time and energy.

_____ You're held responsible (by others or yourself) for things you can't control.

_____ You see that you keep getting into high-risk or no-win situations, but you can't help finding those are the only ones that attract you—safe people and jobs bore you.

_____ You're often worried that the relationship will fall apart, feeling you can keep the peace if you just say and do only the right things.

_____ You keep your partner away from your other friends and family because they don't get along, or you don't think they would.

_____ You spend a lot of time and energy solving other people's problems, over and over, often with little or no appreciation or recognition.

_____ You try hard to impress your partner and keep secrets; you fear that your partner would reject you if they knew about parts of your life or past.

_____ You get into heated arguments that don't make sense to either of you.

_____ The relationship became very intense very fast when you first got together.

_____ One or both of you feel a lot of jealousy and insecurity.

_____ The relationship is never boring, but it's usually stressful.

_____ You go back and forth between feeling abandoned and feeling smothered.

3.   How does this relate to getting and staying clean and sober? Well, common sense tells us there's a strong connection between stress and relapse, and research confirms that link. Looking at the items you checked for question 2, think about how stressful those relationships were or are. How could these stresses lead to a lapse or relapse, or how have they led to relapses in the past?

_____

_____

4.   Most people who get into addictive relationships don't do so just once. What unhealthy patterns do you see in the people you find attractive?

_____

_____

5.   Identify three pros and three cons for continuing this pattern.

_____

_____

6. Identify three pros and three cons to surrounding yourself with safe, more stable, reliable and nurturing people.

   _____

   _____

7. Consider participating in 12-step recovery programs or another support group specifically for ACAs. Identify three reasons this could be beneficial to you.

   _____

   _____

8. Identify one action item to focus on; monitor yourself; and journal about thoughts, feelings, successes, and challenges as you work to disengage from people-pleasing and relying on others to know how to feel about yourself.

   _____

   _____

Be sure to bring this handout back to your next session with your therapist and be prepared to talk about your thoughts and feelings about the exercise.

UNDERSTANDING FAMILY HISTORY

GOALS OF THE EXERCISE

1. Implement a plan for recovery from addiction that reduces the impact of adult-child-of-an-alcoholic (ACA) traits on sobriety.
2. Reduce the frequency of behaviors that are exclusively designed to please others.
3. Identify behaviors that are dangerous to self or others.
4. Eliminate self-defeating interpersonal patterns in occupational and social settings.
5. Choose partners and friends who are responsible, respectful, and reliable.
6. Understand the feelings that resulted from being raised in an addictive environment and reduce feelings of inferiority and/or alienation from others who were raised in nonaddictive homes.
7. Obtain emotional support for recovery from family members.

ADDITIONAL PROBLEMS FOR WHICH THIS EXERCISE MAY BE USEFUL

- Borderline Traits
- Childhood Trauma
- Family Conflicts
- Parent–Child Relational Problem
- Partner Relational Conflicts

SUGGESTIONS FOR PROCESSING THIS EXERCISE WITH THE CLIENT

The "Understanding Family History" activity may be used effectively with clients who are experiencing shame, confusion, or anxiety as a result of seeing themselves repeat negative behaviors seen in childhood caretakers. It may be useful in couples therapy because many ACA individuals form relationships with partners with similar backgrounds. For clients struggling with acceptance and forgiveness of their parents or of themselves, this activity may help in understanding the roles of addiction and powerlessness in distorting values and behaviors. It may also be useful for clients who have parenting issues in recovery to understand the roots of their children's behaviors.

UNDERSTANDING FAMILY HISTORY

It's important to understand the role of family history in addictions—not to blame those who raised us, but for our own recovery and our families' futures. This exercise looks at how family history affects us.

1. As a child, what did you learn about drinking, drug use, or other addictions in your family?

   _____

   _____

2. What problems, if any, did your family have because of these behaviors (e.g., violence, divorce, financial problems, dangerous or illegal activities, lack of stability or other worries)?

   _____

   _____

3. Please describe the typical atmosphere in your family when someone was drinking, using drugs, or engaging in other addictive patterns, and its effects on you then and now.

   _____

   _____

4. The following are some common patterns in families struggling with addictions, related to the unspoken rule "Don't talk, don't trust, don't feel" that develops as other family members try to avoid confrontations or disappointment caused by the inability of adults with substance use disorders to be nurturing and dependable or to cope with the emotional pain that is the result of that inability. For each pattern, give an example from your childhood and an example of how you can make healthy changes now.

   a. Dishonesty/denial

      i. Childhood example:

         _____

      ii. Working for healthy change:

         _____

b. Breaking promises

    i. Childhood example:

_____

    ii. Working for healthy change:

_____

c. Isolating/withdrawing

    i. Childhood example:

_____

    ii. Working for healthy change:

_____

d. Emotional/physical/sexual abuse and neglect

    i. Childhood example:

_____

    ii. Working for healthy change:

_____

e. Influencing others to act in self-destructive ways

    i. Childhood example:

_____

    ii. Working for healthy change:

_____

f. Confused roles and responsibilities (e.g., children taking caring of adults, people blaming others for their own actions, etc.)

    i. Childhood example:

_____

    ii. Working for healthy change:

_____

5. Nearly all of us remember our parents or other adults who raised us doing some good things we want to do for our children in turn. What good relationship patterns from your childhood do you want to continue and pass on?

_____

_____

6. Consider the strengths you obtained from growing up in your house with your family. How can you use these strengths to facilitate your own recovery efforts?

   _____

   _____

7. Often, we found others (inside extended families or outside our family) for support when our family was unable. If you had those folks when you were a child, what did they provide to you at that time? As adults, we have more access and opportunity to reach out to others for support. You hear folks talk about their "chosen family." How will you seek support based on what your current needs are and the available support you have within your family?

   _____

   _____

Be sure to bring this handout back to your next session with your therapist and be prepared to talk about your thoughts and feelings about the exercise.

IS MY ANGER DUE TO FEELING THREATENED?

GOALS OF THE EXERCISE

1. Develop a program of recovery that is free from substance abuse and violent behavior.
2. Terminate all behaviors that are dangerous to self or others.
3. Decrease the frequency of occurrence of angry thoughts, feelings, and behaviors.
4. Verbalize core conflicts that lead to dangerous/lethal behaviors.
5. Recognize the first signs of anger and use behavioral techniques to control it.
6. Think positively and realistically in anger-producing situations.
7. Learn that anger is a secondary emotion responding to fear or anxiety in response to a perceived threat.
8. Learn to self-monitor and shift into an introspective and cognitive problem-solving mode rather than an emotional reactive mode when anger is triggered.
9. Shift from a self-image as a helpless or passive victim of angry impulses to one of mastery and taking responsibility for responses to feelings.

ADDITIONAL PROBLEMS FOR WHICH THIS EXERCISE MAY BE USEFUL

*   Conduct Disorder/Delinquency
*   Dangerousness/Lethality
*   Oppositional Defiant Behavior
*   Posttraumatic Stress Disorder (PTSD)

SUGGESTIONS FOR PROCESSING THIS EXERCISE WITH THE CLIENT

The "Is My Anger Due to Feeling Threatened?" activity is suited for clients who are capable of introspection and who desire to change their reactive patterns of anger. It may be useful when clients describe perceptions of being unable to control their anger, have patterns of impulsive anger disproportionate to the triggering events or situations, or express regrets over their actions when angry. Follow-up can include keeping a journal documenting angry impulses and the client's use of this process to manage their reactions. Teaching strategies of relaxation, mindfulness, and self-soothing can be beneficial in conjunction with the client working on recognizing and managing their anger.

IS MY ANGER DUE TO FEELING THREATENED?

A wise person once said that every problem starts as a solution to another problem. Once we see this, it's easier to let go of the anger and find a better solution for the original problem. What kind of problem makes anger look like a solution? When is anger useful? It's good for energizing and preparing us to fight. It's the "fight" part of the fight-or-flight instinct that is any creature's response to perceived (whether real or not) danger. When we feel angry, chances are that we feel threatened.

This instinct developed in prehistoric people over thousands of generations and is shared by many self-aware animal species. Nearly all the threats they faced were physical (e.g., wild animals, hostile strangers, environmental conditions), and in those situations anger served them well.

Some dangers are still physical, but more often we face threats we can't fight physically. There are threats to our self-images and our beliefs about the world; there are threats brought on by oppression, discrimination, sexism, racism, which can feel just as dangerous as threats to our physical safety or health.

In this exercise, you'll think about a situation that has triggered your anger and identify both the threat that the anger wants to fight and another solution that will work better.

1. It's important to recognize anger as soon as it develops. To do this, you need to watch for the early warning signs of anger, both physical and mental.

    a. Here are some common physical effects of anger. Please *check* any you experience when you are starting to get angry:

    _____ Muscle tension or shaking   _____ Rapid heartbeat

    _____ Rapid, shallow breathing   _____ "Butterflies in the stomach"

    _____ Reddening of the face   _____ Agitation and restlessness

    b. Our thinking changes with anger, often in these ways. Again, *check* any you experience:

    _____ Impulsiveness and impatience   _____ Feelings of power and certainty

    _____ All-or-nothing thinking   _____ Taking things personally

    _____ Inability to see others'   _____ A sense of having been wronged/
          perspectives   feeling criticized/attacked/judged

    _____ Racing thoughts

2.   Now think of a situation that has been a common anger trigger or one that has led to serious consequences because of your angry actions. Briefly describe the situation and the consequences.

_____

_____

3.   Study the situation and identify the threat that triggered your anger. Were you at risk of not getting something you wanted, or of losing something you already had and valued? Were you responding to "programmed" ways to react? The item under threat could be physical well-being, a relationship, a career or life goal, your self-image, or even your values and beliefs about the way the world works. Explain how this situation threatens you.

_____

_____

4.   Think of a solution that will give you better results than acting in anger. Describe the solution and how you'd put it into action.

_____

_____

5.   After you've thought about triggers and solutions, what are your thoughts and feelings about the situation? Do you feel more in control?

_____

_____

6.   There are some situations in modern life where expressing anger is still appropriate, but not with physical violence. Please think of a way you can constructively express anger to be assertive without violence.

_____

_____

7.   When you feel your anger building, pause, take a breath, and ask yourself, "Where's the threat, and what else can I do about it?" This way, you can take control of your feelings and actions. This is difficult at first, but if you keep doing it, the pause and the question become automatic, just as the flash into rage was automatic. When you pause automatically and think this way, you control your anger, rather than it controlling you. Think of someone you trust to help you with this. Explain what you're doing and ask them to watch your mood, and if you start looking angry, remind you to pause and find the threat. Who is that person, and when will you talk with them about this?

_____

_____

Be sure to bring this handout back to your next therapy session and be prepared to talk about your thoughts and feelings about the exercise.

IS MY ANGER DUE TO UNMET EXPECTATIONS?

GOALS OF THE EXERCISE

1. Develop a program of recovery free from substance abuse and dangerous/lethal behaviors.
2. Terminate all behaviors that are dangerous to self or others.
3. Decrease the frequency of occurrence of angry thoughts, feelings, and behaviors.
4. Verbalize the core conflicts that lead to dangerous/lethal behaviors.
5. Recognize the first signs of anger and use behavioral techniques to control it.
6. Think positively and realistically in anger-producing situations.
7. Learn and use stress-management skills to reduce stress and the irritability that accompanies it.
8. Learn to self-monitor and shift to a thinking and problem-solving mode rather than a reactive mode when anger is triggered.
9. Increase self-esteem and sense of purpose for living and learn how to help others in recovery.

ADDITIONAL PROBLEMS FOR WHICH THIS EXERCISE MAY BE USEFUL

- Antisocial Behavior
- Attention-Deficit/Hyperactivity Disorder (ADHD)—Adolescent
- Attention-Deficit/Hyperactivity Disorder (ADHD)—Adult
- Borderline Traits
- Dangerousness/Lethality
- Family Conflicts
- Oppositional Defiant Behavior
- Parent–Child Relational Problem
- Partner Relational Conflicts

SUGGESTIONS FOR PROCESSING THIS EXERCISE WITH THE CLIENT

The "Is My Anger Due to Unmet Expectations?" activity is suited for clients who are capable of introspection and who desire to change their reactive patterns of anger. It may be useful when clients report feeling unable to control their anger, have patterns of impulsive anger disproportionate to triggering events or situations, or express regrets over their actions when angry. Follow-up can include keeping a journal documenting angry impulses and use of this process to identify trigger expectations and manage reactions.

IS MY ANGER DUE TO UNMET EXPECTATIONS?

People in treatment and recovery programs often say that anger always boils down to fear: That they'll lose something they want to keep, or that they won't get something they want. These aren't usually life-and-death matters, but they often react as if they were.

When we look at this closely, we usually see that when possible losses or disappointments have triggered rage, we expect something different and are shocked and disappointed by what actually happened. Sometimes our expectations are based on what we feel is right and fair, what some call the "shoulda-woulda-couldas" (e.g., the person in the next lane *should* let us merge instead of speeding up to crowd us out, or people *should* be honest and considerate). Also, sometimes we just want something badly and convince ourselves that it should happen the way we want it to.

But our expectations are often unrealistic. That's why many old-timers in Alcoholics Anonymous and other recovery programs define an *expectation* as "a premeditated resentment." They mean that when we form expectations, we often set ourselves up for disappointment and anger.

Do you want to avoid getting angry unnecessarily? Anger interferes with our judgment, making us more likely to act impulsively and do things that damage relationships, undermine recovery, and weaken our immune systems. This exercise will help you avoid unrealistic expectations and feel calmer and less angry.

1. Think back to the most recent time you got angry over an unrealistic expectation, a "shoulda-woulda-coulda" experience. Describe what happened and what your expectation was.

   _____

   _____

2. We often expect things that aren't likely (e.g., expecting someone who is usually late to be on time). If experience told you that what you expected was unlikely, what would have been a more reasonable expectation?

   _____

   _____

3. Our expectations are often just mistakes in our thinking. If we learn not to make those mistakes, accepting what happens is easier. Remember, accepting something doesn't mean we like it or believe it's right; it means admitting things are the way they are and deciding to act on reality rather than our fantasies. If you run into the

same situation again but expect what experience tells you is likely to happen, rather than what you hope for or feel should happen, how will you react differently?

_____

_____

Pause. Take a moment to visualize yourself responding this way.

4. Here are some common mistaken expectations that may lead to anger. Please give your own examples:

    a. Expecting people to behave differently than the way they usually act (e.g., expecting love, warmth, and consideration from a person who is normally cold, selfish, and sarcastic)

        Example:_____

    b. Taking things personally or expecting to be the center of someone else's world

        Example:_____

    c. Perfectionism: Expecting ourselves or others to do things perfectly the first time, rather than accepting that we all make mistakes

        Example:_____

    d. Overoptimism (e.g., expecting everything to go the way we want, though it seldom does)

        Example:_____

5. Other emotions that arise when we form unrealistic expectations are self-pity, discouragement, and anxiety. Identify one other emotion that triggers anger. How have these been triggers for your past addictive behaviors?

    _____

    _____

6. These emotions are setups for relapse. Recovery depends on managing them; it helps not to set ourselves up to get angry. The fewer expectations we have, especially unrealistic ones, the easier it is to avoid lapses/relapses and stay in recovery. Please describe a plan to monitor your thoughts and emotions, avoid unrealistic expectations or correct them when they arise, and regain your serenity.

    _____

    _____

7. What is one thing you learned about yourself by completing this exercise?

    _____

    _____

Be sure to bring this handout back to your next therapy session and be prepared to talk about your thoughts and feelings about the exercise.

BENEFITS OF HELPING OTHERS

GOALS OF THE EXERCISE

1. Learn the importance of helping others in recovery.
2. Understand the importance and the benefits of a program of recovery that demands rigorous honesty.
3. Identify the benefits to relationships and self-esteem in taking responsibility for one's own behavior.
4. Develop a program of recovery that is free of addiction and the negative influences of antisocial behavior.

ADDITIONAL PROBLEMS FOR WHICH THIS EXERCISE MAY BE USEFUL

- Attention-Deficit/Hyperactivity Disorder (ADHD)—Adolescent
- Attention-Deficit/Hyperactivity Disorder (ADHD)—Adult
- Conduct Disorder/Delinquency
- Impulsivity
- Legal Problems
- Narcissistic Traits
- Oppositional Defiant Behavior

SUGGESTIONS FOR PROCESSING THIS EXERCISE WITH THE CLIENT

The "Benefits of Helping Others" activity is for clients with patterns of antisocial behaviors. It teaches clients about the benefits they could get from cultivating patterns of generous and dependable behavior. It also teaches clients some ways they can both get guidance from people in recovery with whom they identify and begin to test the waters by trying small positive behavioral changes and monitoring the results. Follow-up may include discussing the issue with the therapist, group, and sponsor, using role-playing activities to rehearse actions the client is considering, and reviewing the outcomes of any behavioral changes the client tries.

BENEFITS OF HELPING OTHERS

When you hear the words "getting out of myself," you may wonder why you should be interested in doing so. How will being more generous and considerate toward others be beneficial to you? One place you can look for answers is to other people who've been in situations like yours and found that being more kind made their lives better. On the most basic level, the way people live their lives in addiction is risky to their personal health, legal situations, relationships, how they feel about themselves, and sometimes their overall survival. People die because of their addictions, whether through accidents, violence, overdose, or their bodies just breaking down a lot sooner than they otherwise would have.

You may find that you like the way your life goes better when you live it in a less self-centered way. Other people may treat you better, you'll get in less trouble, and you might even like yourself better. There are a couple of easy ways to find out: Talk to other people who've been where you are and are doing better and start trying it out in small ways and see what happens. This activity will give you some ideas on how to do that.

1. What benefits could you see to helping others in both service work and/or in a community support group program, like Alcoholics Anonymous (AA) or Narcotics Anonymous (NA)?

    _____

    _____

2. You may have attended meetings and may have a sponsor by now. If not, seek out someone you see in recovery who has been at it a while and whom you can relate to. Ask them or the group about the benefits of helping others in both service work and/or within the program. Write what you learn here: _____

    _____

    _____

3. What do you hear others saying about the benefit of working a program of rigorous honesty, accountability for your own behavior, and accepting and using the emotional and spiritual support of others and a higher power?

    _____

    _____

4. What doubts, reservations, skepticism, or fear do you have about this concept of "getting out of yourself" and helping others?

_____

_____

5. The things we say to ourselves and about ourselves or others and situations (self-talk) have a significant impact on how we feel and act. What self-talk statements do you make that keep you from trusting others, being generous, and taking responsibility for your actions? List five of them.

_____

_____

6. What five positive thoughts challenge those you listed in question 5? If you find it challenging to generate all five on your own, list what you can and ask someone you trust for input.

_____

_____

7. The following is a sampling of some small steps you can take toward increasing the benefits of positive relationships and having healthy self-esteem and self-worth:

   a. Be honest about ways you've hurt, used, disregarded, and manipulated other people.

   b. Keep small commitments and promises to build reliability and trust.

   c. Challenge self-talk that is negative, skeptical, critical, or blaming.

   d. Find a sponsor to begin the practice of establishing a stable and accountable relationship within a program of rigorous honesty.

   e. Avoid therapy-interfering behaviors (i.e., being late for treatment, failing/canceling appointments, not completing assigned tasks, acting guarded in sessions).

   f. Take responsibility for your actions versus blaming others.

   g. Find ways to help others without expectation for praise or reward by volunteering at a meeting, your kids' school, a shelter; donate to a food pantry.

   Please try each of these behaviors in the next two weeks and make notes here about the results so you can talk about them with your therapist, group, home group, or sponsor.

   _____

   _____

8. How would the trust of others benefit you, your recovery, and your relationships?

   _____

   _____

9. After observing, talking with others, and completing this exercise, how might you benefit from actively being more generous and considerate of others?

_____

_____

10. What 12-step work from your community support group meetings (i.e., AA, NA, Adult Children of Alcoholics [ACA], Cocaine Anonymous [CA], Gamblers Anonymous [GA]) would also challenge you to do this work?

_____

_____

Be sure to bring this handout back to your next session with your therapist and be prepared to talk about your thoughts and feelings about the exercise.

TAKING INVENTORY OF DESTRUCTIVE BEHAVIORS

GOALS OF THE EXERCISE

1. Decrease antisocial behaviors and increase motivation to practice more respectful thoughts and behavior toward others.
2. Learn how antisocial behavior and addiction is self-defeating.
3. Develop a program of recovery that is free from addiction and the negative influences of antisocial behavior.
4. Develop a greater willingness to behave in more respectful and considerate ways toward others.

ADDITIONAL PROBLEMS FOR WHICH THIS EXERCISE MAY BE USEFUL

- Attention-Deficit/Hyperactivity Disorder (ADHD)—Adolescent
- Attention-Deficit/Hyperactivity Disorder (ADHD)—Adult
- Conduct Disorder/Delinquency
- Impulsivity
- Legal Problems
- Oppositional Defiant Behavior

SUGGESTIONS FOR PROCESSING THIS EXERCISE WITH THE CLIENT

This activity is for clients with patterns of impulsively destructive, dishonest, or malicious behavior that affects other people. It is framed in terms of self-interest because this is often an effective way to initiate the development of motivation for change in clients who are not invested in the feelings or well-being of others. Follow-up should be ongoing and include discussing the issue with their therapist, group, and sponsor. It is advised to teach basic mindfulness skills or other self-calming strategies that can center them so they can get focused on their thoughts more easily.

TAKING INVENTORY OF DESTRUCTIVE BEHAVIORS

1. Which of the following behaviors have you engaged in?

    _____ Rule or law breaking and/or disregard for rules, often related to alcohol/other drugs

    _____ Blaming others for your problems and actions

    _____ Being dishonest

    _____ Having to tell more lies to cover up previously told lies

    _____ Manipulating and intimidating others with aggressive behavior

    _____ Having a lack of regard for others' feelings (lack of empathy)

    _____ Thrill-seeking without regard for safety of self and/or others

    _____ Self-centeredness and always pushing to get your way

    _____ Seeking power over others

    _____ Having a sense of entitlement

    _____ Intentionally violating the rights of others

    _____ Impulsive decision making without thinking about consequences for others

2. How do these behaviors affect your relationships with others? If you cannot come up with an answer, ask someone close to you for feedback and write it here.

    _____

    _____

3. List three ways these behaviors are self-defeating and backfire on you.

    _____

    _____

4. How are these behaviors related to your addiction or substance use?

    _____

    _____

5. Which of the following negative consequences have you experienced because of these behaviors?

    _____ Loss of or lack of respect from others

    _____ Few or no intimate relationships—many broken relationships

    _____ No sense of achievement or accomplishment

_____ Increased isolation or feelings of alienation

_____ Frequent legal difficulties

_____ Lapse/return to substance use/addictive behaviors

Others (please list in space provided):

_____

_____

6. Select one of the items from question 1 and think about a specific situation related to it. Analyze the chain of events by identifying the decisions you made before your action, the outcome, how others responded, how you felt about yourself, and the negative consequences that followed.

_____

_____

7. The refusal to acknowledge and take responsibility for destructive behaviors leads to making the same mistakes repeatedly, getting more of what you've already gotten. Revisit question 6. What alternative thoughts/behaviors would interrupt the chain or result in a more favorable outcome for you? Identify at least three thoughts and three actions/behaviors.

_____

_____

8. Describe the benefits that would come from practicing alternative thoughts and behaviors like those you listed in question 7 on a more consistent basis.

_____

_____

Spend time imagining yourself engaging in one alternative thought and one alternative behavior. Revisit the benefits of continuing to practice this skill. Remember that making positive changes is challenging and takes time. With more practice you'll get more benefits more often.

Be sure to bring this handout back to your next session with your therapist and be prepared to talk about your thoughts and feelings about the exercise.

ANXIETY TRIGGERS AND WARNING SIGNS

GOALS OF THE EXERCISE

1. Maintain a program of recovery free of addiction and excessive anxiety.
2. Understand the relationship between anxiety and addictive behaviors.
3. Increase insight and awareness related to feelings and processes associated with anxiety.
4. Decrease anxious thoughts, overall stress, and muscle tension and increase positive self-talk.
5. Strengthen belief in the capacity to self-manage anxiety without returning to addictive behavior.

ADDITIONAL PROBLEMS FOR WHICH THIS EXERCISE MAY BE USEFUL

- Childhood Trauma
- Chronic Pain
- Eating Disorders and Obesity
- Panic Disorder
- Posttraumatic Stress Disorder (PTSD)
- Relapse Proneness
- Sleep Disturbance
- Social Anxiety

SUGGESTIONS FOR PROCESSING THIS EXERCISE WITH THE CLIENT

The "Anxiety Triggers and Warning Signs" activity is for clients who experience anxiety but feel helpless to change it. Educating clients about anxiety and normalizing healthy levels of it is important in treating anxiety. This activity helps explain that we all need anxiety for certain things, because it can be adaptive and motivating. There is a point when the benefits of anxiety tip toward more detrimental effects. This is the result of thinking things are more threatening, serious, or worse than they really are; avoiding things that make us uncomfortable; or misreading physical cues. First the exercise asks the client to identify how they experience anxiety physically, behaviorally, cognitively, and emotionally. Second, it asks the client to develop a hierarchy of least-to-most anxiety-producing experiences. Finally, it asks the client to develop a plan for coping with anxiety. Follow-up can consist of teaching relaxation, imagery, mindfulness, and biofeedback techniques to deal with all levels of anxiety.

ANXIETY TRIGGERS AND WARNING SIGNS

Everyone experiences anxiety, ranging from mild worry to intense fear. Some people are very aware of their anxiety; others aren't conscious of it until it's overwhelming; and others are overly aware of their anxiety, which often results in increasing it. Some experience anxiety mainly over specific situations, whereas others have more general feelings of anxiety. We're nervous when we do things for the first time: going on dates, speaking to groups, or starting new jobs. For some, anxiety is short lived and does not interfere in their lives other than causing mild discomfort. For others, anxiety causes panic, stops them from enjoying many activities, and interferes with daily living. For others, anxiety is triggered by reminders of past traumatic events or losses. Anxiety is related to addiction in two ways: We often feel anxiety when we practice new nonaddictive behaviors, and we try to reduce anxiety with addictive behaviors.

This exercise will help you learn about your anxiety so that you can develop strategies to cope with it and avoid returning to addictive behaviors to lessen it.

Anxiety has three components that interact with one another: (a) *physical sensations*, such as heart-pounding, sweating, and dizziness; (b) *thoughts*, such as expecting something terrible to happen, racing thoughts; and (c) *behavioral responses*, such as leaving situations or avoiding places.

1. How have you coped in the past to reduce anxiety or avoid anxiety-producing situations?

    _____

    _____

2. In what ways has your anxiety been linked to your substance use or reliance on other self-defeating behaviors?

    _____

    _____

3. What do you think about when you're anxious? Imagine your anxiety has a mind of its own. What would it say to increase your anxiety? Our anxious thoughts often exaggerate dangers and overlook our coping abilities and resources. Keep a log for 1 week of anxiety-producing situations and the accompanying thoughts and beliefs you have when you feel anxious.

    _____

    _____

4. When we feel anxious, the emotional and physical parts of our brains override the thinking parts. The result is that often we'll do anything that quickly relieves our discomfort. The problem is that this quick fix becomes a habit. Here's a solution to use in your journal:

Following the example provided, list a physical symptom in the left-hand column, the thought connected with it in the center, and a reasonable and positive response in the column on the right. This is best done when calm as the problem-solving part of our brain is online and able to help us. Identify positive responses that are simple and easy to do even when anxiousness is relatively high. Once you are calm, you can do more complex behaviors for longer periods of time.

Physical Sensation	Anxious Thought	Positive Response
I feel warm.	*I'm going to pass out.*	*I'll sit, relax, cool down.*
_____	_____	_____
_____	_____	_____
_____	_____	_____

5. Another way to get to know the level of your anxiety is to create an intensity scale ranging from very low to extremely high. Please identify at least one situation or experience for each level, the physical sensations that are associated with each, and an anxious (related) thought that fuels it.

Level of Anxiety	Situation/ Experience	Physical Sensations	Related Thought
Very low	_____	_____	_____
Low	_____	_____	_____
Moderate	_____	_____	_____
High	_____	_____	_____
Very high	_____	_____	_____

6. In looking back over the information you've collected about your anxiety, what word or phrase would you use to describe or name it?

_____

_____

7. We can decrease our anxiety and fears by mastery. This is a kind of trial-and-error experimentation that occurs as we gradually expose ourselves to things that make us anxious and cope with them by dealing with our physical sensations, challenging our anxious thoughts, and tolerating the anxiety. The secondary result is that our confidence increases. Additionally, we all feel some fear when we do anything new.

That's what can help you get better. You learn that you can approach a situation with nervousness, but those feelings don't hurt you, and you can get a desired outcome. Review the following list for beginning strategies to help you tolerate (insert word/phrase here) until you feel calmer. Which beneficial activity do you believe you could do with little help from someone else?

Pray

Hum your favorite song

Find something soft, smooth, cool, etc., that you could hold while you attend to the attribute that feels good

Hug and sway/rock yourself (as you would to calm an upset child)

Use a weighted blanket

Do something kind for someone else

Prep something that is good for you to drink, focusing on every task that leads up to consuming it (e.g., tea)

Spend time engaging with your petting your pet

Stretch (if physically able) and breathe

Other activities that engage your senses (add them here): _____

_____

8. Avoiding something uncomfortable (when not at risk for harm) will initially reduce a fear response/reaction, AND it tends to increase future avoidance behaviors and make anxiety less manageable. When we avoid uncomfortable feelings with substances, we never condition a response that we can face our fears despite being uncomfortable. This is very challenging when our anxiety has been conditioned to help us survive. In preparation for and while practicing this strategy, imagine yourself doing it and feeling more accomplished, despite the discomfort. What can you say to yourself to push past a desire/tendency to avoid when you are uncomfortable? Who can help encourage you to push past avoidance and what do you want them to know so they can kindly encourage you?

_____

_____

Be sure to bring this handout back to your next session with your therapist and be prepared to talk about your thoughts and feelings about the exercise.

COPING WITH STRESS

GOALS OF THE EXERCISE

1. Maintain a program of recovery free from addiction and excessive anxiety.
2. End the use of addictive behavior as a way of escaping anxiety and practice constructive coping behaviors.
3. Decrease anxious thoughts and increase positive self-enhancing self-talk.
4. Learn to relax and think accurately and logically about events.
5. Identify effective stress-management methods that are already working.
6. Incorporate stress management as part of a lifestyle change and identify areas in which to begin modifying stress responses.

ADDITIONAL PROBLEMS FOR WHICH THIS EXERCISE MAY BE USEFUL

*   Childhood Trauma
*   Chronic Pain
*   Gambling
*   Medical Issues
*   Nicotine Use/Dependence
*   Relapse Proneness
*   Social Anxiety

SUGGESTIONS FOR PROCESSING THIS EXERCISE WITH THE CLIENT

The "Coping with Stress" activity examines the client's existing stressors and habitual responses with the aim of increasing insight and helping them reduce stress and improve coping skills. It includes an imagination exercise aimed at motivating the client to work for improvement and bolstering their confidence in doing so. Follow-up can include homework assignments to practice new stress-management methods; seeking feedback from family, friends, and others on perceived changes in the client's degree of tension; and reporting back on outcomes. Skills training in progressive muscle relaxation, guided imagery, mindfulness, problem solving, and improved communication can improve the success of managing stress. Psychoeducation about benefits of building a regimen for practicing is like building emotional/coping strength muscles and should be pursued. Trying to encourage this for overall well-being in addition to managing addiction is sometimes received better. Starting with small, easily understood tasks while body, mind, and emotions are stabilizing will build more buy-in to try lengthier practices and more complex tasks as recovery progresses.

COPING WITH STRESS

Lapses and relapses in recovery from addictions are often triggered by stressful situations because addictive behaviors have been used as our main tools for handling stress. To stay sober, finding healthier ways to cope with stressors is necessary for our overall well-being and for recovery progress. Stress and stressors are inevitable AND most are transient, which means they come and go, wax and wane. Our abilities to tolerate stress also are transient. At times we can endure significant stress, and other times small stressors send us spinning. This exercise will guide you in learning about your stress management style, your sources of stress, and how you can handle it more effectively.

1.   List three situations that most commonly trigger great stress for you (on a 10-point scale, with 10 being the highest stress level): _____

     _____

     _____

2.   How has an addictive lifestyle, including relationships in addiction and use of alcohol/other drugs and possibly other addictive behaviors, created stress in your life? Identify at least three behaviors.

     _____

     _____

3.   How can you tell when you are experiencing stress in your life? List three reactions each for both physical and emotional stress.

     _____

     _____

4.   What are some positive and negative ways in which have you handled stress?

     _____

     _____

5.   We are often able to bypass stressful situations but don't, and many times we neglect to utilize strategies we know would work. List the two main sources of stress in your life that you can control. What ways will you increase the likelihood that you will act in a way to reduce your stress?

     _____

     _____

6. At other times, a situation may be unavoidable, but we increase the stress we experience because of how we frame the situation (e.g., predicting terrible outcomes and worrying about things we can't change). List two causes of stress you currently cannot control in the first column and possible ways you can change your thinking about them in the second column.

Example: Family mistrust of sobriety effort   **Example: I will continue to work hard**

_____   _____

_____   _____

7. Please describe a stressful situation, big or small, that you handled well and how you did it. How can you use this in continuing to tackle other stressful situations?

   Example: Overloaded at work—talked with supervisor and asked them to help you prioritize tasks—continue to practice advocating for myself.

   _____

   _____

8. You can further reduce stress by avoiding overdoing things. This will allow you to more effectively handle the stress that is unavoidable. Please list at least one thing you can do **each day** to create more balance in each area listed here.

   a. Relationships with family or friends: _____

   _____

   b. Leisure time/activities that bring joy: _____

   _____

   c. Work/school: _____

   _____

   d. Community involvement/doing something for someone else: _____

   _____

   e. Spiritual activities: _____

   _____

   f. Proper nutrition, sleep, and exercise: _____

   _____

   g. Emotions: _____

   _____

h. Self-encouraging affirmation: _____

_____

9. Picture yourself handling a stressful situation using more effective methods. While you picture this future for yourself, pay attention to how it makes you feel. Talk about this with other members of the treatment group or in your next treatment session. How would this improve the results you experience and your quality of life?

_____

_____

Each attempt we make toward doing something positive and different makes us feel more able and motivated to continue. As we increase positive action, more positive things will result.

Be sure to bring this handout back to your next session with your therapist and be prepared to talk about your thoughts and feelings about the exercise.

Therapist's Overview

DEVELOPING A RECOVERY PROGRAM

GOALS OF THE EXERCISE

1. Develop the coping skills necessary to improve attention-deficit/hyperactivity disorder (ADHD) and reduce the impact of a substance use disorder.
2. Understand the relationship between ADHD symptoms and addiction.
3. Identify specific ADHD behaviors that cause the most difficulty in sobriety.
4. List the negative consequences related to continuing a using lifestyle.
5. Develop positive social skills to help maintain lasting, sober peer friendships.

ADDITIONAL PROBLEMS FOR WHICH THIS EXERCISE MAY BE USEFUL

- Attention-Deficit/Hyperactivity Disorder (ADHD)—Adult
- Conduct Disorder/Delinquency
- Gambling
- Peer Group Negativity
- Readiness to Change

SUGGESTIONS FOR PROCESSING THIS EXERCISE WITH THE CLIENT

The "Developing a Recovery Program" exercise is intended to address the needs of adolescents who are attempting to establish sobriety from addiction. It includes looking at the connection between ADHD symptoms and addictive behaviors, improving refusal skills, increasing social skills without the reliance on substances, identifying the importance of other activities, and identifying the benefits of having a sober group of support people. Follow-up could include working with parents to learn the same skills the adolescent is learning so they can reward and provide useful feedback along the way. This exercise can be used with clients who do not have ADHD but who lack skills in refusing offers, seeing the need to change behaviors, and making positive connections with sober peers or identifying alternate activities.

DEVELOPING A RECOVERY PROGRAM

Beginning and maintaining sobriety and ultimately implementing a consistent recovery plan is an ongoing process. All of it is challenging at times, but it can be additionally difficult when managing impulsivity; trying to not rely on substances to socialize or cope with problems; waxing and waning desire to stay connected to peers who are using; having a lack of connection with sober peers; and finding other activities that are appealing. This exercise will walk you through some of the key ingredients in developing an initial recovery plan that is unique to you.

1. What symptoms of your ADHD challenge your attempts at sobriety, and what are you doing about each of them to give yourself the best chance to begin addressing them without substances or other harmful behaviors?

    _____

    _____

2. Sometimes people use substances to assist them in managing their symptoms of ADHD. Which two symptoms of ADHD have you used substances to help manage?

    _____

    _____

3. Often we establish our peer groups based on shared use of substances and other times we have an existing group of friends who all started to use together and stayed together. Breaking these ties can be difficult. What excuses have you made to yourself to stay connected to friends who continue to use?

    _____

    _____

4. What have been the difficulties in refusing offers to use with your established peer group? Difficulties distancing yourself from them? What is your biggest fear about what it would be like or what would happen?

    _____

    _____

5. What excuses have you used that have worked and not worked to get people to stop offering substances to you?

_____

_____

6. Brainstorm with your group, your parents, or your therapist about other alternative strategies for refusing offers in ways that feel comfortable for you and write them here.

_____

_____

7. Fighting urges to use, no longer relying on substances to meet and connect with other people, and not using when you feel alone or stressed are all strategies necessary to maintain sobriety. What are the challenges for you in each of these areas, and in what areas are you having some success? Identify what challenges you and where you have had some success.

_____

_____

8. What are the things that keep you connected to your using peer group? What are those that keep you ambivalent to explore sober relationships with peers?

_____

_____

9. Most people who have found success in recovery have learned that they need other people who support them in that effort. The truth is most people leading sober lives attempted to keep old relationships and told themselves they would be fine continuing to hang with friends who use but not using themselves. Anticipating this change is riddled with justifications, fears, and uncertainty about how to or what will ultimately happen. Identify any of your own justifications, fears, and uncertainties.

_____

_____

10. In what ways can a sober support network (e.g., parents, guardians, teachers, recovering friends) support your efforts at sobriety (e.g., give rewards, provide encouragement, attend a 12-step meeting for parents)? Who would you consider your sober support network that includes those who are not using?

_____

_____

11. Connecting with people who understand substance use and the challenges of choosing sobriety and its benefits is important. We often learn they have other issues they are working on as well (i.e., ADHD, mood issues). In what ways would you benefit from connecting with people like this?

_____

_____

12. Nonusing activities and interests are an important part of any sobriety/recovery plan. First, there's just the matter of filling in the time you used to spend using. Second, you need to find new things that give you a sense of pleasure and satisfaction. What about making social connections that are not based on alcohol or other drug use (e.g., join a club or the gym, new hobbies or something you've always wanted to try, service/volunteer) and list them in the order you would be willing to begin exploring them:

_____

_____

13. New activities can be used to target specific triggers to use. Name three of your triggers and a new activity you can engage in to overcome each trigger you identified (e.g., you use to counter boredom, so you could engage in rigorous exercise).

_____

_____

14. It works for some to begin building sober relationships at the same time they distance from using networks. What is one thing you can do to start and what makes sense to you about how this is beneficial for your recovery process?

_____

_____

Be sure to bring this handout back to your next session with your therapist and be prepared to talk about your thoughts and feelings about the exercise.

STAYING ATTENTIVE AND OTHER NEGOTIATING SKILLS

GOALS OF THE EXERCISE

1. Maintain a program of recovery free from addiction and the negative effects of attention-deficit/hyperactivity disorder (ADHD).
2. Demonstrate sustained attention and concentration for consistently longer periods.
3. Understand the negative influence of ADHD on substance use.
4. Develop positive self-talk when faced with problems caused by ADHD or addiction.
5. Learn positive ways to resolve or manage interpersonal differences.
6. Demonstrate healthy communication that is honest, open, and self-disclosing.
7. Reduce the frequency of behaviors that are designed exclusively to please others.

ADDITIONAL PROBLEMS FOR WHICH THIS EXERCISE MAY BE USEFUL

- Attention-Deficit/Hyperactivity Disorder (ADHD)—Adult
- Impulsivity
- Occupational Problems
- Parent–Child Relational Problems
- Partner Relational Conflicts

SUGGESTIONS FOR PROCESSING THIS EXERCISE WITH THE CLIENT

The "Staying Attentive and Other Negotiation Skills" activity is intended for clients who would benefit from learning negotiation skills to improve their relationships with others. This activity can be incorporated into role-playing in individual sessions or in groups. It can be applied to past problems with intimate, work, or peer relationships or to problems the client is currently experiencing. Follow-up could include assignments to practice the skills learned and report back to the therapist and treatment group on the outcomes. With adolescents, you could involve parents or teachers to help monitor and gently remind and reward with positive feedback when positive strategies are utilized.

STAYING ATTENTIVE AND OTHER NEGOTIATING SKILLS

Attention problems can cause difficulties in many situations, including relationships. Other people may not understand and may be hurt or offended by your having difficulty staying focused and being easily distracted. Either issue, drifting attention or distraction, makes initiating and sustaining relationships difficult. Many people use addictive behaviors to cope with relationship problems caused by these symptoms, and engaging in addictive behaviors creates issues or makes these issues worse.

This exercise will teach you a step-by-step approach to negotiating differences with others and give you some tips on negotiating social situations and relationships. The steps are as follows:

1. Identify the source of the conflict.
2. Provide constructive feedback without criticizing.
3. Receive constructive feedback by actively listening and then clarifying your understanding of the other person's position.
4. Actively listen.
5. Empathize.
6. Compromise.

1. Skill 1 in negotiating is deciding whether you and the other person are having difficulty with each other or if one of you is feeling uncomfortable or unhappy for an unrelated reason. Think of a recent conflict you've had with someone. How did you know that you and the other person were having difficulty or a difference of opinion? Identify any clues.

   _____

   _____

2. Skill 2 in negotiation is telling the other person what you think about the problem without criticizing. While thinking about this last conflict, write down what role you believe you and the person who you were in conflict with played. Identify how you felt in the conflict. Write about who you conveyed this to. If given the chance again, what might you have said differently that would sound less critical?

   _____

   _____

3. Skill 3 in negotiation is asking the other person what they think about the problem. This can help you improve communication and avoid jumping to conclusions or making incorrect assumptions. While thinking about the same conflict, (a) identify one way you understood the person's position, and (b) write a statement/question you could ask to gather more information or better understand where they were coming from.

   _____

   _____

4. Skill 4 is listening openly and actively to the other person's perceptions and feelings.

   a. Identify three things that can hinder you listening to others.

   _____

   _____

   b. We communicate and we are actively listening by not interrupting and asking clarifying questions when it's our turn. This reflects to someone what we heard them say. Give an example of a clarifying question you could ask to get more information about another's perspective:

   _____

   _____

   c. We need to stay present when we are communicating with others. What happens when you get frustrated, upset, or feel personally criticized when someone is talking about how your behavior affected them or they disagree with you/what you did?

   _____

   _____

   Role play with your therapist or in your group how this would go using the information you identified so far in this exercise.

5. Skill 5 is thinking about why other people might feel the way they do. This does not mean judging their thoughts as right or wrong but rather seeing the situation from their point of view. Active listening is critical to get the information we need to start to understand this. Think about a recent discussion or argument about a topic you had a disagreement about. Identify your position and then identify three OTHER ways (not right or wrong) that could explain the other person's position.

   _____

   _____

6. Skill 6 is finding a compromise. Think about typical conflicts you find yourself in with others. Most conflicts have a compromise. Identify a recent disagreement and identify two potential compromises you could have negotiated.

_____

_____

7. Please do some self-evaluation—not to judge yourself but to learn whatever lessons you can. In reviewing your conflict, what did you learn about your negotiation style? What would you like to do differently?

_____

_____

Successfully working through conflicts is beneficial, but not easy or comfortable. Listening better and attending to someone else's perspective help us connect with others.

8. You've just worked on how you can manage conflict differently in current and future relationships. Beginning and maintaining relationships outside conflict situations takes work and follow-through. The following are a few ideas about what you can do to improve attention outside conflict and can lead to fewer conflicts related to people's frustration with us:

   a. Plan regular activities with others around shared interests—avoid frequent requests for last-minute get-togethers.

   b. Learn to listen and pay attention and respond specifically to what is being said.

   c. Pay attention to small courtesies—remember birthdays, call or email to say "hi," and thank people for favors.

   d. Get organized—keep phone lists, use a calendar to log dates and commitments.

   e. What others can you think of?

   _____

   _____

9. Ask someone close to you for feedback about how well you pay attention and follow through in your relationship with them. It is important to note that we can modify behavior that is not working for us or in our relationships; it is not a reflection or judgment of our worth. Write this feedback below and describe how you'll address any issues this person points out. Try to hear feedback as information you can use to help yourself and understand others better.

_____

_____

Be sure to bring this handout back to your next session with your therapist and be prepared to talk about your thoughts and feelings about the exercise.

FROM RECKLESSNESS TO CALCULATED RISKS

GOALS OF THE EXERCISE

1. Maintain a program of recovery from addiction and reduce the negative effects of attention-deficit/hyperactivity disorder (ADHD) on learning, social interaction, and self-esteem.
2. Decrease impulsivity by learning how to stop, think, and plan before acting.
3. Learn the benefits of taking calculated risks rather than acting impulsively.
4. Gain insight into patterns and consequences of reckless behavior and decision making.
5. Learn a method of decision making that leads to more positive outcomes.

ADDITIONAL PROBLEMS FOR WHICH THIS EXERCISE MAY BE USEFUL

- Attention-Deficit/Hyperactivity Disorder (ADHD)—Adolescent
- Bipolar Disorder
- Conduct Disorder/Delinquency
- Impulsivity
- Oppositional Defiant Behavior
- Self-Harm
- Sexual Promiscuity

SUGGESTIONS FOR PROCESSING THIS EXERCISE WITH THE CLIENT

The "From Reckless to Calculated Risks" activity is for clients with a history of impulsivity. The exercise asks the client to review past impulsive decisions and consequences and then guides them through a technique that encourages more calculated responses. Follow-up can include having a client describe a series of self-instructions in situations in which they have acted impulsively. Repetition of this process reinforces the internal problem-solving dialogue necessary for taking calculated risks. If the client is unable to generate personal examples, use scenarios and direct them to develop self-instructions for the person in the scenarios.

FROM RECKLESSNESS TO CALCULATED RISKS

We all take at least some risks in everything we do, but the risks we take in a situation can be reckless—not thinking through the consequences—or calculated. Taking calculated risks involves three steps. First, it means avoiding acting on impulses. Next, it involves thinking through a situation to its possible outcomes. Finally, it calls for making concrete plans before acting. Addictive behavior and ADHD share traits related to recklessness: wanting instant gratification, acting impulsively, and not thinking actions through to their potential consequences.

If we take calculated risks versus reckless risks, we have the best chance of getting the outcomes we want and avoiding preventable problems. In this exercise you'll review your risk-taking patterns and consider changes to give you more control over your life.

1. List three reckless behaviors you have engaged in, the situations in which you did so, and the consequences.

Behavior	Situation	Consequence(s)
_____	_____	_____
_____	_____	_____
_____	_____	_____

2. For one of the behaviors you listed in question 1, choose a situation with which you continue to struggle. Complete the following formula to learn how to take more calculated risks.

    a. The situation is:_____

    _____

    b. What outcome do you want to achieve?

    _____

    c. What are three things you can tell yourself in this situation to avoid impulsive responses, such as "slow down," "don't take it personally," or "relax and think for a minute"?

    _____

    _____

d. Write out concrete instructions to yourself in the following format.

- What is the problem?

  _____

  _____

- What has been my typical pattern?

  _____

  _____

- What are my options—what other things can I do?

  _____

  _____

- What do I want to have happen?

  _____

  _____

- The approach that will give me the best chance of the result I want and will minimize difficulty will be (name three specific, observable steps) . . .

  i. _____

  ii. _____

  iii. _____

- What can I say to myself to help me cope and stay more focused?

  _____

  _____

- To avoid this problem in the future, I need to focus on . . .

  _____

  _____

e. What benefits can you identify that would come from handling situations and emotions this way?

_____

_____

_____

_____

Imagine step by step a substance/addictive behavior related scenario and a nonsubstance related scenario with the help of your therapist following the preceding steps. Take 10 minutes to imagine each. Sometimes it helps talking through this out loud in a confidential, private space with your therapist so there is an outside perspective. Think about using other people to help you work through things when you get stuck, think of this as using your phone-a-friend option—calling for assistance from someone who has either done it before or knows what you're trying to do or will give you support you need when feeling stuck.

Be sure to bring this handout back to your next session with your therapist and be prepared to talk about your thoughts and feelings about the exercise.

GETTING ORGANIZED

GOALS OF THE EXERCISE

1. Maintain a program of recovery free from addiction and the negative effects of attention-deficit/hyperactivity disorder (ADHD).
2. Demonstrate sustained attention and concentration for consistently longer periods.
3. Understand the negative influence of ADHD on substance use.
4. Structure a recovery program that is sufficient to maintain abstinence and reduce the negative effects of ADHD on learning and self-esteem.
5. Develop positive self-talk when faced with problems caused by ADHD and/or addiction.
6. Identify coping strategies that have worked to sustain attention in the past.
7. Develop new skills to cope with inattention and difficulties with concentration.

ADDITIONAL PROBLEMS FOR WHICH THIS EXERCISE MAY BE USEFUL

*   Attention-Deficit/Hyperactivity Disorder (ADHD)—Adolescent
*   Living Environment Deficiency
*   Psychosis
*   Self-Care Deficits—Primary
*   Self-Care Deficits—Secondary

SUGGESTIONS FOR PROCESSING THIS EXERCISE WITH THE CLIENT

The "Getting Organized" activity is for clients who are struggling with inattention, distractibility, or difficulty completing tasks. It can be used with other clients who generally need assistance getting organized. Follow-up can include having the client keep a journal or log of distractions or instances of inattention and then self-monitor improvement through use of newly learned skills. It is important to reinforce small successes to create and sustain therapeutic momentum and build further successes. With adolescents, ask the clients' parents, teachers, coaches, etc., to help them organize the pieces relevant to areas in which they struggle and provide positive feedback and rewards for small and larger successes. Explore technology to assist with reminders, electronic forms, or plans that can be taken with a client for reference in real time.

GETTING ORGANIZED

Managing daily life is a key part of recovery. Addictive lifestyles interfere with being organized, and people who live with attention-deficit/hyperactivity disorder (ADHD) often struggle with the same things. You may have used substances to cope with symptoms of ADHD, often resulting in more problems and then even more use of substances. There are many reasons we forget to do things or don't complete tasks. We may get distracted, get tired, lose interest, jump from task to task, procrastinate, or lack confidence. Substance use creates a great deal of disorganization but getting organized is a learnable skill that improves with practice. Completing any task involves four steps: (a) deciding what you need to do, (b) spotting cues to catch your focus slipping, (c) using techniques to stay calm and focused, and (d) checking progress and rewarding yourself. This exercise will help you identify barriers to getting organized and finishing tasks. It also provides coping strategies for you to practice.

1. For the next week, please monitor the following items and write what you learn here.

   a. What tasks do you have trouble completing?

   _____

   b. Specifically, when do the breakdowns occur (time of day, after a certain length of time, etc.)?

   _____

   c. Specifically, what gets in the way of being organized or completing things (i.e., not enough time, boredom, distractions, lack of plan)?

   _____

   d. Identify specific distractions (i.e., phone, cravings, anxious thoughts, physical symptoms, other responsibilities that seem more important) and an idea for how to get around them.

   _____

   e. What tasks can you usually complete?

   _____

   f. What has helped you so far in getting organized or completing what you set out to do (e.g., frequent reminders, no distractions, notes to yourself)?

   _____

2.   Please choose a task you have difficulty completing. It's helpful to pick one that you do often and will have many chances to practice (e.g., laundry, shopping, homework). Write it here.

_____

Start writing about every time you complete this task and how you succeed. If you have a method that works for this task, you can use it for others.

3.   Here are four suggested strategies.

   a.   *Chunking:* Break an activity into short time segments (e.g., 15-minute intervals) or small steps (e.g., (1) get to the bank, (2) get quarters, (3) sort clothes, versus (1) do laundry today). This makes it easier to stay on task. Identify how you can do this with your activity.

_____

_____

   b.   *Visual cues:* Use concrete, visible reminders of deadlines. You can do this by writing lists, using a calendar, or using a scheduling app on your phone to set daily goals. Don't overcommit: That increases stress and fatigue, which make ADHD symptoms worse and could prevent you from finishing what you started. Please describe how you can use this strategy for your activity.

_____

_____

What might you consider doing if you feel your stress level building?

_____

_____

   c.   *Set yourself up for success:* Start with tasks you know you can complete. Doing those tasks first will increase your motivation to follow through on harder ones. Or you may want to work on tougher tasks first while you're focused and fresh, whichever works best for you. Outline five concrete steps for each on two separate sheets of paper for the tasks you would like to/need to accomplish. Try them both and assess which method seems to work best and for what activities. Trying something before judging its effectiveness is an important part of testing strategies.

_____

_____

   d.   *Build structure:* Develop a written daily and weekly routine and stick to it. Having a routine, including daily tasks, meals, sleep/wake times, medications, meetings, and time for relaxation and fun, will help you manage time and improve your chances of accomplishing the things you need to do. When our lives get busy and there are more demands on our time, adding new things to our existing schedules helps us stay organized so we don't neglect these necessary daily tasks. How can you use this strategy? In the beginning of recovery or testing this strategy, start with one day at a time and reassess at the end of each day, plan for the next. As you build more bandwidth and skill, you can tackle longer periods of time.

_____

_____

4. Set a date to begin trying out each of these strategy suggestions. Evaluate your success, struggles, and lessons learned after 2 weeks of practice. Record the results here:

Strategy A (chunking):

_____

_____

Strategy B (visual cues):

_____

_____

Strategy C (set yourself up for success):

_____

_____

Strategy D (build structure):

_____

_____

5. List specific ways you will reward yourself for success.

_____

_____

6. Inevitably, you will lose focus, get distracted, get stuck. Identify one positive affirmation (to replace criticism or self-blame) you can say to yourself to get back on track.

_____

_____

Be sure to bring this handout to your next session with your therapist and be prepared to discuss your thoughts and feelings about this exercise.

SELF-SOOTHING: CALM DOWN, SLOW DOWN

GOALS OF THE EXERCISE

1. Maintain a program of recovery from addiction and reduce the negative effects of attention-deficit/hyperactivity disorder (ADHD) on learning, social interaction, and self-esteem.
2. Develop the skills necessary to bring ADHD symptoms under control so that normal learning can take place.
3. Learn and demonstrate safe stress-reduction techniques as alternatives to addictive or risky behaviors, including substance abuse, gambling, overspending, and sexual promiscuity.
4. Reduce the impact of medical and other problems on recovery and relapse potential.
5. Reduce feelings of alienation by learning about similarities to others.

ADDITIONAL PROBLEMS FOR WHICH THIS EXERCISE MAY BE USEFUL

*   Anger
*   Anxiety
*   Borderline Traits
*   Chronic Pain
*   Eating Disorders and Obesity
*   Gambling
*   Grief/Loss Unresolved
*   Medical Issues
*   Posttraumatic Stress Disorder (PTSD)
*   Social Anxiety
*   Suicidal Ideation

SUGGESTIONS FOR PROCESSING THIS EXERCISE WITH THE CLIENT

The "Self-Soothing: Calm Down, Slow Down" activity is useful to help clients learn to recognize signs that their agitation is escalating and improve their skill at calming themselves. This exercise can be used as a check-in and review at the initiation and/or conclusion of every individual or group therapy session. This activity can be used with clients who do not have ADHD but need improved coping strategies for distress tolerance, anger, frustration, or acting impulsively.

SELF-SOOTHING: CALM DOWN, SLOW DOWN

For people coping with issues of attention and/or impulsive decision making, learning to calm themselves can often help them avoid negative outcomes. It can improve learning, relationships, and self-esteem. It can replace self-destructive behaviors they may have used to cope with anxiety, restlessness, boredom, irritability, frustration, and negative reaction from others, as well as reducing impulsivity, distractibility, and other problems related to ADHD. There are numerous healthy ways to calm down. You may already have some that work—if so, keep using them! This exercise will give you more tactics you can practice and use in your day-to-day activities.

1. Identify healthy tactics you have found useful in calming yourself when you're agitated (continue to use these as you learn additional methods).

    _____

    _____

2. List three self-destructive activities or practices you have engaged in to calm yourself, to cope with boredom or when you found yourself agitated/frustrated/irritable.

    _____

    _____

3. The following is a list of calming-down strategies. Choose three from the list and practice each for 5 minutes at different times, at least three times each day for a week. Keep a record of how calm you feel before and after. Use the following rating scale: very calm (1), calm (2), no change (3), less calm than when you started (4), more upset than when you started (5). Practice them at different times of the day and note whether they work better at some times than at others.

    a. Concentrate on breathing slowly and deeply.

    b. Relax in a quiet place.

    c. Use an external cue for focus (e.g., wrap yourself in a weighted blanket, hold a recovery token, gaze at a candle flame, pet your dog, play or listen to soft music).

    d. Develop a calming mantra or message to repeat to yourself.

    e. Imagine a peaceful scene full of relaxing details, utilizing all your senses.

    f. Take a walk.

g. Pray or meditate.

h. Take you shoes off and walk on something smooth, soft, and attend to how the surface feels on your feet.

i. Use a phone/computer app focused on relaxation or breathwork.

_____

_____

Challenge yourself to try something you've not done before to build a repertoire of tools. It is advised that you try them out before needing them to see if they are worth exploring when you need them most.

Remember that repetition is the key—the more you practice any of these techniques, the better they will work and the more competent you will feel to manage your emotions. Sometimes other people can help us calm down, but we need to have skills in doing this for ourselves in case those people aren't available.

4. What worked well (those items you ranked a 1 or 2)? What didn't work as well as you would have hoped? Identify any ways you could combine items to increase their efficacy. Being open to exploring a range of options is a recovery strategy.

_____

_____

5. Ask some people you trust what they do to calm themselves. Practice their methods yourself five times before assessing its efficacy; write the results here.

_____

_____

6. Write the specific steps you will incorporate into a self-soothing ritual. It is important to remember that some strategies work well sometimes and other times they may not work as well. Having a variety of strategies and combining when necessary may make them work better for you. Which strategies will you use first, second, third, . . . and so on?

_____

_____

_____

7. What body cues will indicate that you are calm and can stop the self-soothing ritual for the time being?

_____

_____

8. What physical signs will tell you that you are getting agitated and need to calm yourself again?

_____

_____

9. If you find yourself in a bind and need to reach out for help, do so! This is not a failure; some situations and experiences require more sometimes. What signs will tell you it's time to reach out for support?

_____

_____

Be sure to bring this handout back to your next session with your therapist and be prepared to talk about your thoughts and feelings about the exercise.

EARLY WARNING SIGNS OF MANIA/HYPOMANIA

GOALS OF THE EXERCISE

1. Maintain a program of recovery that incorporates management of manic/hypomanic behavior and addiction symptoms.
2. Understand the importance of early detection and intervention in manic/hypomanic episodes.
3. Identify early warning signs of mania/hypomania, create plans to self-monitor for these early warning signs, and plan who to ask for help and how to ask if they occur.
4. Establish and maintain compliance with prescribed regimen of mood stabilizer(s), antidepressant(s), and any other psychotropic medications.
5. Alleviate manic/hypomanic mood and return to previous level of effective functioning.

ADDITIONAL PROBLEMS FOR WHICH THIS EXERCISE MAY BE USEFUL

- Dangerousness/Lethality
- Gambling
- Impulsivity
- Psychosis
- Relapse Proneness
- Sexual Promiscuity

SUGGESTIONS FOR PROCESSING THIS EXERCISE WITH THE CLIENT

The "Early Warning Signs of Mania/Hypomania" activity is useful for clients diagnosed with bipolar disorder or for those at risk for these disorders (e.g., clients diagnosed with depression, attention-deficit/hyperactivity disorder, or attention deficit disorder) who may be having manic/hypomanic symptoms including those induced by use of substances. It is crucial to watch for these signs in patients starting antidepressant medications! These medications may trigger previously latent mania, which can lead to behaviors that endanger the client or others. This exercise identifies warning signs related to (a) thinking and emotions and (b) observable behaviors. It offers a checklist for both types of warning signs and helps the client create routine self-monitoring and an action plan for use if they experience one or more early warning signs for longer than 1 day. Follow-up can include referral to support groups and reviewing outcomes with the therapist and group. Couples or family work could also include identifying strategies to assist clients who do not see early warning signs themselves.

EARLY WARNING SIGNS OF MANIA/HYPOMANIA

Mania and hypomania can be hard to detect when they start, and they can feel so good that we don't *want* to do anything about them. However, the time to get help is before they lead to actions with painful results. Another reason to catch a manic or hypomanic episode early: If it runs its course, it usually ends with a sudden plunge into dangerous depression and certainly puts people at risk of relapse. This exercise will help you spot the warning signs so you can get some help before your mania or hypomania leads you to grief. This problem can look different depending on the person, or in the same person at different times, so you probably won't experience all the early warning signs on this list. If you experience more than one for a day, call your therapist or physician and talk about what is going on. Ask family members or others with whom you live to do the same on your behalf and give them permission to do so.

1. Some of the early warning signs of mania or hypomania are changes in our *thoughts and emotions*. Be alert for any of the following in your own thinking. You may notice them yourself, or someone close to you may point them out. Use this handout as a checklist.

   _____ Suddenly improved mood when nothing in your life is significantly better

   _____ Suddenly feeling more irritable and impatient than usual

   _____ A sudden burst of creative thinking, with lots of new ideas

   _____ Feeling more restless than usual

   _____ Your mind jumping from one subject to another more than usual

   _____ Becoming more easily distracted by things going on around you

   _____ Suddenly feeling more impulses to do things that feel good (using alcohol/ other drugs, sex, spending, traveling, etc.)

   _____ A sudden and significant increase in self-confidence and self-esteem

2. Other early warning signs show up as changes in *behavior*. These are the ones other people may be more likely to see and comment on:

   _____ Suddenly feeling more energetic and needing less sleep than usual

   _____ Increased sex drive and sexual activity

   _____ Talking more/faster, interrupting more, having a harder time than usual being quiet

_____ Snapping at people or blurting out things you wouldn't usually say

_____ Unusual bursts of physical activity, such as walking, pacing, exercise, fidgeting

_____ Decreased appetite and eating less

_____ Increased impulsive behavior in areas like spending money, using substances, gambling

_____ Suddenly working harder and becoming more productive at work, school, or hobbies

_____ If treating, desire or actual discontinuation of prescribed medications

3. Describe your plan for monitoring the early warning signs listed here. For you, what are the earliest indicators?

   _____

   _____

4. Describe your plan of action if you see two or more of these things happening for longer than a day. Include who you will reach out to.

   _____

   _____

5. What ways could the people closest to you be involved in this plan? As mentioned, sometimes others see early signs before we see them ourselves. What roles would you like each to play in helping you access the most appropriate resources and care?

   _____

   _____

6. Early detection and action will assist in stabilizing quicker and minimizing negative consequences. List ways that increased mood stability, decreased impulsivity, less risk of relapse, and avoidance of negative consequences that can accompany a manic episode would be beneficial to you.

   _____

   _____

Be sure to bring this handout back to your next therapy session and be prepared to talk about your thoughts and feelings about the exercise.

MANIA, ADDICTION, AND RECOVERY

GOALS OF THE EXERCISE

1. Maintain a program of recovery that is free of bipolar behavior and addiction.
2. Understand the relationship between bipolar states and addiction.
3. Understand the biopsychosocial aspects of bipolar states and addiction and accept the need for continued treatment, including medication.

ADDITIONAL PROBLEMS FOR WHICH THIS EXERCISE MAY BE USEFUL

- Depression–Unipolar
- Grief/Loss Unresolved
- Impulsivity
- Posttraumatic Stress Disorder (PTSD)
- Psychosis
- Readiness for Change
- Substance-Induced Disorders
- Substance Use Disorders
- Suicidal Ideation

SUGGESTIONS FOR PROCESSING THIS EXERCISE WITH THE CLIENT

The "Mania, Addiction, and Recovery" activity is meant for clients with co-occurring disorders suffering from depression, dysthymia, bipolar disorder, cyclothymic disorder, and addiction. It guides clients to awareness of the role of self-medication for emotional distress in their addictions and to exploration of healthier alternatives. Follow-up could include bibliotherapy related to the client's mood disorder(s), homework assignments to engage in healthy alternative activities identified through this exercise and then report back to the therapist and/or a treatment group on the results, and assignment to a treatment support group for a mood disorder.

MANIA, ADDICTION, AND RECOVERY

What is the connection between substance use addictions and emotional issues? Many people suffer from both addictive problems and mood disorders such as depression or bipolar disorder and are unable to overcome either problem alone. Others find that when they are faced with painful losses or other stressful events, they feel they can't cope without blocking their pain with alcohol, another drug, or some addictive behavior. This exercise will help you identify and plan for these issues.

1. People who abuse alcohol or other drugs may be more likely to struggle with depression or other mood disorders, because they can become depressed or manic as a result of their drinking or drug use. Identify ways you feel substance use is related to problems with your moods.

    _____

    _____

2. Sometimes the connection between addiction and moods works in the other direction: The mood problems come first, and when people do things to try to improve their mood or escape their emotional pain, they end up with a substance use disorder, either on a substance (e.g., alcohol) or on a behavior (e.g., excessive spending). Identify how your mood problems may have led you to seek substances or act impulsively.

    _____

    _____

    It is important to understand and accept the following without harsh self-criticism: starting substance use may have been an attempt to cope at the time, coupled with an underappreciation that it could cause additional painful consequences or that you would end up with another problem to manage.

3. What are the potential consequences that would come (have come) from untreated bipolar symptoms?

    _____

    _____

4. What have been the challenges to accepting your diagnosis of bipolar disorder?

_____

_____

5. Many people find that some of the methods they use to overcome chemical dependence and other addictions, such as participating in recovery programs, learning new coping skills, and finding replacement activities, also help them with mood problems. What recovery tools might help you deal with bipolar, depression, or other mood problems?

_____

_____

6. On the other hand, some techniques used with mood disorders may not seem to fit into recovery from substance abuse, such as the use of prescribed mood-altering medications.

   a. If you are under a doctor's instructions to take medications for a mood disorder, have you talked about your substance abuse issues with the doctor who prescribed the medications? If you have, what did the doctor tell you about this?

   _____

   _____

   b. If you haven't, what keeps you from sharing this information, and what is the potential risk to your recovery efforts of keeping this secret?

   _____

   _____

7. If you are taking prescribed mood-altering medications, what might happen to you and your recovery from addiction to substances if you stopped taking those medications?

_____

_____

8. What are the three things you value the most that would be compromised if you didn't treat your problems in a way that sustains stability and absence of substance use or other impulsive/high-risk behavior?

_____

_____

9. Others often recognize we are heading for trouble before we do. We may feel too good and too productive to want to make changes or believe we need to. Please name three people who can help alert you to behaviors that would indicate your mood is becoming problematic and you may be heading toward relapse. Identify one way each person can assist you.

_____

_____

10. There are a few strategies that work well for co-occurring mental health issues. Accepting them as part of a prevention, safety, and treatment plan is critical to maintaining stability and aligning with a life consistent with personal values. Examples of these strategies include consistent and adequate sleep regimen, stress management, adhering to recommended treatments, and avoiding use of substances. Please describe the tools you will use to cope with the combined problems of substance abuse and mood disorders.

_____

_____

Be sure to bring this handout back to your next therapy session and be prepared to talk about your thoughts and feelings about the exercise.

FORMING STABLE RELATIONSHIPS

GOALS OF THE EXERCISE

1. Develop a recovery program that reduces the impact of borderline behavior traits on substance use, mood stability, and interpersonal relationships.
2. Understand connections between addictive thinking patterns and unhealthy relationships.
3. Learn strategies to form stable and healthy relationships that promote recovery.

ADDITIONAL PROBLEMS FOR WHICH THIS EXERCISE MAY BE USEFUL

- Adult-Child-of-an-Alcoholic (ACA) Traits
- Dependent Traits
- Partner Relational Conflicts
- Sexual Promiscuity
- Substance Use Disorders
- Suicidal Ideation

SUGGESTIONS FOR PROCESSING THIS EXERCISE WITH THE CLIENT

The "Forming Stable Relationships" activity is for clients whose recovery is compromised by chaotic, painful, and unstable relationships. It guides clients in exploring similarities between addictions and the dynamics of unhealthy relationships, then studying the qualities of healthy relationships. The exercise concludes by offering actions to help clients form healthier relationships and prompting them to identify the steps to take during the following month. The exercise is suited for individual or group use, in session, or as homework. The quality of the therapeutic relationship should set the stage for exploring and modeling stable, safe relationships with healthy boundaries.

FORMING STABLE RELATIONSHIPS

Healthy relationships promote healthy living. Troubled relationships often trigger relapses. Safe and secure relationships support recovery in the face of other stressors. Forming stable relationships is a useful life skill. Do you keep finding yourself in painful relationships but don't know how to get it right?

1. Unhappy relationships can be like addictions to drugs or such behaviors as gambling, overworking, or overspending. Here are some traits of negative relationships. Please give an example of each if you've experienced it in your relationship history:

    a. *Rapid high-intensity involvement:* As with drugs, seeking instant gratification from intense experiences.

        Example: _____

    b. *Dishonesty, distrust, manipulation, and controlling behavior:* Trying to control the moods, thoughts, and behaviors of others; blaming them for our moods, thoughts, and behaviors. Hiding things or avoiding certain topics. "Mind-reading," assuming, and hinting instead of being open and direct.

        Example: _____

    c. *Desire for total union and social/emotional isolation:* Fearing losing our partners or feeling incomplete when apart. This leads to clinging and smothering. The result is not to have other close relationships. Resenting what friends and family say about these relationships.

        Example: _____

    d. *Desire to "fix" the other:* Seeing ourselves as rescuers, drawn to people with many problems. It distracts from problems and lets us feel generous, superior, and needed.

        Example: _____

2. Some of the traits of stable and positive relationships are listed here.

    a. *Gradual, step-by-step development:* It's wise to be cautious and not get too vulnerable, physically or emotionally, until you know it's safe. Relationships develop as safety and trust develop.

    b. *Honesty, trust, respect, and acceptance:* These partners don't try to control each other. They can ask for what they want instead of hinting or manipulating.

c. *Separateness, independence, and a full social life:* Healthy partners accept that they're separate people. They're together by choice, not because of need.

d. *Expectation that each will solve their own problems:* No rescuing! Each is supportive without taking on the other's responsibilities.

3. Here are some ways to begin the development of healthier relationships. How can you act on each one? These apply to all relationships, including friendships and intimate relationships.

a. *Work on yourself first:* We attract, and are attracted to, people who are as healthy and stable as we are. To attract healthy people, you have to be healthy yourself.

What is one thing I can do to improve myself? (i.e., anger management, emotional regulation):

_____

_____

b. *Be yourself:* To find a partner who accepts you as you are, you must let others see the real you. If you put on an act, no one has a chance to know and accept you. This requires both safety and vulnerability.

What can I do to be more vulnerable with and feel safe with people?

_____

_____

c. *Be selective:* You have the right to be treated well—don't settle for less or give less in return. Never get involved with someone out of pity or a sense of obligation.

What can I do to understand what I want and ask for it?

_____

_____

d. *Don't try to change people:* People don't change unless they choose to. You can't have a relationship with someone's potential, only with the person who exists now.

What can I do to accept what I can't change?

_____

_____

e. *Take your time:* Go step by step. Be cautious and check the other person out as you go. Increase your vulnerability and involvement slowly as you see that each step is safe.

What can I do to self-monitor?

_____

_____

f. *Get feedback:* Seek out someone you know who has good relationship skills and whose wisdom you trust.

What can I do/who can I talk to about this and how I can increase my acceptance of kind/constructive feedback from others?

_____

_____

g. *Listen to your gut:* Think about past relationship choices that went badly; think back to your inner voice or gut feelings at the time. Pay attention to any uneasy feelings.

What can I do to learn from my mistakes and trust myself?

_____

_____

4. Identify three challenges in relationship development and three ways it will positively benefit you and your recovery.

_____

_____

_____

Be sure to bring this handout back to your next session with your therapist and be prepared to talk about your thoughts and feelings about the exercise.

SEEING THAT WE'RE ALL JUST HUMAN

GOALS OF THE EXERCISE

1. Develop a program of recovery from addiction that increases abilities to tolerate ambiguity and regulate emotional intensity without self-destructive behaviors.
2. Replace all-or-nothing thinking, unmanaged anger, and fear of abandonment with undistorted perceptions about relationships.
3. Learn that fear, anxiety, and self-doubt are normal and universal human emotions.
4. Increase identification with both strengths and weaknesses of other people.
5. Correct distortions in self-perception.

ADDITIONAL PROBLEMS FOR WHICH THIS EXERCISE MAY BE USEFUL

- Adult-Child-of-an-Alcoholic (ACA) Traits
- Anger
- Dependent Traits
- Narcissistic Traits
- Partner Relational Conflicts
- Self-Harm
- Social Anxiety
- Substance Use Disorders

SUGGESTIONS FOR PROCESSING THIS EXERCISE WITH THE CLIENT

The "Seeing That We're All Just Human" activity is aimed at clients whose exaggerated perceptions of differences between themselves and others, devaluing themselves and idealizing others, or vice versa interfere with empathy, relationships, and a healthy self-image. It addresses either/or, good/bad thinking, and judgment of self and others by guiding clients to see both others and themselves as a mixture of strengths and areas to learn/grow and to identify ways in which relationships offer complementary strengths and mutual learning. This exercise is suitable for individual or group use, in session, or as homework. Follow-up can include keeping a journal on this topic and reporting to the therapist and group on insights and outcomes. Both skills-based and insight-oriented strategies can be incorporated into treatment depending on ability and capacity. Consider using in conjunction with exercises that increase skill building in assertive communication, managing anger reactions, improve self-worth, control impulsive behavior, increase compassionate self-talk, and identify benefits of strength- and value-based behaviors.

SEEING THAT WE'RE ALL JUST HUMAN

Many people working on recovery feel they're uniquely flawed, with weaknesses and problems no one else can understand. But they may also feel they're special in ways that others aren't (smarter, stronger, more sensitive, more talented). Either way, these beliefs interfere with recovery and get in the way of forming healthy friendships that will help healing and growth.

1. If you sometimes feel that you are too different from others for them to accept and understand you, or for you to be comfortable becoming close to them, identify three of those differences.

    _____

    _____

2. In 12-step and other support programs, you may hear cautions against "comparing your insides with other people's outsides." What does this phrase mean to you? Provide an example where this caused difficulties.

    _____

    _____

3. The way most people use "comparing your insides with other people's outsides" means thinking, "I must be crazy, sick, or weak, because other people appear to have it all together, while I feel confused, anxious, scared, or overwhelmed." If you've felt this way, describe a relationship in which you experienced this. How did it affect you?

    _____

    _____

4. Feeling confused, anxious, fearful, and overwhelmed are normal emotions that every person feels at times. Describe a situation in which you felt that you coped with substances, self-injury, isolation, or some other self-destructive behavior.

    _____

    _____

5. Think about a person you respect and admire. What do you respect and admire about them specifically? Imagine that they may have experienced similar feelings of confusion, anxiety, or fear. How would you benefit from feeling similarly about yourself to the way you feel about the person you admire?

_____
_____

6. What five strengths or personal qualities do you value most?

_____
_____
_____
_____

7. For the five qualities you listed, please give an example of a time you've shown each in something you've done:

_____
_____
_____
_____

8. Describe a time where you felt validated, appreciated, or sought out for something you could positively contribute to.

_____
_____

9. What opportunities or experiences have you avoided because you didn't feel worthy?

_____
_____

10. Identify two activities that would support your strengths and put you in more contact with people who could both be helped by you and be a help to you?

_____
_____

11. Who do you know that could assist you in beginning to focus more on your strengths? Describe what you might say to ask for assistance in this area.

_____
_____

12. What can you do daily to focus more on your strengths and address uncomfortable feelings without self-destructive behaviors?

_____

_____

Be sure to bring this handout back to your next session with your therapist and be prepared to talk about your thoughts and feelings about the exercise.

CORRESPONDING WITH MY CHILDHOOD SELF

GOALS OF THE EXERCISE

1. Learn how childhood trauma can result in interpersonal problems and addiction.
2. Reduce fear, anger, and depression and increase self-esteem and confidence.
3. Overcome denial, minimization, and intellectualization of the effects of childhood trauma.
4. Reduce anxiety by reframing childhood perceptions of childhood situations using adult insights.
5. Overcome feelings of emotional isolation by providing a corrective experience.

ADDITIONAL PROBLEMS FOR WHICH THIS EXERCISE MAY BE USEFUL

*   Adult-Child-of-an-Alcoholic (ACA) Traits
*   Grief/Loss Unresolved
*   Parent–Child Relational Problem
*   Posttraumatic Stress Disorder (PTSD)
*   Self-Harm

SUGGESTIONS FOR PROCESSING THIS EXERCISE WITH THE CLIENT

The "Corresponding with My Childhood Self" activity is for clients who are stuck in modes of reaction formed in response to childhood trauma (e.g., denial, minimization, or intellectualization used to block painful feelings). It may be useful after incidents in which clients respond inappropriately to situations related to childhood trauma. Follow-up may include other therapeutic techniques for addressing unresolved trauma and/or learning and using healthy coping mechanisms. It will be important before assigning this activity or doing it within the therapy visit to have clients have strategies to address uncomfortable experiences. Clients should be allowed to engage in this activity on their time and terms. This may be more suited for those who have some time sober, have an engaged social support network, and are actively engaged in a therapeutic relationship. It will be important to assess ongoing for thoughts of nonsuicidal self-injury (NSSI), suicidal ideation, or ideation indicating relapse proneness.

CORRESPONDING WITH MY CHILDHOOD SELF

If you sometimes feel like a child pretending to be an adult, with a grown-up body but a child's feelings and reactions, it's important to know that most people feel this way at times.

If memories of hurtful things that happened in your childhood sometimes feel as fresh and painful as if they had just happened, you need to know that this is a common experience too. People who were traumatized as children often feel "stuck," unable to get over long-ago events. Many have relied on substances to cope, prolonging the healing process.

This exercise will help you get "unstuck" by understanding and beginning to resolve painful experiences that may still haunt you and help you use adult strengths to heal the pain of the child within you.

1. Think of a childhood experience that still bothers you, one you'd like to put to rest. If no one event stands out to you, you can think about a period of time, perhaps a difficult year.

2. Try to find a picture of yourself at the time of this event or period, or one taken within a year or so before or after. If you don't have a photo, you can still do the exercise; the picture may simply help you focus.

3. Set aside at least an hour for this exercise, without distractions, in a place where you have privacy and feel safe. You'll need some paper, a pen or pencil, and the picture you chose.

4. Draw a line down the center of a page to make two columns. Over the column on the left, write the first name your friends call you now. Over the right-hand column, write the name you went by as a child. If it's the same name, add your ages now and then for both columns.

5.   Focus on the photo. Think about what is going on in this child's world at the time of your life that you're remembering. What are they thinking and feeling? In the left-hand column, write the first thing you would say to this child if you had the chance to talk with them. Stop after a sentence or two.

6.   Now switch your pen or pencil to your opposite or weak hand—your left hand if you're right-handed or vice versa. Look at the photo: Recall what it felt like to be that child. Imagine having the adult you are now talking with you then, saying the things you wrote in the first column. As that child, what would your answer be? With your weak hand, write a reply in the right-hand column.

7.   Switch back to the left-hand column and your strong hand; write your adult's answer to what your child just said. Keep writing back and forth with your strong hand for your adult self and your weak hand for your child self. Don't worry about what words or feelings come out. Just write whatever comes to mind. This may feel awkward; that's normal too. Being a child often feels awkward, so using your opposite hand helps to get in touch with how it felt and may still feel at times. You can stop any time; there are no prefixed number of times to do this.

8.   Stop after half an hour. You may want to plan a time to continue the conversation. Now read through both columns and think about what you wrote. What would it have been like as a child to have an adult with whom you could talk this way? When you were writing for your child, how did it feel to have someone paying attention?

_____

_____

Take time to acknowledge the wisdom of your adult self that came from and despite the childhood experiences you had.

9.   What issues, needs, wishes, or desires that went unmet and are still unresolved could you meet for yourself now? If you are more aware of significant traumatic experiences or reactions, bookmark this and talk to your therapist about reasonable therapeutic next steps and a plan to address it.

_____

_____

10. Think about therapy, community support group meetings, spiritual mentorship, or family and friends. How could people support you in taking care of those needs, wishes, and desires?

_____

_____

Close any part of this activity with an awareness that abuse, neglect, and household dysfunction have profound impacts on kids and do persist into adulthood. It is vital to exercise self-compassion for both the child you were and the adult you are now. Before we can heal deep wounds, we need to put our present self in a position to address them by dealing with current problems. These feelings may come up throughout treatment and recovery; make a commitment to attend to them the best you can while keeping yourself safe in your recovery from substances, other addictive behaviors, and other mental health issues.

Be sure to bring this handout back to your next session with your therapist and be prepared to talk about your thoughts and feelings about the exercise.

SETTING AND MAINTAINING BOUNDARIES

GOALS OF THE EXERCISE

1. Learn how childhood trauma may have resulted in interpersonal problems and addictive behavior patterns.
2. Resolve past childhood/family issues leading to less fear, anger, and depression and greater self-esteem and confidence.
3. Gain an understanding of personal power to set boundaries for oneself and the right to protect oneself emotionally and physically.
4. Learn to find balance and flexibility regarding roles or boundaries in relationships.

ADDITIONAL PROBLEMS FOR WHICH THIS EXERCISE MAY BE USEFUL

- Adult-Child-of-an-Alcoholic (ACA) Traits
- Borderline Traits
- Dangerousness/Lethality
- Dependent Traits
- Family Conflicts
- Parent–Child Relational Problem
- Partner Relational Conflicts
- Peer Group Negativity
- Sexual Promiscuity
- Social Anxiety

SUGGESTIONS FOR PROCESSING THIS EXERCISE WITH THE CLIENT

The "Setting and Maintaining Boundaries" activity should be preceded by a discussion to ensure the client understands the concept of boundaries in relationships and to probe what they consider healthy, keeping cultural considerations in mind when examining norms and mores with the client. When a client has a clear, functional goal, this exercise is useful in conducting a relationship inventory and identifying areas for growth. Follow-up can include planning strategies for difficult situations described in work on this activity and sharing those plans with the therapist, treatment group, and program sponsor.

SETTING AND MAINTAINING BOUNDARIES

When we have healthy personal boundaries, we can accept positive people and actions in our lives and protect ourselves from those that are harmful. In trying to protect ourselves, we may have learned not to trust or allow anyone to get close emotionally. On the other hand, in our search for love and acceptance we may have made ourselves too vulnerable and let others hurt us too easily. Healthy boundaries let us choose whom to trust, how far to trust them, and what actions to accept from them. We also learn to respect the boundaries of others in what we do or say to them.

1. List some people with whom you have difficulty setting or maintaining healthy boundaries, along with situations where you have trouble with them and what the results have been.

Person	Situation	What Happens	How You Are Affected

2. If there are people, situations, or actions about which you can set and maintain healthy boundaries, please list them here.

Person	Situation	Action or Behavior

3. What are the reasons you can set and maintain boundaries with the people, situations, or actions on the second list, but not with those on the first list?

4. How can you use the same methods that work with the second list for the people, situations, or actions on the first list, or use other methods to get the same healthy results?

    _____

    _____

5. List five ways substance use/other addictive behaviors/untreated mental health issues have affected your ability to set and maintain boundaries for yourself and/or respect the boundaries of others (i.e., think of intimate relationships, family relationships, your relationship with your children, your friends, coworkers).

    _____

    _____

6. What changes would you like to make in your boundaries to help you live a more interpersonally satisfied life??

    _____

    _____

7. How might these changes affect your recovery efforts? Your self-esteem? Your overall emotional well-being?

    _____

    _____

8. What do you need to do to make these changes (e.g., increased confidence, more assertiveness, etc.)? Be as specific as you can.

    _____

    _____

9. What will you do if others resist accepting your boundaries?

    _____

    _____

10. In starting new relationships, it is important to share personal thoughts, feelings, and experiences in a graduated way to see if what you share is dealt with respectfully. As more trust develops, more personal and vulnerable information can be shared. Identify five experiences from less personal to more personal you could share with someone you are trying to get to know better. What are the indicators that may cue you that it would be safe to share more? Indicators that additional sharing is not warranted?

    _____

    _____

Be sure to bring this handout back to your next session with your therapist and be prepared to talk about your thoughts and feelings about the exercise.

COPING WITH ADDICTION AND CHRONIC PAIN

GOALS OF THE EXERCISE

1. Practice a program of recovery, including 12-step program participation and appropriate use of pain management skills.
2. If a pain management regimen includes continued use of potentially addictive medications, ensure the prescribing physician is aware of the client's history of addiction and has experience working with patients in recovery.
3. If a pain management regimen includes potentially addictive medications, ensure the client takes precautions against abuse, including keeping their 12-step sponsor informed of medication use and taking medications only, and exactly, as prescribed.
4. Develop healthy options to cope with chronic pain.
5. Reduce daily suffering from pain and substance abuse.
6. Acquire and utilize necessary pain management skills.

ADDITIONAL PROBLEMS FOR WHICH THIS EXERCISE MAY BE USEFUL

- Medical Issues
- Relapse Proneness
- Substance-Induced Disorders
- Substance Use Disorders

SUGGESTIONS FOR PROCESSING THIS EXERCISE WITH THE CLIENT

The "Coping with Addiction and Chronic Pain" activity is designed, as the title indicates, for clients who suffer from both addictions and severe and/or persistent pain. It addresses the perceived dilemma many clients face of reconciling participation in 12-step recovery programs with the need to use prescribed medications that have a high potential for addiction, as well as noting other sources of emotional and practical support. Follow-up can include referral to appropriate medical professionals and to one or more of the chronic pain support groups cited in the exercise. It is helpful for the psychotherapist to coordinate work on this issue with any other health care providers from whom the client is receiving services, after ensuring that you and the other providers have each received the client's consent to share treatment information. Additional referrals to support groups for those with similar conditions should be encouraged to reduce isolation and increase feelings of connection and understanding. Ongoing assessment of relapse potential and suicidal ideation is warranted.

COPING WITH ADDICTION AND CHRONIC PAIN

People with both addictions and severe or chronic pain face a dilemma: Doctors tend to treat pain using medications that carry the risk of addiction. Pain often led these patients to use addictive drugs in the first place. On the other hand, doctors may be reluctant to prescribe these meds for fear of patients getting addicted. How do you find relief from both addiction and pain? This activity will help you find solutions.

1. How does chronic pain affect your daily life? (Consider all areas, e.g., mood, recovery efforts, recreation, attitude, social connections, work/school, family/relationship roles, spirituality, self-esteem/self-worth, sexual health):

    _____

    _____

2. What tools do you utilize to address chronic pain or acute flare-ups?

    _____

    _____

3. Outside of medical treatment, how do you take care of other areas of physical and emotional health?

    _____

    _____

4. In what ways does your chronic pain condition potentially challenge a stable recovery plan?

    _____

    _____

5. Do your medical providers have specialized knowledge in pain management and addictions? If not, can they refer you to a pain management specialist? As part of this exercise, please check on this and let your therapist know. Also, have you talked with them about your addiction history? If not, what keeps you from sharing that information?

    _____

    _____

6. Research has found that even drugs that are normally addictive don't lead to physical addiction if a patient takes no more than needed, for no longer than needed, to control severe pain. If you and your doctor plan to manage your pain this way, what is your plan to avoid taking more than you need and to stop taking these medications (say, by switching to something safer and not so strong) as soon as appropriate, to avoid getting addicted?

    _____

    _____

7. Many people struggling with addiction find that when they use narcotics or equivalent drugs, even if they don't abuse those drugs, their judgment and inhibitions are affected, and they relapse into drinking or using other drugs. How will you avoid falling into this trap? What thoughts, feelings, and behaviors will you need to monitor?

    _____

    _____

8. Medical professionals have a central part to play in pain treatment, but other people also play key roles in helping you manage the situation (e.g., your sponsor if you're in a recovery program, family, and friends). How can they help you avoid falling into addictive thinking and behaviors when you're using potentially habit-forming drugs to manage your pain?

    _____

    _____

9. If you are participating in a 12-step program, what is your program's philosophy about the use of prescribed medications?

    _____

    _____

10. In addition to 12-step or other recovery programs focusing on addictions, you may find help from support groups for chronic pain sufferers. These include local organizations, which you may find via local media (many newspapers publish lists of support groups of all kinds). You may also want to investigate the following online groups:

    a. American Chronic Pain Association: www.theacpa.org

    b. National Pain Advocacy Center: nationalpain.org

    c. Others you or your treatment providers know/recommend:

    _____

    _____

11. If not, please explore the websites listed and talk with your therapist about what you learn. Identify how you can incorporate them into a recovery/treatment plan and the benefits to you.

_____

_____

12. At times people feel discouraged by having two chronic conditions and can have negative thoughts about their lives (e.g., "my life is limited," "what's the point in trying?" etc.). These thoughts can lead to relapse and/or depression, hopelessness, and most seriously, suicidal thinking. What ways will you challenge these thoughts and beliefs, and what pleasurable activities will you engage in to live your most meaningful life?

_____

_____

Be sure to bring this handout back to your next session with your therapist and be prepared to talk about your thoughts and feelings about the exercise.

MANAGING PAIN WITHOUT ADDICTIVE DRUGS

GOALS OF THE EXERCISE

1. Practice a recovery program, including 12-step program participation and learning necessary pain management skills.
2. Regulate pain without addictive medications or substances of abuse.
3. Develop healthy options to cope with chronic pain.
4. Reduce daily suffering from pain and substance abuse.
5. Achieve improved quality of life with relief from pain and build renewed contentment and joy in performing activities of life.

ADDITIONAL PROBLEMS FOR WHICH THIS EXERCISE MAY BE USEFUL

- Medical Issues
- Posttraumatic Stress Disorder (PTSD)
- Self-Harm
- Substance Intoxication/Withdrawal
- Substance Use Disorders

SUGGESTIONS FOR PROCESSING THIS EXERCISE WITH THE CLIENT

The "Managing Pain Without Addictive Drugs" activity is intended for clients who are suffering from severe and/or chronic pain but who cannot use potentially addictive pain medications. The exercise offers several alternative approaches to managing pain and restoring quality of life without running the risk of relapse, which may accompany either use of traditional pain medications or trying to "gut it out" and cope with pain through willpower, risking relapse. Follow-up may include assignments to investigate local service providers or support groups, as well as investigation of online resources, including the support groups identified in the handout. Concurrently, clients should be assessed for emotional reactions to chronic pain and behaviors they engage in to address them, including depression, helplessness, burdensomeness, hopelessness, irritability, anger, isolation, self-harm, and suicidality.

MANAGING PAIN WITHOUT ADDICTIVE DRUGS

If you suffer from severe or chronic pain and need to manage it without addictive pain medications, this exercise will help you find ways to do so. Chronic pain tends to command full attention. It is important to note that our physical health is intimately tied to our emotional, relationship, and spiritual health. Any condition that taxes our bodies and potentially affects our quality of life must be monitored and treated so a quality of life is nurtured and restored.

1. How does the chronic pain you experience affect your daily life?

    _____

    _____

2. What have you shared about your addiction with the professionals who treat your chronic pain? If you have not shared, what are the benefits of doing so, and how will you do this?

    _____

    _____

3. What methods of pain management other than medications have you tried, and how have they worked?

    _____

    _____

4. There are many nonaddictive ways of managing pain. Please talk with your doctor and your therapist about each of the ones listed here and find out what opportunities exist in your community for you to try. Briefly write about what you find in the space at the end of this exercise.

    a. *Over-the-counter (OTC) pain medications.* These are mild pain-relieving drugs with no mind-altering effects. If you use these medications, be careful not to exceed safe dosages.

    b. *Other non-mind-altering medications.* This category includes drugs such as glucosamine chondroitin and MSM, which help the body rebuild damaged tissues.

c. *Topical (external) medications.* These ointments relieve pain from musculoskeletal problems such as arthritis and joint injuries. They include pain-relieving ingredients, and some also have ingredients that reduce swelling and soreness. Some contain steroid compounds. Talk to your doctor about using these drugs.

d. *Diet modifications.* Sometimes pain is caused by unhealthy elements or deficiencies in a person's diet. Other problems may be caused by food allergies. You may choose to work with a registered dietician or nutritionist.

e. *Acupuncture.* Acupuncture has been proven to give fast and effective pain relief in many cases.

f. *Therapeutic massage.* This is another technique that, provided by trained professionals, can give quick and lasting relief for many cases of chronic musculoskeletal pain.

g. *Hypnosis.* This treatment is very effective for many people.

h. *Meditation.* Many pain sufferers find that meditation using mindfulness or guided imagery can help them detach from their pain. Soothing music can increase the effectiveness of meditation.

i. *Moderate cardiovascular exercise.* Before starting an exercise program, talk with your doctor to ensure that it's safe, and ask how to get the most benefit from your workouts.

j. *Stretching and progressive muscle relaxation.* The key here is to avoid pushing the stretch itself too far, causing pain or injury. As with exercise, get your doctor's guidance first.

k. *Laughter.* Hearty laughter boosts levels of the same neurotransmitters as cardiovascular exercise, relieving pain and emotional distress. Laughter also strengthens your immune system.

l. *Pet therapy.* Spending time with an affectionate animal also provides some relief from physical and emotional distress. Hospitals often include pet therapy in treatment.

m. *Spiritual and/or religious activity.* Prayer and the company of others who share our beliefs can reduce the isolation that often comes with pain and help make sense of an experience that seems senseless. The emphasis on forming a relationship with a higher power of one's own understanding makes this a good fit for using a 12-step program.

n. *Participation in pain management support groups.* You may get useful advice and support from groups for chronic pain sufferers, which you can find through newspapers or magazines or at local hospitals. You can find several pain management groups online.

5. Please use this space to briefly describe your plan for coping with your chronic pain using nonaddictive methods. Include what you already have in place, identifying any gaps and areas for more consideration and research.

    _____

    _____

6. You are more than your chronic pain or health condition. At times it seems to take center stage due to necessary treatments, physical discomfort, etc. However, there are benefits to reducing our preoccupation with chronic pain and focusing on engaging in our life despite it. Additional areas to explore outside those identified in question 1: helping others, gratitude/spiritual/faith practice, engaging with others that are important to us, identifying what we can do versus what we can't, etc. Write about how this makes you feel and what might be some considerations for further exploration.

    _____

    _____

7. When feeling discouraged, I can commit to saying this to myself:

    _____

    _____

    When feeling discouraged, I can commit to doing this to support my recovery:

    _____

    _____

    When feeling discouraged, I can commit to engaging in this to shift my mindset:

    _____

    _____

Be sure to bring this handout back to your next therapy session and be prepared to talk about your thoughts and feelings about the exercise.

HOW DO YOU DO THAT?

GOALS OF THE EXERCISE

1. Comply with rules and expectations in the home, school, and community consistently.
2. Eliminate all illegal and antisocial behavior.
3. Terminate acts of violence or cruelty toward people or animals and stop destruction of property.
4. Demonstrate marked improvement in impulse control.
5. Express anger in a controlled, respectful manner on a consistent basis.
6. Resolve the core conflicts that contribute to the emergence of conduct problems.
7. Demonstrate empathy, concern, and sensitivity for the thoughts, feelings, and needs of others on a regular basis.

ADDITIONAL PROBLEMS FOR WHICH THIS EXERCISE MAY BE USEFUL

- Anger
- Antisocial Behavior
- Attention-Deficit/Hyperactivity Disorder (ADHD)—Adult
- Dangerousness/Lethality
- Impulsivity
- Legal Problems
- Oppositional Defiant Behavior
- Self-Harm

SUGGESTIONS FOR PROCESSING THIS EXERCISE WITH THE CLIENT

The "How Do You Do That?" activity is designed for the client who has a pattern of aggression or indifference toward social norms and the rights and well-being of others. It can also be used with clients who have problems with impulse control and recklessness, resulting in legal, financial, occupational, and/or family/marital problems. Follow-up can consist of presenting the client's completed exercise in individual, family, or group therapy to consistently review and reinforce gains that result from recovery, attitude, mental health, coping, behavior changes.

HOW DO YOU DO THAT?

We've all done things we've regretted. We can't stop having negative emotions and impulses—they're part of being human—but we can avoid sabotaging our own brains by abusing alcohol or other drugs. This is a choice we have to make in advance. When we find ourselves in tough situations, by then it's too late to decide it's a bad time to be impaired by substances. And we can change our thinking, which takes equal effort as giving up substance abusing/addictive behaviors.

People who need their bodies fit for challenging events have to prepare in advance by working out and eating right and having the right tools and mindset. We also need a kind of mental fitness to resist letting our emotions and impulses choose our actions for us. This activity will help you build an effective mental "fitness" plan.

1. You may know people who have a hard time staying out of trouble. Think of two people with this pattern. Try to see any patterns that exist in their actions that get them in legal, financial, relationship, or other trouble, including relapses into substance abuse or other addictive patterns. What do those actions of theirs have in common?

   _____

   _____

2. Now think of a couple of people who never seem to get in those kinds of jams. What do they do differently?

   _____

   _____

3. Your answer may have been something like, "They just don't do ___," which leads into another question: "How do they not do ____?" At first it may seem they just use will-power, but that's not enough. Many people who want to stay out of trouble, but don't, have achieved things in other parts of their lives that they could never have done without tremendous willpower. So, what else is different between the actions of people who get in trouble and those who don't?

   _____

   _____

4. One way to change behaviors that bring you unwanted consequences is to think about how what you do affects other people, and how they'll feel about you and treat

you as a result. You can ask one or two people you trust to help by watching you, signaling you if you're starting to do something that will cause trouble, and giving you some recognition when you show more thoughtfulness of others. That applies here, but we want to give you another tool called *mental rehearsal*.

Mental rehearsal means that before you take an action, you stop for a moment, take a slow and meaningful breath, and picture yourself doing it, then picture what would happen as a result. For example, you might feel like telling your boss that they are an idiot. Then you would picture the result, which might be you getting fired. What behavior that resulted in a negative consequence can you reimagine?

_____

_____

5. For many, it's very hard to stop and think when we're upset. Comparing mental fitness to physical fitness again, stopping and thinking when emotions run high, or controlling strong impulses, is like bench-pressing your own weight. No athlete can do that on their first day in the gym. What behavior do you struggle with that gets you in more trouble than it's worth? Imagine two alternatives to get a different, more positive result and write them here:

_____

_____

6. How can you increase your strength, stamina, and performance, starting with something easier and working up to something more challenging?

_____

_____

7. Here's a way that works for many people. To start with easier things, think about the results of choices that don't bring up strong feelings for you—little things that don't matter much. Try it with parts of your daily routine, like what to eat for breakfast, what movie to go see, what time to go to bed. The key is thinking about choices instead of acting without considering what will happen next. As for the practice part, try to stop at least 10 times a day before you choose an action and think about the results. Keep a little notebook handy and write these choices down as you make them. It may feel silly, but this builds the habit of prethinking. As you keep doing this with more and bigger decisions, it will become more automatic, until you're the one other people ask, "How do you. do that?" What do you think about this idea, and what small decisions will you start with?

_____

_____

Be sure to bring this handout and your notebook entries to your therapy sessions, and be prepared to discuss any questions, thoughts, and feelings you may have had in completing it.

TRADING PLACES

GOALS OF THIS EXERCISE

1. Comply consistently with rules and expectations in the home, school, and community.
2. Eliminate all illegal and antisocial behavior.
3. Terminate acts of violence or cruelty toward people or animals and stop destruction of property.
4. Demonstrate marked improvement in impulse control.
5. Express anger in a controlled, respectful manner on a consistent basis.
6. Resolve the core conflicts that contribute to the emergence of conduct problems.
7. Demonstrate empathy, concern, and sensitivity for the thoughts, feelings, and needs of others on a regular basis.

ADDITIONAL PROBLEMS FOR WHICH THIS EXERCISE MAY BE USEFUL

- Anger
- Antisocial Behavior
- Attention-Deficit/Hyperactivity Disorder (ADHD)—Adolescent
- Attention-Deficit/Hyperactivity Disorder (ADHD)—Adult
- Dangerousness/Lethality
- Impulsivity
- Legal Problems
- Narcissistic Traits
- Oppositional Defiant Behavior
- Self-Harm

SUGGESTIONS FOR PROCESSING THIS EXERCISE WITH THE CLIENT

The "Trading Places" activity is designed for clients who have a pattern of aggression or indifference toward social norms and the rights and well-being of others. It can also be used with clients who have problems with impulse control and recklessness that affect others in their lives, resulting in legal, financial, occupational, and/or family/marital problems. Before giving this homework assignment, the clinician should discuss it with the client and carry out the cognitive/role-playing practice described in item 10. Follow-up can consist of having the client describe, in individual, family, or group therapy, examples of their use of the technique outside of the therapeutic setting and the results. Assignment of the activity "How Do You Do That?" (Exercise 11.A) is also a useful follow-up.

TRADING PLACES

We've all been hurt or offended by things other people did: cutting us off in traffic, making harsh remarks, taking or destroying our possessions, breaking promises. We can list many hurtful and offensive things people have done to us. However, there is another way to look at this.

A member of a recovery program met with his sponsor. The sponsor saw that he was upset and asked why. The person said he was angry about something a friend had done to him. The sponsor replied, "I don't think he did that to you. Probably, no one's ever done anything to you." The sponsee began to argue, but the sponsor went on, "Have you ever been so focused on doing something or getting something you wanted or felt you needed very much that you ran roughshod over someone else while you were trying to get what you wanted? Was your motive to hurt them?"

The sponsee answered, "No, I just wasn't thinking about that."

The sponsor concluded, "We're all that way. Most of the time, people aren't doing what they do *to us*, they're doing it *for themselves*, and we happen to be in the way. Even some people's hostile, abusive actions are more about making themselves feel stronger, smarter, etc., than hurting us. They'd do the same things to anyone who happened to be in their path. There are two things to learn here. First is to not take others' actions personally. Second is to build a habit of asking ourselves how our actions will affect others and whether we'd want to be affected that way."

This activity will help you explore whether it benefits you to practice thinking this way and building the habit of putting yourself in the place of others whom your actions will affect.

1. Please name a time when someone did something that hurt you and write why you believe they did it.

   _____

   _____

2. Now describe a time when you did something that hurt someone and explain why you did what you did.

   _____

   _____

3. As a result, in both situations, what did the person who was hurt think of the one who hurt them?

_____

_____

4. In the situation you thought of for question 2, would you have acted differently if you'd thought first about how your actions would affect someone else? If so, what would you have done instead?

_____

_____

5. If you had taken the different action you described, how would it change the way someone else thinks about you?

_____

_____

6. Please briefly describe how you would like to have others see you—what qualities and strengths would you like to have others see in you?

_____

_____

7. In addition to having a different outcome related to how others experience us, it has a profound impact on who we feel and think about ourselves. Would taking the action you described in question 4 change the way you see yourself and feel about yourself? If so, how?

_____

_____

8. Please list a few pros and cons of following your impulses without worrying about how others feel or are affected, then do the same for thinking about these things before deciding what to do:

Acting without worrying about effect on others	*Thinking about effect on others before acting*
_____	_____
_____	_____
_____	_____

9. If these pros and cons make it seem that thinking of others might improve your quality of life, identify an actionable item you could commit to be more deliberate in your actions.

_____

_____

10. Here's a method that works for a lot of people, called *trading places*. It's a good idea to practice first in a session with your therapist.

To begin, describe a time when you hurt someone unintentionally with an action you took to get what you wanted. Once you've described it, mentally trade places with that person—tell how you think they were affected and how they felt. Next, think about how you'd feel in their place. Finally, get feedback from your therapist about how they think someone might feel if you did to them what you described.

Now think of what else you might have done if you'd thought about your action's impact on someone else and put yourself in their place and describe that. Now describe how you'd feel and be affected if someone in your life took the action you thought of this time and get another person's thoughts about how they believe a person would feel as a result of that action.

To continue, talk with one or two friends or relatives you trust, explain that you're trying to build the habit of thinking of others before you act, and ask them to keep an eye on you and let you know how they see your actions changing. You could think of an inconspicuous signal for them to give you if they see you starting to slip up and act without thinking how you're affecting others. They should also let you know what positive changes they see and congratulate you for the work you're doing. You'll probably also see results in more people liking and respecting you in general.

11. After a week, identify three ways this has gone well and its impact on you. Also name three ways you've been challenged and how you handled them. What ways does making improvements in this area help you in your recovery process?

_____

_____

Be sure to bring this handout to your next therapy session, and be prepared to discuss questions, thoughts, and feelings you may have had in completing it.

ANGER AS A DRUG

GOALS OF THE EXERCISE

1. Maintain a program of recovery that is free of addiction and violent behavior.
2. Decrease the frequency of occurrence of angry thoughts, feelings, and behaviors.
3. Think positively in anger-producing situations.
4. Learn and implement stress-management skills to reduce stress and irritability.
5. Learn to self-monitor and shift to a thinking and problem-solving mode rather than a reactive mode when anger is triggered.
6. Shift from viewing anger as something beyond control to a view of anger, particularly rage, as a chosen way of coping that can be changed.

ADDITIONAL PROBLEMS FOR WHICH THIS EXERCISE MAY BE USEFUL

- Anger
- Antisocial Behavior
- Conduct Disorder/Delinquency
- Impulsivity
- Oppositional Defiant Behavior

SUGGESTIONS FOR PROCESSING THIS EXERCISE WITH THE CLIENT

The "Anger as a Drug" activity may be especially useful with angry clients who have also engaged in non-substance-abusing addictive behaviors. It is suggested for use with clients who have some insight into their own feelings or who are willing to be introspective. Follow-up can include coping skills training in communication, relaxation, conflict resolution, and problem solving to provide alternative behaviors. Self-monitoring of angry thoughts, feelings, and behaviors should be ongoing. An additional benefit would be obtained in teaching clients about identifying, challenging, and replacing thoughts and learning how anger is a relapse concern if it is not managed better. Teaching them basic diaphragmatic breathing before working through this exercise and having the practice throughout would be beneficial.

ANGER AS A DRUG

Does it seem strange to call anger a drug? We usually think of drugs as chemicals, like alcohol, cannabis, cocaine, and heroin. We talk about being addicted to a drug if we keep using it when the consequences are more negative than positive, but we find it hard to quit. People also behave addictively with activities like gambling, sex, eating, spending, work, and with some emotions. Addictive activities and emotions can cause as much trouble as any substance.

What do these things have in common? They can change the way we feel, quickly, on demand. Physically and emotionally, we can use them to block pain or to feel great. We can become addicted to anything that makes us feel good quickly and easily.

Anger can feel good. If we're anxious or depressed, we may feel weak, uneasy, and ashamed. When we get angry, we feel strong and sure of ourselves. Anger also makes us feel more alert, awake, and energetic. So, we may use anger to cope with uncomfortable feelings. Fear, anxiety, or shame can trigger anger so fast we may not realize what else we are feeling.

Like other drugs, anger has negative consequences. It leads to destructive actions. In this exercise, you'll look at your anger to see if you've used it as a drug and to find better ways to handle painful feelings.

1. List 10 negative consequences that have resulted from your anger.

    _____

    _____

    _____

    _____

    _____

    _____

    _____

    _____

    _____

    _____

2. When you've been very angry or in a rage, have you felt weak or strong? Uneasy or sure of yourself? How does anger feel to you?

_____

_____

3. In what ways have you used anger to avoid or escape negative feelings like hurt, shame, inadequacy, anxiety, and depression?

_____

4. In what ways have you justified your angry reactions? Give examples of justifications you've made to yourself and to others.

_____

_____

5. Think about a recent time you got very angry. Start at the "eruption" and work backward. Trace it backward to the triggering event, situation, or feeling. What were you thinking and feeling before you recognized feeling rage? Did your feelings change over time? Can you recognize if you attempted to say to yourself or do anything to calm down? Write about each of them here:

_____

6. Another characteristic of many drugs is a rebound effect when they wear off. You may have found that when the anger wore off, painful emotions returned or you felt extra guilt, regret, shame. What rebound effects have followed your anger?

_____

_____

7. The next time painful emotions start to trigger your rage, what early signs will you look for, and how can you redirect that reaction to something else that gives you better results?

Cues (in your body, thoughts, sensations)

_____

_____

Before you have access to problem solving and logical parts of your brain, you have to calm down. At the first signs of those cues, what can you do to calm down?

_____

_____

8. There are several situations and circumstances where anger is appropriate, and it is a normal and appropriate feeling. Identify a plan to manage, express, and tolerate without escalation. A solid preparedness plan is key to not resorting to out-of-control behavior or substance use. When I feel anger, I will

    a. tell myself

    _____

    _____

    b. distract myself with

    _____

    _____

    c. call

    _____

    _____

    d. calm myself by:

    _____

    _____

9. If other people can help, what can they do? List two people who can help and describe when and what you would like their help with.

    _____

    _____

Be sure to bring this handout back to your next session with your therapist and be prepared to talk about your thoughts and feelings about the exercise.

MANAGING RISK

GOALS OF THE EXERCISE

1. Develop a program of recovery free of addictive patterns and dangerous/lethal behaviors.
2. Terminate all acts that are dangerous to self and/or others.
3. Increase insight into the core motivations that lead to dangerous/lethal behaviors.
4. Recognize the benefits of respect and detriments of fear from others.
5. Increase self-esteem and self-respect.

ADDITIONAL PROBLEMS FOR WHICH THIS EXERCISE MAY BE USEFUL

- Anger
- Antisocial Behavior
- Impulsivity
- Oppositional Defiant Behavior
- Partner Relational Conflicts
- Posttraumatic Stress Disorder (PTSD)

SUGGESTIONS FOR PROCESSING THIS EXERCISE WITH THE CLIENT

The "Managing Risk" activity is designed for the client who has exhibited dangerous behavior that appears to have the aim or effect of intimidating others as a frequent or primary way of relating to those others. It asks clients to look at their own dangerous behavior and inquire about their desire to relate to others in ways that are more beneficial. Follow-up can include processing the exercise with the therapist or group, guided experimentation with behavioral changes suggested by the content of the exercise, and the assignments titled "Anger as a Drug" (Exercise 12.A) and "Is My Anger Due to Feeling Threatened?" (Exercise 2.A).

MANAGING RISK

Addictive behaviors often include risking serious trouble or danger without regard for whether it hurts us or others. The challenge is that in sobriety we may continue to take significant risks, interact with people in ways that lead them to fear us (e.g., being quick to anger, unpredictable, and threatening, engaging in violent outbursts when angry, etc.), or use others' fear to get our way. The other side is that when people fear us, they don't respect us. Wanting the respect of others, especially those important to us, is healthy. Feeling respected is important for self-esteem, and healthy esteem is important for sustained recovery. This exercise will help you look at ways addictive or dangerous behaviors have affected your life and begin to look at alternatives.

1. List five dangerous behaviors associated with your substance abuse.

   _____

   _____

   _____

   _____

   _____

2. What are the negative consequences of engaging in behaviors that are dangerous to yourself and others?

   _____

   _____

3. How has anger/threats altered feelings you didn't want to feel? Which ones can you identify?

   _____

   _____

4. How have others responded to your dangerous behaviors?

   _____

   _____

5. One way engaging in dangerous behavior affects us negatively is that people fear us rather than respect us, and then we feel discouraged and isolated. Describe your experience of this reaction.

_____

_____

6. Let's analyze what it means to fear other people. This differs from respect. Describe personal examples of the qualities described.

   a. When people fear someone, they feel tense and unsafe around them; they are cautious and don't relax around that person, and they may try to avoid being around them. Give a personal example:

   _____

   b. When a person is feared, others don't trust them to treat them appropriately or feel that they respect or care about them. Example:

   _____

   c. If we fear a person, we may try to keep our children or others away from that person. Example:

   _____

7. If you would rather be respected than feared, resulting in better relationships and feeling better about yourself, you must consistently practice behaviors that earn respect and not fear. Please think of a way you can do each of these behaviors in your daily life.

   a. How can I be honest and dependable?

   _____

   b. How can I be kind, generous, and considerate?

   _____

   c. How can I think about other people's feelings and dignity and treat them with care?

   _____

   d. How can I control my words and actions even when I'm angry?

   _____

8. You may find yourself around dangerous people and think you need to be feared to be safe; you may have grown up with relationships that were based on fear. Some points to consider:

   _____

a. People who are feared are lonely. Your loved ones, friends, and others will be more willing to maintain close and supportive relationships if they respect you rather than fear you.

b. If your loved ones need help with a problem, they're much more likely to let you know if they trust you and aren't afraid of you.

c. Your children will probably follow your example in how they deal with people. They will have much happier lives if you teach them to be the kind of people others respect.

9. What positive impact do you hope to experience by eliminating dangerous behavior?

_____

_____

10. What initial steps can you take in terminating behaviors dangerous toward yourself or others? Name five alternative coping strategies you can try.

_____

_____

_____

Don't be discouraged if you slip back into old patterns under stress. Make amends to anyone you've hurt, learn what lessons you can, and keep working on it. If you're active in a 12-step program, use the steps on this, because they work.

Be sure to bring this handout with you to your next individual and/or group session and be prepared to discuss your thoughts, feelings, and questions about the exercise.

BUILDING MY SUPPORT NETWORK

GOALS OF THE EXERCISE

1. Demonstrate increased interdependence and self-confidence through autonomous decision making, honest expression of feelings and ideas, and reduced fear of rejection.
2. Demonstrate healthy communication that is honest, open, and self-disclosing.
3. Identify and get help from supportive others at home, work, and in other settings.
4. Reduce feelings of alienation by learning about similarities to others.
5. Engage in a program of recovery, to reduce the impact of dependent traits on self and an addictive lifestyle.

ADDITIONAL PROBLEMS FOR WHICH THIS EXERCISE MAY BE USEFUL

- Adult-Child-of-an-Alcoholic (ACA) Traits
- Chronic Pain
- Depression–Unipolar
- Grief/Loss Unresolved
- Living Environment Deficiency
- Medical Issues
- Peer Group Negativity
- Posttraumatic Stress Disorder (PTSD)
- Relapse Proneness
- Self-Care Deficits—Primary
- Self-Care Deficits—Secondary
- Social Anxiety
- Substance Use Disorders
- Suicidal Ideation

SUGGESTIONS FOR PROCESSING THIS EXERCISE WITH THE CLIENT

The "Building My Support Network" activity is intended for clients who are socially and emotionally isolated, or who have formed unhealthy dependent relationships with other people. It works by guiding the client to see interdependence as normal and desirable and to reflect on the positive effects for both helper and "helpee." The exercise goes on to lead the client to make concrete plans to break out of isolation and seek help and support from a network of others in a healthy way.

BUILDING MY SUPPORT NETWORK

When people are actively abusing alcohol or other drugs, or engaging in other addictive behaviors, they often isolate themselves. Reversing that trait is an important part of recovery. Most people who succeed in achieving long-term abstinence do so with the help of others.

1. When people enter a treatment program or therapy for addiction, they may have great difficulty asking anyone for information or help. Name some situations that you needed support or help but didn't reach out. What kept you from asking for help? What was the outcome of these situations?

    _____

    _____

2. If you meet others who are new to a task in which you have knowledge and experience, how do you respond if they ask you for help or advice?

    _____

    _____

3. Write about how you feel and what you think when you observe others in treatment or recovery getting help and support from other people in recovery specifically when they feel stuck and need help.

    _____

    _____

4. What are some areas where you could use information, support, and feedback?

    _____

    _____

5. Who knows a lot about these areas? List some people who you think might be helpful to you by name in each of the following categories.

Categories	Names
Family members	
Friends	
Coworkers	
Support group members	
Mental health professionals	
Clergy or spiritual advisors	
Medical professionals	

6. Think about how you might ask each of these people for help and support in your recovery. You will probably want to communicate these things:

   a. What you are trying to do to stay clean and sober and change your life.

   b. What goals you have set. These can be things like staying sober for a year, working the 12 steps, finding six new activities to replace drinking and using, being more assertive or self-compassionate, and so on.

   c. What challenges you are currently having.

   d. How you feel these people can help you achieve your goals and help solve your problems (don't ask them to do it for you unless it's a special problem and that's their job).

   e. Why you chose them to ask for help.

7. When you have identified people who will help you work on your recovery, the next step is to establish a routine with each of them, because most of us are so busy that we fail to get around to things unless they are scheduled, or our avoidance keeps us from doing it. For example, you might meet with a therapist at a set time each week; have family dinners on certain nights; call a friend at about the same time each weekend; go to a particular meeting daily or weekly; or have lunch with a sponsor regularly. For each person you named earlier, when will you meet or talk with them?

   Name   **When/where/how I will connect with them**

   _____   _____

   _____   _____

8. It can also be an important part of your recovery work to help others in whatever way you can. For example, you might volunteer a few hours a week to do some sort of service work. If you belong to a 12-step group, you can volunteer for chores such as making coffee, setting up furniture, cleaning up after meetings, and so on. What

service work will you include in your recovery program, and when and where will you do it?

Service Task	For Whom	Time	Place
_____	_____	_____	_____
_____	_____	_____	_____
_____	_____	_____	_____
_____	_____	_____	_____

Be sure to bring this handout back to your next session with your therapist and be prepared to talk about your thoughts and feelings about the exercise.

HOW INTERDEPENDENT AM I?

GOALS OF THE EXERCISE

1. Demonstrate increased independence and self-confidence through autonomous decision making, honest expression of feelings and ideas, and reduced fear of rejection.
2. Gain an understanding of what is a healthy and realistic degree of independence.
3. Analyze the client's areas of independence, potential independence, and need to depend on others to get their needs met.
4. Decrease the client's dependence on relationships while they begin to meet their own needs, build confidence, and practice assertiveness.

ADDITIONAL PROBLEMS FOR WHICH THIS EXERCISE MAY BE USEFUL

- Living Environment Deficiency
- Self-Care Deficits—Primary
- Self-Care Deficits—Secondary

SUGGESTIONS FOR PROCESSING THIS EXERCISE WITH THE CLIENT

The "How Interdependent Am I?" activity is for clients with boundary issues and a pattern of being overly dependent on others. It guides clients in examining what an appropriate degree of independence looks like, and then in making an inventory of things that they do independently, things that could be done interdependently with others, and things for which they must go on depending on others. It concludes by guiding the client in the creation of a plan to increase autonomy. Follow-up can include keeping a journal and sharing outcomes with the therapist and treatment group.

HOW INTERDEPENDENT AM I?

What do the terms *independence* and *interdependence* mean to you, and how interdependent should you be? American culture tends to teach us unrealistic and unhealthy things about this subject. Men may have been taught that they should be able to handle any problem without help or emotional support—in other words, to be 100% independent all the time. Women may have been taught that it is not feminine to be strong and they should always depend on others to take care of them. Neither attitude makes sense. Human beings are interdependent; we all need to be somewhat able to solve our own problems but also able to get help when we need it because we can't do some things alone, like overcoming an addiction. This exercise will help you figure out your own balance between independence, interdependence, and relying on others.

1. Do you feel you are:

    _____ too dependent on others

    _____ about right

    _____ It was intense and exciting from the start.

    _____ don't know

2. List the first five things you can think of that you routinely do for yourself without anyone's help (e.g., paying bills, transportation, cooking, keeping appointments).

    _____

    _____

    _____

    _____

3. Next, list five significant things you consistently do with the help of others but play an equal role yourself.

    _____

    _____

    _____

    _____

4. Now, list five significant things you mostly or completely depend on others to do for you.

    _____

    _____

    _____

    _____

5. Of the items you listed for questions 3 and 4, which do you feel you will always need others to help you with or do for you?

    _____

    _____

6. If you didn't list anything for question 2 or for question 3, what do you think is the root of this lack of independence and interdependence (e.g., a major disability; a belief that you can't do anything, or must do everything, on your own; lack of knowledge or resources)?

    _____

    _____

7. What things from questions 3 and 4 do you think you could and should do by yourself, for yourself?

    _____

    _____

8. What things from question 4 do you think you could and should do in teamwork with others? What is the benefit to recovery? To your feelings about yourself?

    _____

    _____

9. On the items from question 6, what would it take for you to start doing these things for yourself, rather than in cooperation with others or depending completely on them to do them for you?

    _____

    _____

    _____

10. For the items you listed for question 7, what would it take for you to start doing these things interdependently with others rather than depending on them completely?

    _____

    _____

11. What has contributed to the over-reliance on others for things you can do yourself? Fear? Guilt? People pleasing? Uncertainty about your own skills/capabilities?

    _____

    _____

12. What has been the impact of this over-reliance on others to your feelings about yourself?

    _____

    _____

13. Briefly describe a plan to start doing, on your own, one item on your list from question 6. What do you hope you will gain from doing so?

    _____

    _____

14. Briefly describe a plan to start doing, interdependently with others, one item from question 7.

    _____

    _____

15. What self-statements will you utilize to keep you engaged in this process and push you out of your comfort zone? What is the benefit to you in gaining more independence?

    _____

    _____

16. After answering these questions and making the plan for question 7, has your answer to question 1 changed? If so, how?

    _____

    _____

    _____

Be sure to explore with your therapist any cultural considerations regarding the roles of independence, interdependence, and dependence.

Be sure to bring this handout back to your next session with your therapist and be prepared to talk about your thoughts and feelings about the exercise.

CORRECTING DISTORTED THINKING

GOALS OF THE EXERCISE

1. Decrease distorted thinking and increase positive self-talk.
2. Learn how addictive patterns are related to distorted perceptions and thinking.
3. Identify personal patterns of distorted perceptions that are related to addictive patterns.
4. Learn and use tools to identify and correct distorted thoughts and see situations more accurately.

ADDITIONAL PROBLEMS FOR WHICH THIS EXERCISE MAY BE USEFUL

- Anger
- Anxiety
- Borderline Traits
- Dangerousness/Lethality
- Dependent Traits
- Narcissistic Traits
- Social Anxiety
- Suicidal Ideation

SUGGESTIONS FOR PROCESSING THIS EXERCISE WITH THE CLIENT

The "Correcting Distorted Thinking" activity is intended primarily for depressed clients, to address Beck's depressive triad of cognitive distortions (i.e., self, situation, and future), and other depressive symptoms. It teaches the client about several common forms of cognitive distortion and guides them in seeking examples in their own lives. It follows by offering strategies for overcoming these distortions and asks the client to test them and report the results. This exercise is suitable for individual or group use, in session, or as homework. Follow-up could include an assignment to use the corrective strategies at least once a day, write about the results, and report outcomes back to the therapist or treatment group.

CORRECTING DISTORTED THINKING

Distorted thinking is a basic problem in both depression and addiction. Denial is a good example—not seeing or understanding things that are obvious to others. Minimizing or exaggerating problems or achievements is another example. Misinterpreting other people's words and actions and seeing our own as better or worse than what is accurate are yet other examples. To solve any problem, the first step is to see it clearly. This exercise will help you see how addictive problems distort our views of ourselves, other people, and our situations and futures, and will give you tools to overcome these distortions.

1. *Denial/minimization.* We don't see or remember our destructive behavior and its negative results, or we don't admit to ourselves how serious it is. We think we may have missed work three or four times in the last 2 months when it's really 12 times. We blame arguments with our loved ones on them and don't take our share of the responsibility. We don't admit that medical, financial, or relationship problems may be linked to our drinking, drug use, gambling, or other compulsions.
    Ways I see this in my life:

    _____

    _____

2. *All-or-nothing thinking.* We see things as completely good or bad, perfect or awful. Events are wonderful or disastrous; nothing is just okay or average.
    Ways I see this in my life:

    _____

    _____

3. *Overgeneralization.* If one thing goes wrong, we conclude that it's a terrible day; if we make one mistake, we believe we are mistakes; we often use the words *always* or *never*.
    Ways I see this in my life:

    _____

    _____

4. *Negative focus.* We exaggerate the negative and overlook the good. This feeds self-pity, which is an excuse to act out.

Ways I see this in my life:

_____

_____

5. *Predicting without facts.* We leap to conclusions, which are usually negative. We give definite meanings to events or actions that aren't clear, such as thinking people are mad at us when they don't act happy, and we neglect to check to see whether our interpretations are right before we believe them.

    Ways I see this in my life:

    _____

    _____

6. *Emotional reasoning.* We assume our emotions or suspicions reflect the way things really are: "If I feel it, then it's true."

    Ways I see this in my life:

    _____

    _____

7. *"Should" statements.* We judge our actions by what we think we should or shouldn't do and beat ourselves up with guilt and shame when we fail to meet those standards. We may do this to other people, getting angry and judgmental when they don't do what we think they should, even if we never told them our expectations.

    Ways I see this in my life:

    _____

    _____

8. *Judgment and labeling.* We judge ourselves and others instead of our actions or their actions. If we lose at something, we call ourselves losers. If others fail, we call them failures.

    Ways I see this in my life:

    _____

    _____

9. *Taking things personally.* We see others' actions as being aimed at us and feel responsible for things we don't control.

    Ways I see this in my life:

    _____

    _____

10. Here's a strategy to correct distorted thinking: Check it out with someone you trust. When you're upset about a situation, talk with your sponsor or someone else you trust who isn't emotionally involved. Tell them what happened. Tell only what you saw and heard, not what you believe others were thinking or feeling. Ask your sponsor or friend what they think, and share your thoughts and feelings. Ask them whether it seems you're making one of the mistakes in questions 1–9. Try this and describe what happens:

_____

_____

11. Here's another strategy. When you feel upset, take a piece of paper, and draw five columns. In the first column, describe the situation. In the next column, list your emotions (e.g., anger, fear, despair, worry, confusion, embarrassment, shame) and rate the strength of each on a 10-point scale, with 10 the most intense. In column three, write what you think about the situation. Now review the distortions described earlier. In column four, write a nondistorted, reasonable replacement thought that is probably true for each distorted thought in column two. Think about this thought briefly. Then, in the last column, rate the believability of the replacement thought (0% to 100%). How will you handle the situation differently?

_____

_____

12. Self-monitor upsetting situations for the next week and keep a log following the outline in question 11. Write what you recognized or gained from this activity.

_____

_____

Be sure to bring this handout and the self-monitoring log back to your next session with your therapist and be prepared to talk about what you learned about yourself and your thinking.

GRATITUDE

GOALS OF THE EXERCISE

1. Elevate mood and develop a program of recovery free from addiction.
2. Understand affective disorders and how these symptoms increase vulnerability to addiction.
3. Alleviate depressive symptoms and return to the previous level of effective functioning.
4. Develop healthy thinking patterns and beliefs about self, others, and the world that lead to alleviation and help prevent the relapse of depression.

ADDITIONAL PROBLEMS FOR WHICH THIS EXERCISE MAY BE USEFUL

- Adult-Child-of-an-Alcoholic (ACA) Traits
- Anxiety
- Chronic Pain
- Grief/Loss Unresolved
- Medical Issues
- Narcissistic Traits
- Peer Group Negativity
- Posttraumatic Stress Disorder (PTSD)
- Relapse Proneness
- Self-Harm
- Spiritual Confusion
- Suicidal Ideation

SUGGESTIONS FOR PROCESSING THIS EXERCISE WITH THE CLIENT

The "Gratitude" exercise is designed for clients who are struggling with negativity, high levels of daily stress, and learned helplessness. By shifting cognitive focus to positive factors in their lives, it disrupts the downward spiral of anxious and depressive thinking about problems and fears. With repeated use, the client develops the habit of attending to more positive phenomena throughout the day, big and small, countering the cognitive distortions. Follow-up could consist of sharing the content of the gratitude journal with a group and opening groups by asking each client to identify one thing for which they are currently grateful. Clients will have to be coached on the practice of being grateful even in times of distress, loss, and difficulty.

GRATITUDE

The ways we view, perceive, and think about the world and ourselves has a significant impact on how we feel and cope. When our mood is low, when we experience significant loss, or when we have many troubles, it is easy to focus on the things that make us unhappy. We can hold on to things that cause us a great deal of pain and stress, try to control things, blame, repetitively think about our fears—what others want, think, or expect from us—or all the ways we don't measure up. Thinking in these ways will only get us stuck. We get stuck in a polluted, negative, self-defeating mindset that is hard to break. There are specific disciplines and ways of seeing the world that people subscribe to in order to attempt to have a simple, happy, uncomplicated life. Simple, happy, and uncomplicated does not generally describe a life of active addiction, depression, or chronic pain, but no matter where we are in any of this, there are some ways of thinking about things and responding that are better for us than others.

One way to short-circuit this negative cycle is to practice gratefulness. When you appreciate what you have, what you have appreciates in its value to you. So basically, being grateful for the goodness that is already evident in your life will bring you a deeper sense of happiness. Sounds too simple to work, doesn't it? We're going to have a hard time ever being happy if we aren't thankful for what we already have. There's no harm in trying.

For the next 14 days, practice gratitude. Keep a daily gratitude journal. The instructions are listed as follows.

1. Get a notebook or use your laptop or other device. Sometimes writing on nice paper with a nice pen feels good but recording in a way that makes the most sense to you. The whole point is to make this entire experience focused on feeling good about your life.

    _____

    _____

2. Each day for a few minutes sit by yourself someplace quiet and write down five things you are grateful for this day. If you forget one day, don't berate yourself; simply start again when you remember.

    _____

    _____

3. Start each entry with the statement "Today I feel grateful. . ." There are no hard-and-fast rules. Each of your five points can be one word or one paragraph. No matter how bad a day you've had, you can always find five things, even if they are things like "I have a job," "My kids are healthy," "I'm sober," "The sun was shining."

    Before getting started, we can exercise gratitude for the same five things every day. As your mindset changes and you get better at this strategy, you may notice you attend to different things. Don't get too hung up on doing it "right"; just do it.

    Start your first entry here:

    _____

    _____

4. Count your blessings often. Reviewing what you've written can be very helpful. If you want to have more things in your life to feel grateful for, start acknowledging them today. Some people review them the next morning to start the day out positively, but this is not necessary to obtain the benefit of focusing on what you're grateful for each day.

    _____

5. Share your gratitude journal with someone else. This is helpful for two reasons. Sharing with others may bring joy into their life, especially knowing that you appreciate their friendship or support and that you think about them. Also, sharing with someone makes it real. It acknowledges that you value your blessings. Don't believe it? Try it. It works!

    Share one of your items with a trusted other and write how it made you feel.

    _____

    _____

6. After the 14 days, journal about any changes to your thoughts and feelings.

    _____

    _____

Be sure to bring this handout back to your next session with your therapist and be prepared to talk about your thoughts and feelings about the exercise.

CREATING A PRELIMINARY EATING AND HEALTH PLAN

GOALS OF THE EXERCISE

1. Extinguish overeating, restricting, purging, use of laxatives, and/or excessive exercise or other compensatory behaviors.
2. Learn and demonstrate constructive strategies to cope with dysphoric moods.
3. Use support from others and decrease interpersonal isolation.
4. Determine what people and services will be involved in the treatment process.
5. Take greater responsibility for practicing positive health-related behaviors.

ADDITIONAL PROBLEMS FOR WHICH THIS EXERCISE MAY BE USEFUL

- Anxiety
- Borderline Traits
- Medical Issues
- Obsessive-Compulsive Disorder
- Self-Care Deficits—Primary
- Self-Care Deficits—Secondary
- Self-Harm
- Sexual Abuse

SUGGESTIONS FOR PROCESSING THIS EXERCISE WITH THE CLIENT

The "Creating a Preliminary Eating and Health Plan" activity is suited for clients who could benefit from making changes to their current eating patterns or health maintenance behaviors. It can also be used with people whose eating-disordered behaviors are no longer providing the anesthetic effect or relief they once did and who are looking for ways to normalize their self-care, particularly related to relationship to food, weight, and body image. It may be useful to have the client create a time frame for completing the assignment's tasks (e.g., physicals, nutritionist/dietician consults) to allow them to have more awareness of control over important aspects of recovery. Depending on their financial situation and available resources, the client may need more assistance in accessing community-based resources. A referral for specialized eating disorder treatment should be made to a practice that practices as a multidisciplinary treatment team.

CREATING A PRELIMINARY EATING AND HEALTH PLAN

Recovery from eating disorders spells self-control, freedom from obsession with food and weight, and gaining the energy and ability to deal with people and situations without the distractions of weight, anxiety, and self-hate blocking the way. Successful recovery includes giving up eating-disordered and compensatory behavior, addressing other problems (e.g., mood disorders, addictive and/or compulsive behaviors, other psychiatric illnesses, trauma, suicidal or self-injurious behaviors), using positive coping techniques (e.g., adequate nutrition, exercise, support, management of relapse triggers, anxiety/stress management), knowing what triggers eating-disordered behavior, correcting distorted thinking, and planning to deal with relapses.

This exercise will help you identify key issues in planning for recovery and creating an initial plan that is both comprehensive and concrete. As you work in recovery, you will be able to use the same format to address new issues that come up in middle and later recovery stages.

1. People seek help for disordered eating for a variety of reasons (e.g., shame, disruption to their lives, the urgings of others, illness, etc.). What motivates you to seek help for this issue now?

   _____

   _____

2. What are the specific behaviors you're looking to change?

   _____

   _____

3. What **emotions** do you feel before, during, or after these behaviors (e.g., guilt, fear, anger, shame, depression, anxiety)?

   _____

   _____

4. What are you avoiding dealing with that engaging in these behaviors soothes?

   _____

   _____

5. What **thoughts** support or help maintain your disordered eating patterns (e.g., "I'm too fat," "I need to be thinner," etc.)?

_____

_____

6. What **situations or events** trigger or cue you to engage in disordered eating (e.g., stress, conflict, social situations, holidays)?

_____

_____

7. What medical issues do you need to address, either due to past eating patterns or to decrease your risk of returning to using eating or avoidance of eating to cope? If you don't know, when would you be willing to get a physical to check for problems? How will you encourage yourself to do this rather than continue to avoid?

_____

_____

8. What are the other related issues you'll need to address (e.g., alcohol/other drug abuse, depression, anxiety, suicidal thoughts/behavior, self-harm, perfectionism, self-loathing, trauma) as part of your recovery?

_____

_____

9. Which people can you rely on for support? These can include doctors, family, friends, counselors, spiritual advisors, etc. What will you have to challenge within yourself to ask?

_____

_____

10. Research what is available locally and/or online and list three potential benefits for using community support groups. What support groups are available in your community? With your therapist, vet these options to avoid recovery-interfering groups.

_____

_____

11. Please place your answers for questions 2 through 5 in the column labeled "Disordered Responses." Next, in the column labeled "Recovery Responses," list alternatives. Work to include more than one response for each disordered response. Many people need assistance with the recovery boxes. If you do, ask for that help. Sometimes we need help with disordered responses as well due to distortions, lack of awareness, a strong desire to avoid, secondary gains from behaviors, shame.

	Disordered Responses	**Recovery Responses**
Behaviors (Question 2)	_____	_____
Emotions (Question 3)	_____	_____
Thoughts (Question 4)	_____	_____
Triggers (Question 5)	_____	_____

Finally, please remember that recovery involves continually learning more ways to manage triggers and lapses. Keep thinking of options for dealing with feelings of being overwhelmed, uncomfortable, or stressed by relationships and/or social situations involving food, drink, and challenges to body image. You wrote down some ideas under "Triggers" (Question 5) in the table. Keep adding to the list. Here are some strategies you may find useful. *Circle* those that you've tried and had some success. *Check* those you'd be willing to try. Add any that are missing:

_____ Attend events that *you want* to attend, not those that you feel you *should* attend.

_____ Use affirmations (e.g., *I see myself handling this situation positively*), and visualize yourself carrying them out in specific ways.

_____ Set aside quiet time during stressful periods (e.g., weddings, holidays).

_____ Plan and practice verbal responses to comments about your weight or eating.

_____ Know your lapse and relapse triggers and continually refine how to manage them.

_____ Distract yourself with an alternate activity and/or remove yourself from the triggering situation.

_____ Practice delaying the time you respond to an urge to binge or purge. The longer you delay the urge, the greater the likelihood that the urge will pass. Do something productive while you are delaying (rather than sitting and watching the clock or focusing on your urge, discomfort).

_____ Rehearse comfortable ways to change the subject or exit an uncomfortable situation.

_____ Practice meditation, relaxation daily (not just in times of stress or anxiety).

_____ Focus on the reasons you came to treatment this time and why it matters to get into recovery.

Others: _____

_____

Be sure to bring this handout back to your next session with your therapist and be prepared to talk about your thoughts and feelings about the exercise.

EATING PATTERNS SELF-ASSESSMENT

GOALS OF THE EXERCISE

1. Increase awareness of disordered eating patterns and motivation to begin a recovery program.
2. Identify the relationship between eating-disordered behavior and addictive behavior.
3. Develop nutritious eating habits and healthy, realistic attitudes about body image and weight that prevent a relapse of the eating disorder.

ADDITIONAL PROBLEMS FOR WHICH THIS EXERCISE MAY BE USEFUL

- Borderline Traits
- Medical Issues
- Self-Care Deficits—Primary
- Self-Care Deficits—Secondary
- Self-Harm

SUGGESTIONS FOR PROCESSING THIS EXERCISE WITH THE CLIENT

The "Eating Patterns Self-Assessment" activity is suited for clients with unhealthy eating patterns who nevertheless express frustration with others' view that their eating is problematic, who say everything is "under control," or who know their behavior is problematic but feel intense shame and guilt and may deny problems to maintain secrecy. Getting someone with an eating disorder into treatment can be difficult. They often believe they need their eating-disordered behaviors either to cope with emotional distress or to maintain a sense of personal control in their lives. This exercise is appropriate at the outset of assessment or treatment to paint a concrete picture of what is problematic regarding eating patterns, thought processes, relationships with food, and coping styles and mechanisms. It can be used as a baseline to revisit later in treatment to assess progress. It is not an all-inclusive list of symptoms or behavioral characteristics, but rather a sampling of many observed in eating-disordered patients. It is not designed as a substitute or replacement for a thorough bio-psychosocial assessment.

EATING PATTERNS SELF-ASSESSMENT

People living addictive lifestyles often have neglected their health in many ways. For others, the relationships they have had with food (e.g., how and what they have eaten, how and why they have focused on their weight) has affected their health for the worse. Eating disorders such as bulimia, anorexia, and binge eating are not simply about food and weight. Like other addictive behaviors, people use eating and the pursuit of perfect body shape as ways to handle stress, anxiety, and other difficult emotions. Like other addictive behaviors, it becomes compulsive and preoccupying, and this may lead to eating rituals or rules that eventually take over their lives.

Also, as with other addictive behaviors, people trying to overcome eating disorders must learn healthy ways to get their needs met, cope with difficult feelings, and develop new relationships in order to succeed. Additionally, people with eating disorders sometimes use substances and develop difficulties with alcohol/other drugs as well. If not substance problems, then other problems may need to be resolved, including trauma, self-injury, anxiety, and mood issues.

As with anything, knowing that a problem exists and what the problem is comes before taking action to solve it. We need to know exactly what we're working against and toward. This exercise will help you start the process of creating a recovery plan.

1. Following is a list of behaviors associated with eating disorders. Please put a *check* next to those that are part of your experience. Completing this exercise may be difficult, particularly listing items that you may not have shared with anyone else. Remember that recovery is the goal, and any fear or shame you may feel about sharing this information is just part of the problem you are working to overcome.

    _____ Dieting, restricting, fasting, or skipping meals

    _____ Binge eating (episodes of rapidly eating large amounts of food coupled with fear that you will not be able to stop eating during each episode)

    _____ Purging (use of self-induced vomiting, laxatives, diet pills, diuretics, and/or compulsive overexercise to lose weight, maintain weight, or compensate for perceived overeating)

    _____ Obsessively counting calories and/or fat grams

    _____ Rituals related to food, such as cutting or arranging food in a particular way on the plate or refusal to eat certain items

    _____ Eating in secret, hoarding food, or discomfort when eating around others

_____ Fear of inability to stop overeating

_____ Constant preoccupation with food, appearance, weight, body shape, and/ or body size

_____ Wearing layered or loose-fitting clothing to hide your body

_____ Substance use disorder

_____ Excessive activity, insomnia, and/or restlessness

_____ Fatigue

_____ Obsessing about "good" and "bad" food groups or rigidly avoiding/restricting self to particular foods, food groups

_____ Isolation due to appearance or avoiding situations/activities/interactions all together because of anxiety, fear, mood

_____ Suicidal feelings or suicide attempts

_____ Poor impulse control

_____ Self-injurious behavior

_____ Intense fear of becoming fat

_____ Perfectionism or overachieving behaviors at the cost of everything else

_____ Guilt after eating

_____ Feeling a sense of accomplishment/control the less you eat/drink

_____ Irregular or absent menstruation or other medical complications

_____ Avoiding eating when hungry/restricting food intake

_____ Low frustration tolerance and/or irritability

_____ Difficulty handling stress/anxiety

_____ Problems with intimacy

_____ Difficulty identifying and expressing feelings

_____ Difficulty asking for help

_____ People-pleasing behaviors

2. Please review this list and the items you've checked. What thoughts come to mind when you look at those items as fitting your experience? In assessing yourself with this information, what conclusions would you draw?

_____

_____

3. How have the items that you've marked led to negative consequences for you (e.g., medically, others' comments, negative feelings about yourself)?

_____

_____

4. In addition to eating and body image issues, what other co-occurring issues will need to be addressed (e.g., alcohol, other drugs, mood problems, trauma, etc.)?

_____

_____

5. What activities that used to bring you joy, calm you, or that fulfilled you have you avoided or limited as eating disorder symptoms developed?

_____

_____

6. What thoughts about yourself are most pronounced as you think about daily life with your eating disorder?

_____

_____

7. What role, if any, has substance abuse and/or addictive behaviors played in keeping your eating disordered behaviors active?

_____

_____

8. Name three action items that feel most important to explore with your therapist or physician. For each, what will be the benefit of addressing them?

_____

_____

Be sure to bring this handout back to your next session with your therapist and be prepared to talk about your thoughts and feelings about the exercise.

CREATING POSITIVE FAMILY RITUALS

GOALS OF THE EXERCISE

1. Learn and demonstrate healthy communication and conflict management skills, leading to greater harmony within the family and cessation of addictive behavior.
2. Forgive family members' past actions and begin a life of harmony with each family member.
3. Learn and use positive coping tactics and enjoyable/pleasurable activities with family members.
4. Reframe family conflict as an ordinary problem that has a solution.
5. Increase the number of positive interactions within the family.

ADDITIONAL PROBLEMS FOR WHICH THIS EXERCISE MAY BE USEFUL

- Adult-Child-of-an-Alcoholic (ACA) Traits
- Childhood Trauma
- Conduct Disorder/Delinquency
- Oppositional Defiant Behavior
- Parent–Child Relational Problem
- Partner Relational Conflicts
- Relapse Proneness
- Substance Use Disorders

SUGGESTIONS FOR PROCESSING THIS EXERCISE WITH THE CLIENT

The "Creating Positive Family Rituals" activity is designed for clients who experience frequent negative interactions with family members or remain isolated/distant from their families and who want to have closer and more positive interactions. Processing of this assignment may include identifying ways that addictive behaviors have contributed to conflicts or emotional distance. It may be useful to have the client facilitate a family meeting to complete this assignment and practice other important recovery skills (e.g., negotiation, problem solving, communication, stress management, and accountability for behavior). Note: although a key goal is inducing the client to take responsibility for their part in conflict with other family members, the clinician must keep in mind that cessation of conflict is not completely under the client's control and that the family system may resist the client's efforts to change its dynamics. Additionally, thorough assessment of any current domestic violence will be important to address to keep clients safe. Exploring culture around family values, customs, expectations, and how aligned clients are with them is important.

CREATING POSITIVE FAMILY RITUALS

Many people in recovery have missed important events in their families' lives due to their addictive behaviors or the negative consequences of addictive lifestyles. When families are enmeshed (interfering with each other's lives too much, not allowing family members to solve their own problems when that would be best) or disconnected (not interested, involved, dependable, or present enough for each other), then conflict and misunderstanding occur more often, and resolution of either is difficult.

When family members get busy, they sometimes forget how important they are to each other, so family time needs to be scheduled like other important events (e.g., sports practices, support group meetings, and medical appointments). The benefits of scheduling family events are continuity, predictability, meaningfulness, and mutual support without being overly controlling.

The purpose of this exercise is to focus on healthy ways for family members to enjoy being together, to increase stability, to communicate better, and to solve problems together. The more positive interactions that a family has, the more supported its members feel. For you, the person in recovery, this helps you stay clean and sober. In this exercise, the word *ritual* doesn't necessarily mean a formal or rigid event; it means an activity that you engage in on a regular, scheduled basis.

1. How did substances or other addictive behaviors or unaddressed co-occurring issues affect your time, availability, connection, nurturing, commitments to family?

    _____

    _____

2. What will be the benefit of changing family interactions toward more consistent engagement with each other for you? For your family? For your recovery?

    _____

    _____

3. Review all family members' schedules for mandatory commitments. Identify possible days and times when everyone is available. Additionally, consider prescheduled events at school, church, and extended family celebrations you could attend together. Write potential shared activities here.

    _____

    _____

4. Together, make a list of activities that you could share. If you pick activities that everyone likes to do, it will probably be easier to get the whole family to participate. Write them here.

    _____

    _____

5. Decide whether you will develop a ritual for the whole family (e.g., eating dinner together, going to church together) and/or different rituals for you and the children alone, to give your significant other a break and give each child more of your attention during that time, and for you and your significant other alone (e.g., a date night). Write your thoughts here.

    _____

    _____

6. Write a script for how you will talk with your family about this and why it is important to you. Ask for participation and talk about any perceived gains you think it has for the family. Consider the age and development level of your family members and how this will affect engagement. How will you introduce this to them? Prepare for any potential reactions.

    _____

    _____

    _____

7. Make a final decision about what each ritual will be, schedule when you will start the ritual, who will be involved, and how often.

    Activity: _____

    Start Date: _____

    Participants: _____

    Frequency: _____

    Make this activity a priority and commit to it. If you don't, other family members will follow your example and will not take it seriously. Also, if you have never done this, your family will need time to adjust. Attempting to make something consistent when it hasn't been so, takes patience. You may want to start with a monthly or weekly ritual and make it as much fun as you can. As positive experiences increase, your family will become more enthusiastic.

8. How will you and the other members of your family handle arguments, complaints, criticism, or no-shows at the beginning of this ritual? What will you do to address your own growing pains (feeling frustrated, overwhelmed, discouraged, or unmotivated).

_____

_____

_____

9. What length of time will you practice your ritual and then check its success? (For a weekly ritual, you may want to give it more than a month before you evaluate. For less frequent family activities, you will need to allow more time.)

_____

_____

10. At evaluation time, what adjustments, if any, need to be made?

_____

_____

Consider a means to share the calendar so everyone can see, plan, anticipate, make edits as things will invariably come up. Reschedule the time you planned to be together as opposed to canceling.

Be sure to bring this handout with you to your next session with your therapist and be prepared to discuss your thoughts and feelings about this exercise.

IDENTIFYING CONFLICT THEMES

GOALS OF THIS EXERCISE

1. Learn and demonstrate healthy communication and conflict management skills, leading to increased harmony within the family and cessation of addictive behavior.
2. Implement healthy coping behaviors to deal with conflicts within the family.
3. Take responsibility for one's own part in conflict initiation and resolution.
4. Learn to identify conflict as healthy or unhealthy and make decisions about how to resolve it.
5. Learn about conflict triggers to avoid unhealthy conflicts when possible.

ADDITIONAL PROBLEMS FOR WHICH THIS EXERCISE MAY BE USEFUL

- Adult-Child-of-an-Alcoholic (ACA) Traits
- Anger
- Childhood Trauma
- Dangerousness/Lethality
- Occupational Problems
- Oppositional Defiant Behavior
- Parent–Child Relational Problem
- Partner Relational Conflicts
- Posttraumatic Stress Disorder (PTSD)

SUGGESTIONS FOR PROCESSING THIS EXERCISE WITH THE CLIENT

The "Identifying Conflict Themes" activity is used to help the client assess patterns in conflicts (e.g., topics of conflict, times conflicts are likely to happen, and with whom). It guides the client in looking at initiation or maintenance of a conflict as something in which they have an active part, assisting them in taking active steps to resolve conflict in healthy ways. This exercise can be used in groups to role-play conflict situations the client has difficulty handling in positive ways. This can be a useful activity for family therapy sessions, gathering data of how any individual family member perceives conflict and hearing others' perspectives to help identify solutions. If parents/guardians are not available when working with adolescents, assign the adolescent the task of interviewing family members and reporting the results. Teaching clients basic stress management skills alongside conflict management is critical. Preparing for all the ways conflict, building conflict, anticipated conflict feel and having a relapse prevention strategy before embarking on the exercise is advised.

IDENTIFYING CONFLICT THEMES

Conflict in families is inevitable. Resolving conflict in negative ways (e.g., ignoring, being physically or emotionally abusive, refusing to admit wrongs, blaming others, leaving) creates more problems and further isolates each person involved from the other(s). On the other hand, resolving conflict in positive ways helps family relationships grow stronger and more supportive. One thing positive conflict management requires us to do is to ask ourselves what responsibility we have in initiating, maintaining, and resolving any conflict, so we can change those actions and improve the situation. This exercise asks you to start keeping a conflict journal to gather information about what conflict looks like in your family relationships. Follow this format and record the conflict in your home for 2 weeks.

- Date and time
- Intensity of the conflict (1 = very low to 10 = very high)
- Where did it happen?
- What was going on?
- Who was present?
- What was my behavior during the conflict?
- What feelings can I identify
- What did I want to have happen?
- What was the outcome?

Review your conflict journal after 2 weeks and reflect on the following questions.

1. What did you notice about the conflicts in your family? Look for themes or patterns. (Were they about a particular topic? What affected intensity? Who was involved? How did they resolve?)

_____

_____

_____

_____

_____

2. What times of the day were conflicts or arguments most likely to occur (e.g., upon waking, bedtime, after work/school)?

    _____

    _____

3. List any conflict situations that came up more than once.

    _____

    _____

4. What role(s) do you play in conflicts (e.g., instigator, victim, peacemaker, rescuer, etc.)? What role did you plan in initiating, fueling, working to resolve?

    _____

    _____

5. Describe the range of feelings you experienced in the conflicts that did arise.

    _____

    _____

6. To what degree/extent did you believe conflict was triggered by old "stuff" (family of origin, trauma reaction, past using/addictive behavior)?

    _____

    _____

7. For any conflict with a positive outcome, what was different (e.g., intensity lower, got my way, everyone got to express themselves, no name calling, a compromise, etc.) from those conflicts that did not have a positive outcome?

    _____

    _____

8. Do you tend to see arguments as right/wrong, win/lose? How do you think this affects conflict?

    _____

    _____

9. What difficulties did you notice as patterns in resolving conflicts?

    _____

    _____

10. What do you feel needs to change to reduce negative conflict in your family?

    _____

    _____

11. Do you tend to get into conflicts with some members of your family more often than others? If so, why do you think this is?

    _____

    _____

12. Discuss with a counselor or trusted support person helpful ways they or others they know deal with conflict in their families and get positive results. Write about the main points you learn; pay particular attention to any information you could use to help yourself engage differently, be present differently, help resolve with better outcomes.

    _____

    _____

13. Write down one thing you can begin to work on in the next week to approach conflict in your family differently.

    _____

    _____

Be sure to bring this handout with you to your next therapy session and be prepared to talk about your thoughts and feelings about this exercise.

CONSEQUENCES AND BENEFITS

GOALS OF THE EXERCISE

1. Assist the client to accept the fact that compulsive behavior is a problem and to actively participate in a recovery program.
2. Lead the client to compare their stated values with the actions and experiences of an addictive lifestyle.
3. Challenge the client to establish their own measure for consequences that would convince them addictive behaviors have become an unacceptable problem.

ADDITIONAL PROBLEMS FOR WHICH THIS EXERCISE MAY BE USEFUL

- Antisocial Behavior
- Nicotine Use/Dependence
- Readiness to Change
- Relapse Proneness
- Sexual Promiscuity
- Substance Use Disorders

SUGGESTIONS FOR PROCESSING THIS EXERCISE WITH THE CLIENT

The "Consequences and Benefits" activity is designed for clients who minimize the impact of addictive behavior. It challenges the client to decide what hitting bottom would mean to them and to consider what negative consequences they are willing to go through rather than quit. Follow-up can consist of discussing answers with the therapist or group, self-monitoring for ongoing negative consequences of addictive behaviors, and discussion of their significance. Consider assigning Step 1 and 2 reading material and return to discuss before assigning or in interim between assigning and return to process.

CONSEQUENCES AND BENEFITS

This assignment will help you clarify your beliefs about any behaviors that are so unacceptable that you want to avoid those effects at any cost, even if that means permanently giving up those behaviors. Many people consider changing their behavior(s) when their behavior conflicts with their personal goals/values and/or the negative consequences begin to outweigh the benefits. Sometimes, they find that despite disliking the behavior and wanting to change, they are unable to stop. This can apply to the effects of any behavior, including substance use, compulsive gambling, overspending, or high-risk sexual behavior. Appreciating the consequences of addictive behavior isn't always enough to motivate us to make changes. However, it can provide information for us to consider the impact of continuing the behavior.

1. You may have heard someone say that for someone with an addiction to give up an addictive behavior, they have to hit bottom. To some, hitting bottom means losing everything or going to prison. It may not mean that for you. It can mean we can't let some experience happen, or happen again, no matter what. Think about these questions:

   a. Have you observed someone experience a consequence of addictive behavior and you thought that you could not tolerate that same consequence in your own life, and if so, what was it?

   _____

   _____

   b. What promise have you made to yourself that you would give up your gambling behaviors if a certain thing happened because of it? What was the experience you told yourself you couldn't tolerate?

   _____

   _____

2. What consequences have you experienced because of your compulsive behavior? Please *check* any you've experienced. *Circle* any you've experienced more than once; write the number of times after the item.

   _____ Spent more time or money than you intended.

   _____ Spent money on the behavior that you needed for something else.

_____ Given up another activity you liked because it interfered with the behavior.

_____ Embarrassed or hurt your family.

_____ Been asked to quit by loved ones.

_____ Hidden it from family/friends.

_____ Lied/deceived others.

_____ Felt ashamed/guilty/regretful.

_____ Hoarded food/pornography/other things related to the behavior.

_____ Been unfaithful to your partner.

_____ Terminated a relationship/divorced due to gambling behavior.

_____ Lost time from work to engage in the behavior or to cope with the aftermath.

_____ Lost a job because of it.

_____ Sold or traded important possessions to get money for it.

_____ Traded sex or committed a crime to get money for the compulsive behavior.

_____ Been arrested, in jail, or in prison because of compulsive behavior.

_____ Considered/attempted suicide while practicing a compulsive behavior or due to its consequences.

_____ Accidentally or intentionally harmed or killed someone while practicing compulsive behavior.

_____ Used substances in conjunction with the behavior.

_____ Other(s): (please list)_____

3. Now look back at question 2. Have you experienced any consequences you once said would be unacceptable (question 1b)? If so, which ones? If you have others, please list them also.

    _____

    _____

4. If a close friend or family member told you about experiencing the events you listed in question 2 and 3, and asked your advice, how would you feel? What advice would you give them?

    _____

    _____

5. Which consequences in question 2 and 3 that you've experienced once would mean your behavior was out of control if they happened again?

    _____

    _____

6. Which events from question 3 that you've never experienced would tell you that you'd hit bottom and needed to quit permanently?

_____

_____

7. Make an argument (whether you agree or not, and maybe including things you've heard from others) listing 10 benefits that would come from being abstinent from current addictive behaviors.

_____

_____

8. How do identified consequences put you in conflict with things that matter most to you?

_____

_____

9. To what degree do you believe current behaviors have resulted in things that are undesirable or feeling as if your life has become unmanageable?

_____

_____

10. Reflect what brought you into treatment this time. How is it related to the items you identified?

_____

_____

Be sure to bring this handout back to your next session with your therapist and be prepared to talk about your thoughts and feelings about the exercise.

UNDERSTANDING NONCHEMICAL ADDICTIONS

GOALS OF THE EXERCISE

1. Accept powerlessness over gambling and participate in a recovery program for compulsive behavior other than substance use.
2. Acquire the necessary skills to maintain long-term abstinence from compulsive behavior.
3. Gain an understanding of compulsive behaviors not involving use of alcohol or other drugs.
4. Reduce the risk of relapse by applying techniques that work for substance use disorders to other addictive behaviors.
5. Avoid switching from substance-using addictions to nonchemical behaviors that do not involve alcohol or other drugs but may be equally disruptive to daily life and relationships.

ADDITIONAL PROBLEMS FOR WHICH THIS EXERCISE MAY BE USEFUL

*   Narcissistic Traits
*   Readiness to Change
*   Relapse Proneness
*   Substance Use Disorders

SUGGESTIONS FOR PROCESSING THIS EXERCISE WITH THE CLIENT

The "Understanding Nonchemical Addictions" activity is designed for clients whose primary addiction is nonchemical (e.g., gambling, high-risk sex, workaholism, spending, etc.). It is also meant for recovering addicts and alcoholics who are at risk for switching addictions. Follow-up may include participation in appropriate 12-step programs, keeping a journal to self-monitor for signs of nonchemical addictive behavior and/or switching, and reporting back on insights and progress. Additionally, relapse prevention planning and recovery planning have the same components. Consider assigning psychoeducation or reading material on Step 1 of the 12-step program to help draw insight that it's not about the "what."

UNDERSTANDING NONCHEMICAL ADDICTIONS

Some people suffer from addictions that don't involve alcohol or any other mind-altering drug. They can be just as addicted, just as out of control, as any person with a substance use disorder, and they can lose most of the same things (e.g., jobs, self-respect, money, relationships, their freedom, and their lives). Newly recovering alcoholics and addicts are at high risk for becoming addicted to other behaviors. The goal of this assignment is to increase your awareness of this danger and suggest some tools you can use to avoid or overcome it.

1. What is the connection between substance addiction and nonchemical addictions? Nonchemical addictions are also called *compulsive behaviors*. People do these things for the same reasons they use alcohol or other drugs—to quickly make them feel better, to help them cope with a situation or solve a problem, or to impress others and gain social status. For some, these behaviors, like addiction to alcohol or other drugs, take on a life of their own. Describe the initial how, why, for what reason, in relation to other addictive behaviors or substances you involved yourself in your nonchemical addiction.

   _____

   _____

2. What are five consequences that you've experienced related to your nonchemical addiction? If you've worked through the previous exercise, Consequences and Benefits, identify five from your list.

   _____

   _____

3. If you have a co-occurring substance addiction, describe how the two seem related and connected. Do they create the same or different experiences, feelings, and consequences?

   _____

   _____

4. Some of the same methods that people use to overcome chemical addiction (e.g., participating in support groups, learning new coping skills, and finding replacement methods and activities for things they can't safely do anymore) can also help them deal with compulsive behaviors outside the realm of drinking and other substances. After all, as those who are involved with Alcoholics Anonymous or another 12-step program soon learn, the idea is "to practice these principles in all our affairs."

What substance abuse recovery tools might help you deal with your own nonchemical problems, and how would they help? Identify an example for each of the following tools:

a. Sources of support you'll use to cope with any addictive problem not involving alcohol or other drugs that you might have now or in the future:

_____

b. Coping skills to handle triggers without returning to substance use or compulsive behavior (e.g., stress management, relaxation training, anger management, financial management, conflict resolution, problem solving):

_____

c. Understanding cues, cravings, triggers, high-risk situations, feelings, events, people:

_____

d. Replacement activities for socializing and pleasure; managing down time and boredom:

_____

e. Skills for handling relationship issues:

_____

f. Addressing interactions with former "using" friends without being lured or pressured into old behaviors:

_____

g. If you are participating in a 12-step recovery program, are you aware of the policies such programs, and the groups you attend, have developed about addressing other issues in meetings? Some groups are more open and accepting of a variety of topics than others.

_____

h. If your group discourages you from talking about problems that are threatening your recovery but deemed "other issues," what other groups can you attend where you can feel accepted bringing up those problems?

_____

i. Other tools (work with your therapist or sponsor to identify appropriate self-help manuals, books, apps):

_____

Be sure to bring this handout back to your next session with your therapist and be prepared to talk about your thoughts and feelings about the exercise.

AM I HAVING DIFFICULTY LETTING GO?

GOALS OF THE EXERCISE

1. Maintain a program of recovery free from addiction and unresolved grief.
2. Move toward resolution of feelings of anger, sadness, guilt, and/or abandonment surrounding a loss and make plans for the future.
3. Accept a loss and increase social contact with others.
4. Develop and demonstrate coping skills by renewing old relationships and forming new ones.
5. Identify any areas in which the client will need additional assistance in achieving resolution.

ADDITIONAL PROBLEMS FOR WHICH THIS EXERCISE MAY BE USEFUL

- Borderline Traits
- Childhood Traits
- Dependent Traits
- Depression–Unipolar
- Posttraumatic Stress Disorder (PTSD)
- Suicidal Ideation

SUGGESTIONS FOR PROCESSING THIS EXERCISE WITH THE CLIENT

The "Am I Having Difficulty Letting Go?" activity is designed for clients having trouble understanding their issues of unresolved grief or loss. It also can be useful with clients who are very aware that they have grief issues to resolve but don't know how to begin. The exercise can be tailored to address losses other than bereavement. It is important to examine the client's views about death, dying, and loss in general, as these are influenced by spiritual belief systems and other cultural factors. Follow-up can include processing the exercise with the therapist/group, designing and conducting a mourning and letting-go ritual, and the "Moving on After Loss (18.B)," "What Would They Want for Me? (18.C)," and "Finding a Higher Power That Makes Sense (44.B)" exercises. *Note: You must intervene immediately and effectively if a client reports suicidal ideation, intent, or behavior.*

AM I HAVING DIFFICULTY LETTING GO?

Grief and sorrow can be related to the death of a loved one, the end of a relationship, losing a job, a major illness, a big financial loss, or any other serious setback or loss, whether expected or unexpected. For people coping with addictions, these losses might be related to their addictive behaviors, or unrelated. Sometimes losses occur well into a person's recovery, and inability to cope with loss can increase the risk of relapse into addiction to deal with painful emotions. Also, losses that occurred while actively engaged in addictive behaviors may not be resolved and may act as relapse triggers in early, late, or middle recovery if healing does not occur. Healthy resolution of grief is a process that begins with seeing whether we have unresolved losses. This exercise will guide you in reflecting on whether unresolved grief is a recovery issue for you, what your unresolved losses might be, and how to cope with them.

1. Here are some signs that may mean you're dealing with unresolved loss. These are common reactions, which many people experience. Please *check* any that apply for you:

    _____ Inability to stop talking about the loss

    _____ Feeling anger and resentment

    _____ Avoiding talking or thinking about certain subjects that remind you of the loss

    _____ Mentally replaying, over and over, what you believe you should have done differently

    _____ Inability to accept that the loss occurred

    _____ Withdrawing from others or isolating

    _____ Becoming overwhelmed and disorganized

    _____ Having trouble sleeping or eating

    _____ Feeling apathetic or numb

    _____ Having difficulty concentrating

    _____ Feeling guilty about the loss

    _____ Feeling as if you're "falling apart"

    _____ Feeling a lack of control in other areas of your life

    _____ Feeling betrayed by other people

    _____ Having suicidal thoughts (*If you are thinking about killing or hurting yourself, share this with your therapist immediately and ask for help to stay safe.* These thoughts will pass if you do whatever it takes to avoid acting on them.)

_____ Feeling hopeless that the situation, or your feelings, will ever change

_____ Feeling or believing that if you express an emotion about the loss, it will take over (e.g., feeling that if you start crying you won't be able to stop, or if you express anger, you'll lose control)

_____ Feeling dissatisfied with everything or everyone

_____ Consideration or use of substances/addictive behavior (new or old) to help forget, numb, avoid

_____ Feeling a lack of purpose

_____ Having a sense of failure or worthlessness

_____ Anger at God, loss of faith, or questioning one's spiritual belief system

Other: _____

Review the list again and (*) those items that you believe are related to a loss you can identify easily.

2. What loss or losses do you believe are related to the signs you checked in question 1?

_____

_____

3. What methods of coping with these losses have you attempted that were helpful and positive?

What methods of coping with these losses have you attempted that were self-destructive?

_____

_____

4. What has been the most difficult aspect of thinking about letting go (e.g., do you feel you would be abandoning or betraying someone you lost if you let yourself heal and move ahead with life)?

_____

_____

5. Please list any fears or questions you may have about letting go.

_____

_____

_____

_____

6. Many people entering recovery are skeptical about religion or spirituality and uncomfortable with the references in 12-step programs to a higher power, the prayers said at the beginnings and endings of meetings, and hearing other group members talk about their relationships with the higher power of their understanding. However, coping with pain and loss is one of the most important roles of spirituality in recovery. Can you find a higher power that makes sense for you, and if so, how could you seek the help of that higher power in coping with a loss? Please talk about this with a sponsor or other friends in recovery and write here about your thoughts after those conversations.

_____

_____

Be sure to bring this exercise back to your next session with your therapist and be prepared to discuss your thoughts and feelings about the exercise.

MOVING ON AFTER LOSS

GOALS OF THIS EXERCISE

1. Normalize the experience and process of grief.
2. Learn that grief can be addressed and resolved in several ways.
3. Move toward resolution of feelings of anger, sadness, guilt, and/or abandonment surrounding a loss and make plans for the future.
4. Accept a loss and obtain increased social support from others.
5. Develop and demonstrate coping skills by renewing old relationships and forming new ones.

ADDITIONAL PROBLEMS FOR WHICH THIS EXERCISE MAY BE USEFUL

- Childhood Trauma
- Depression–Unipolar
- Posttraumatic Stress Disorder (PTSD)
- Spiritual Confusion
- Suicidal Ideation

SUGGESTIONS FOR PROCESSING THIS EXERCISE WITH THE CLIENT

The "Moving on After Loss" activity is suited for clients who are experiencing loss or losses. It offers suggestions for action to resolve grief and loss. Grief over a particular loss can be new or old. This activity asks the client to take an active role in determining how they will continue living their life and regain as much quality of life as possible despite the loss. It can be helpful to process family and cultural issues and identify barriers and resources specific to the client's situation.

This exercise may be useful for skill training in individual and/or group settings; that is, the therapist would teach a skill in session, then have the client or group practice the new skill as homework for a set length of time and report the outcomes at a future session. Follow-up can include processing this exercise with the therapist/group and assigning the "Am I Having Difficulty Letting Go?" (18.A), "What Would They Want for Me?" (18.C), and "Finding a Higher Power That Makes Sense" (44.B) exercises. *Note: You must intervene immediately and effectively if a client reports suicidal ideation, intent, or behavior.* Prior to assigning or working on this assignment, it would be useful to teach and practice mindfulness meditation or other self-soothing strategies.

MOVING ON AFTER LOSS

Many feelings and thoughts may be attached to loss. Grief is a normal and natural reaction to losing someone or something important. Depending on how meaningful a loss is, the feelings related to it may vary from mild to very intense and may be easy or difficult to resolve. Unresolved grief can keep us from being fully present in our day-to-day lives. Part of recovery is learning to manage our feelings, both pleasant and painful, with positive skills and without addictive behaviors. Until we resolve any loss, it can remain a trigger for relapse. It is important to remember that recovery is about action, and just waiting for time to pass will not heal what's unresolved. Sometimes old losses resurface after a period of sobriety, particularly if it occurred while active in addiction behaviors.

Furthermore, to recover from loss, we must *expect* to recover. It does not mean to push ourselves and force instant resolution either; this can be just as dangerous. Therapeutic and recovery-focused action over time resolves grief and loss. This exercise gives you suggestions for resolving grief, and it will give you alternatives to leaving a loss unresolved and avoiding dealing with it or staying stuck in grief. It will guide you through steps that others have found useful, so that you can generate your own personal plan for moving on with your life.

EXERCISES FOR GRIEF AND LOSS

Caution: If you start to feel overwhelmed during this assignment, stop and take care of yourself. Calm your body and emotions, write in a journal about what is causing you difficulty and what is too painful to tackle alone, then work with your therapist on moving past those parts of this process. Facing it is better than avoiding it; but the time and pace of it is up to you. Make sure to be kind to yourself as you will feel more vulnerable. Lean on others, and the passing of time does help some.

1. Write about the messages or lessons you've learned from the person who has died or left, or another part of your life that you've lost. Reflect on these gifts that you'll always have with you.

2. Give your pain a voice by recording or listing all the ways you feel the pain. This activity helps express and release some of your pain.

3. Write a letter to the person or other part of your life you are grieving, telling how you feel about the loss and the ways in which it has affected your life. Include any questions you have about this loss. Next, write a letter back to yourself from the person or part of your life you are grieving, answering your questions. You may want to do this exercise in two parts with the help of your therapist.

4. Practice a relaxation strategy to calm stress, sadness, anxiety, and pain. Do this for a few minutes until you feel calm. Then picture yourself making whatever positive changes you want to make in your life. Think of who will be in your life, where you will be, and what you will be doing daily.

5. Spend time with understanding and supportive people. Find and join a bereavement support group and/or work with your sponsor. Reconnect with old, positive acquaintances.

6. Write positive, nurturing memories about your loved one or your previous experience. Grieving doesn't mean forgetting the good stuff.

7. Add a pet or a plant to your environment so you can take care of and nourish life.

8. Lean on spiritual beliefs or philosophies that give you comfort. Finding a relationship with a higher power of your understanding in a 12-step program can be a great help, even for people who have never been religious or have had bad experiences with faith groups.

9. Write about positive ways you coped with past losses that you can try applying this time.

10. Donate some time to help others. Getting out of our own selves sometimes provides some needed respite and interjects joy while actively grieving. Volunteer to help kids or animals; make donations to causes you feel committed to.

    After reviewing the above list, write your thoughts about which you are willing to try.

    _____

    _____

    _____

    _____

MY "MOVING ON" PLAN

1. Using these suggestions or others you have gathered on your own, please make a simple plan for how you will cope and live with the losses you have experienced:

   _____

   _____

2. What suggestions would you make to others who are either beginning to grieve a loss or are avoiding dealing with a loss?

   _____

   _____

3. What was the hardest part in completing this activity?

   _____

   _____

4. What questions do you still have? What barriers?

   _____

   _____

5. Sometimes we think we can't do anything to resolve a loss or that we'll never feel better because a loss is too great. Please record any thoughts like this here, then talk about them with your therapist, a spiritual advisor, and/or a friend who has experienced a loss and now seems to be feeling better.

   _____

   _____

6. Do you see ways a relationship with a higher power can help you live with the loss you're facing? How?

   _____

   _____

7. Identify any cultural variables that may assist in understanding and moving on and talk about this with others.

   _____

   _____

8. Plan for dates and occasions that have a lot of memories attached to them, so they don't take you by surprise.

    _____

    _____

9. Make a plan for the objects/items that surround you and remind you of your lost one. You may want to keep things close, and you may want to give away items that would mean something to someone who loved them too. There is no rush or right time so think about how you might know when you're ready.

    _____

10. What are the events, people, places, items that you tend to associate with the loss (different from the positive memories of your loved one)? Create an internal mantra to shift your mind away from being overtaken by the feelings of loss/your perceived inability to move on to one in which you feel grateful, more hopeful.

    _____

Be sure to bring this exercise with you to your next therapy appointment. This may be an exercise that you work on and then rework more than once as you address each loss. Please write about and then discuss with your therapist any problems you encounter and your general feelings about this activity.

WHAT WOULD THEY WANT FOR ME?

GOALS OF THIS EXERCISE

1.   Challenge beliefs about grief, loyalty, and/or abandonment of lost loved ones that prevent resolution of bereavement.
2.   Learn that grief can be addressed and resolved in several ways, over time.
3.   Move toward resolution of feelings of anger, sadness, guilt, and/or abandonment related to loss and plan for the future.
4.   Accept a loss and increase social contacts with others.
5.   Demonstrate a commitment to moving ahead in life with renewed positive activities and relationships.

ADDITIONAL PROBLEMS FOR WHICH THIS EXERCISE MAY BE USEFUL

- Adult-Child-of-an-Alcoholic (ACA) Traits
- Borderline Traits
- Posttraumatic Stress Disorder (PTSD)
- Self-Harm
- Spiritual Confusion
- Suicidal Ideation

SUGGESTIONS FOR PROCESSING THIS EXERCISE WITH THE CLIENT

The "What Would They Want for Me?" activity is suited for clients experiencing loss or losses, primarily losses of people or pets. It asks the client to shift their perspective to that of the person or pet being mourned. Starting from the premise that the lost loved one loved the client and wanted them to be happy, it challenges the view that loyalty to that lost loved one means refusing to resolve grief and move ahead with life. This exercise may be useful for skill training in individual and/or group settings; in group, it may be therapeutic to allow other members to offer their thoughts about what the lost loved one might say. Follow-up can include processing this exercise with the therapist or group and the "Am I Having Difficulty Letting Go?" (18.A) and "Moving on After Loss" (18.B) exercises. *Note: You must intervene immediately and effectively if a client reports suicidal ideation, intent, or behavior.* Teaching self-soothing strategies to aid in managing ebbs and flows of strong emotions is a critical part of the recovery plan.

WHAT WOULD THEY WANT FOR ME?

For many people, part of the pain of grief is the experience that feelings of connection, loyalty, and attachment to lost loved ones are just as strong as when they were alive, but it is impossible to see them again, to talk to them, to hug them, and to share activities with them. It's normal in such times to feel regret or guilt over missed opportunities for shared times or over occasions when we may have let them down, though we are only human and that's a normal part of every relationship. Under these conditions, we may find that if we catch ourselves having fun and not feeling grief, we feel guilty and disloyal to the loved ones we've lost. The idea of letting go and moving on with life may feel wrong, as if it would mean we were abandoning them, or they weren't significant in our lives.

The reality is that whatever the situation may have been, when we grieve, it is for our own loss, and once we've allowed those feelings to run their course at whatever pace is natural for us, the healthiest thing we can do—and the best way to honor the ones we've lost—is to live the best life we can. If the ones we've lost loved us in return, they would want us to be happy, not to spend the rest of our lives in sadness and regrets. It is true that along the way, you will have a range of emotions, both good and bad. Your ability to feel confident in managing them is the key, not to not have them at all.

This exercise will guide you in thinking through these ideas and exploring any conflict you may be feeling about resolving your grief and moving on with your life.

1. First, think about the best times you had with your lost loved one(s). Think about how you felt while sharing those times with them and about the feelings you believe they experienced. Please pick one of those times to symbolize what was good about the relationship and briefly describe it here, including the way you and the loved one(s) you are grieving were feeling during that time:

    _____

    _____

2. Was your enjoyment increased by your seeing that they were happy then too? Do you think they felt the same about you, happier because of seeing your enjoyment?

    _____

    _____

3. If the situation were reversed, you were gone from their lives, and they were mourning the loss of being able to see you and spend time with you, would you want their sadness to go on and on, or would you rather that they regained their happiness and returned to enjoying their lives? If there was a way for you to leave a message for the people who love you to hear when you're gone, what would you want to say to them about this? Please briefly write what you'd want to tell them.

    _____

    _____

4. Now let's return to the actual situation you are experiencing. Please imagine your lost loved one(s) being asked the same question you just answered. What do you think they would want to say to you? Write **two** brief messages. The first will be from you to whomever you've lost, telling them what you loved most about having them in your life and how you feel about losing them. Please take a few minutes and write that message here.

    _____

    _____

5. For the second message, please imagine them answering the one you just wrote, telling you in turn what they valued most about their relationship with you, and what they would want for you in your life from now on. Again, please take a few minutes and write the second message here.

    _____

    _____

6. Finally, please think about the kinds of activities that would bring you happy memories of the loved one(s) you've lost. List some activities here that make you smile because they bring up good memories of times you shared. Try to capture what brought the most joy.

    _____

    _____

7. If there are meaningful anniversaries connected with this loss (e.g., a birthday, a wedding anniversary, a holiday like Mother's Day or Father's Day, or any other day that stands out in your memory) how could you engage in one or more of the activities you just listed to celebrate your appreciation for having had them in your life? Please list three ideas here.

    _____

    _____

Be sure to bring this exercise with you to your next therapy appointment. This may be an exercise that you rework more than once as you address different losses. Please write about and discuss with your therapist any problems you encounter and your general feelings about this activity.

HANDLING CRISIS WITHOUT IMPULSIVITY

GOALS OF THE EXERCISE

1. Maintain a program of recovery free from impulsive behavior and addiction.
2. Reduce the frequency of impulsive behavior and increase the frequency of behavior that is carefully thought out.
3. Gain confidence in one's ability to handle or prevent crises without addictive coping behaviors.
4. Create a written quick reference for use in a crisis.

ADDITIONAL PROBLEMS FOR WHICH THIS EXERCISE MAY BE USEFUL

- Attention-Deficit/Hyperactivity Disorder (ADHD)—Adolescent
- Attention-Deficit/Hyperactivity Disorder (ADHD)—Adult
- Bipolar Disorder
- Borderline Traits
- Medical Issues
- Relapse Proneness
- Self-Harm
- Substance Use Disorders
- Suicidal Ideation

SUGGESTIONS FOR PROCESSING THIS EXERCISE WITH THE CLIENT

The "Handling Crisis Without Impulsivity" activity is a relapse prevention tool for clients who feel that they might be unable to cope with some crisis without returning to addictive behaviors. It guides the client in anticipating crises that might occur and planning healthy responses for each. Follow-up can include sharing crisis management plans with the therapist, a treatment group, and sponsor; keeping a journal and reporting on preparations made; and keeping a journal and reporting back about crises that do occur and how the client copes with them. This assignment is useful in conjunction with the activities titled "Relapse Prevention Planning" (Exercise 36.C) and "Personal Recovery Planning" (Exercise 47.C) in this manual.

HANDLING CRISIS WITHOUT IMPULSIVITY

Dealing with unexpected, uncomfortable, and stressful events is a normal part of life; these things will occur throughout the recovery process and the rest of our lives. Some crises are preventable, and all crises can be managed without addictive behaviors. For many people dealing with substance abuse issues or other addictive patterns, their addictions have been a key tool in coping with crises. In recovery, a crisis can tempt them to return to their old patterns. Crises can make us feel overwhelmed by intolerable stress, and mood swings and intense emotions are often part of early recovery, making any stressful situation more likely to feel like a crisis. This exercise will help you think ahead today to prevent and/or cope with crisis so that you have a completed quick-reference action plan.

1. A crisis is often not a total surprise. Sometimes it builds over time, and there are signs that things are beginning to get overwhelming. What physical, emotional, and behavioral signs have you noticed in yourself in past situations that could tell you when a crisis was building? Name three of each.

    Physical:_____

    Emotional:_____

    Behavioral:_____

2. Please list three events that would be particularly distressing and overwhelming for you. Think about situations that make you want to immediately escape them, numb your feelings, avoid facing what is happening, or punish yourself or anyone else. Identify how you plan to cope with them if they happen.

    Event   **Plan**

    _____   _____

                                        _____

    _____   _____

                                        _____

    _____   _____

                                        _____

3. Situations that are easily manageable if we face them early often become crises because we procrastinate and neglect doing things that we know we need to do sooner or later, such as paying bills. Are there situations and feelings you avoid dealing with or other ways you set yourself up for crises? If so, what are the ones you most often avoid?

    _____

    _____

4. What steps can you take today to prevent crises from building up in your life?

    _____

    _____

5. How can you slow things down? Sometimes time and distance give us needed perspective. They let logic and knowledge of potential consequences from the behavior kick in and can deescalate a developing crisis. Here's a partial list of what others do. Identify those you could use from the list and add three that are not included:

    Talk to someone

    Take a time-out

    Call my sponsor

    Take a walk/exercise

    Pray

    Relax by breathing

    _____

    _____

We need the logical part of our brain to help us solve problems. This is negatively affected as our stress levels increase. What calming strategies can you use to keep stress at manageable levels? If you need assistance, this is a good activity to walk through in therapy, and you can continue to get practice at home by using calming, relaxation, guided meditation apps.

6. If you run into an unexpected and/or distressing life event that's a crisis for you, what steps will you take to cope? Include people you'll contact and what help you can get from them, places you may go, and resources, skills, or information you'll use.

    a. Who I can contact and what help I need from them:

    _____

b. Places to go:

_____

c. Resources available to me:

_____

d. Personal skills/strengths I can rely on:

_____

e. Information to use and remember:

_____

f. Self-talk I can use to avoid escalating:

_____

Remember that there will always be stress so getting good at calming ourselves and tolerating it when we can't make it go away is of great benefit to us. If substances or addictive behaviors were used to avoid, block, escape stressful feelings, learning alternative strategies that work will just take some time.

Be sure to bring this handout back to your next therapy session and be prepared to talk about your thoughts and feelings about the exercise.

LEARNING TO THINK THINGS THROUGH

GOALS OF THIS EXERCISE

1. Maintain a program of recovery free from impulsive behavior and addiction.
2. Learn to stop, think, and plan before acting.
3. Learn self-observation skills to identify patterns of impulsive behavior.
4. Decrease antisocial behaviors and increase prosocial behaviors.

ADDITIONAL PROBLEMS FOR WHICH THIS EXERCISE MAY BE USEFUL

- Anger
- Attention-Deficit/Hyperactivity Disorder (ADHD)—Adolescent
- Attention-Deficit/Hyperactivity Disorder (ADHD)—Adult
- Borderline Traits
- Conduct Disorder/Delinquency
- Dangerousness/Lethality
- Oppositional Defiant Behavior
- Self-Harm
- Suicidal Ideation

SUGGESTIONS FOR PROCESSING THIS EXERCISE WITH THE CLIENT

The "Learning to Think Things Through" activity is designed for clients who would benefit from observing their own behavior, assessing it, and developing and implementing new behavioral approaches. It may be useful to work through a few of the exercises together in session and have the client practice alternative coping methods outside of the session and record the results. You may or may not want to give the example provided until the client has worked through one successfully on their own.

If a client gets stuck, you may show video clips of people acting impulsively (e.g., from TV programs or popular films) and walk through the steps with them regarding the characters in the clips. The outcome of impulsive behavior is often positive in the short-term, but the long-term consequences are negative. The goal is to get the client to improve their insight regarding achieving desired outcomes with fewer negative results. This is a useful adjunct to relapse-prevention work in discussing and managing actual cravings, urges, and desires to engage in addictive behaviors.

LEARNING TO THINK THINGS THROUGH

Impulsivity means having difficulty resisting urges or delaying behavior. Some people think of it as being impatient or not thinking things through. Acting impulsively can cause social, legal, academic, relationship, work-related, self-esteem, and other types of problems. It can lead to physical fights, addictive behavior, and alienation from others. Acting and reacting less impulsively is a skill that can be learned and used to avoid these painful consequences and to get the outcomes you desire.

Acting less impulsively involves two components: (a) It requires being able to observe your own thoughts, emotions, and behavior, and (b) it involves developing self-management habits and skills. This exercise will help you work through the steps of self-observation and find ways to get what you want without the painful consequences that often accompany acting without thinking first.

1. Identify a situation in which you acted impulsively. You may want to pick an event related to addiction, because this is often connected with acting impulsively. Describe the event as follows:

    a. What happened first (what you did, said; how did you feel; or what happened to you or around you that got you started)?

    _____

    b. Then what?

    _____

    c. Next, and so on, to its conclusion.

    _____

    Sometimes it can be helpful to work backwards from the conclusion. Either way, this task is designed to get you to slow things down and think more about each step along the way.

2. Now assess your motivation for your behavior by asking yourself, "What was I attempting to resolve, address, modify?" Think about how you felt, and your initial thoughts related to the situation to get at this. Write it here.

    _____

    _____

3. Third, analyze the consequences by asking yourself, "What were the outcomes or results of this behavior?" and "Were they what I wanted to happen?"

_____

_____

_____

_____

4. Fourth, assess alternatives. Ask yourself, "What would have been a more ideal outcome and what else could I have done to get what I wanted?" List as many other options as you can think of.

_____

_____

_____

_____

5. Lastly, pick one of the alternatives you listed and five actions you will take to practice this alternative.

_____

_____

_____

_____

6. Take a moment to imagine yourself doing it and anticipating any obstacles. What obstacles do you believe you may encounter?

_____

_____

_____

7. Identify one self-affirming thought you can say to yourself when you begin to recognize a desire to engage in something for instant gratification.

_____

_____

Be sure to bring this worksheet back to your next therapy session and be prepared to discuss any questions you may have and to talk over your thoughts and feelings about this activity.

HANDLING TOUGH SITUATIONS IN A HEALTHY WAY

GOALS OF THE EXERCISE

1. Maintain a program of recovery free from addiction and proactively address any legal conflicts resulting from past addictive behaviors.
2. Accept responsibility for legal problems without blaming others.
3. Learn to cope with the uncertainty that is associated with legal problems.
4. Identify nonaddictive coping strategies to deal with any outcome of legal problems.
5. Create a plan to cope with each possible legal outcome.
6. Decrease antisocial behaviors and increase prosocial behaviors.

ADDITIONAL PROBLEMS FOR WHICH THIS EXERCISE MAY BE USEFUL

- Antisocial Behavior
- Conduct Disorder/Delinquency
- Living Environment Deficiency
- Oppositional Defiant Behavior
- Self-Care Deficits—Secondary

SUGGESTIONS FOR PROCESSING THIS EXERCISE WITH THE CLIENT

The "Handling Tough Situations in a Healthy Way" activity is designed for the client who is having difficulty coping with current legal issues (pending or resolved) or unresolved legal issues. It can be used as an adjunct to basic problem-solving strategies or to a cost/benefit analysis.

HANDLING TOUGH SITUATIONS IN A HEALTHY WAY

A big part of recovery from addictions, and a healthy coping skill, is taking responsibility for our past and current behaviors. If you're working a 12-step program, this is also part of that work. Handling legal problems without resorting to old negative coping patterns is vital to recovery. Sometimes the outcomes of legal issues are not in our hands, and we must learn to cope with the possibility of serious consequences (e.g., prison time) without addictive behaviors. Other times the consequences of legal situations are known (e.g., fines, child support/alimony, loss of a driver's license).

Whether the outcome is known or unknown, it's normal to feel anxiety, depression, confusion, guilt, shame, anger, and fear. Still, we can handle pending, current, or settled legal situations in healthy ways by using new skills. The goal of this exercise is to help you look at the legal issues you face, explore your feelings about them, identify techniques to cope with those legal issues, and begin planning to maintain your recovery no matter what happens.

1. List your pending legal charges, known current legal issues, and unresolved legal issues.

   _____

   _____

2. What are the possible consequences for the items you listed in question 1 (e.g., jail/prison, criminal record, stigma, court-ordered treatment, fines, community service, probation/parole/separation from loved ones)?

   _____

   _____

   _____

3. What are your worries and fears about your pending legal issues or the legal issues you have not resolved?

   _____

   _____

4. With whom could you consult to get more information and insight regarding what you are facing (e.g., probation, attorney, police, court official, etc.)?

_____

_____

5. For each pending or unresolved legal issue, what would be the best and worst possible outcome? Considering all these potential outcomes, what is a strategy to deal with each issue?

Legal Issue	Best Outcome	Worst Outcome	Strategy
_____	_____	_____	_____
_____	_____	_____	_____
_____	_____	_____	_____
_____	_____	_____	_____
_____	_____	_____	_____

6. How can you begin to assume responsibility for your legal problems? Name one action you can take for each legal problem.

_____

_____

7. Name three ways failing to address these unresolved legal issues put you at risk for relapse.

_____

_____

8. Write a beginning plan for how you will cope with possible painful consequences of future legal problems without relapsing. Include the following: (a) how you will manage a range of feelings, and fears, anxiety; (b) how you will manage triggers, temptations to resort to old behaviors; and (c) what you will share with others about this plan.

_____

_____

9. How would you benefit from living without the stress of legal problems?

_____

_____

10. If you've been court-ordered to participate in treatment or to attend recovery meetings, how can you make the most out of this experience?

_____

_____

11. Talk with people who have had legal problems and resolved them without returning to addictive behaviors. Ask them how they were able to do it, and list three things they did that could work for you in dealing with your current legal issues.

_____

_____

Be sure to bring this handout to your next therapy session, and be prepared to discuss questions, thoughts, and feelings you may have had in completing it.

WHAT'S ADDICTION GOT TO DO WITH MY PROBLEMS?

GOALS OF THE EXERCISE

1. Maintain a program of recovery free from addiction and proactively address any legal conflicts resulting from past addictive behaviors.
2. Accept responsibility for legal problems without blaming others.
3. Identify the connections between legal problems experienced and addictive behaviors.
4. Identify thought patterns that created legal difficulties.
5. Understand the need to maintain abstinence from addiction and to remain free of negative consequences that include legal problems.
6. Decrease antisocial behaviors and increase prosocial behaviors.

ADDITIONAL PROBLEMS FOR WHICH THIS EXERCISE MAY BE USEFUL

- Antisocial Behavior
- Conduct Disorder/Delinquency
- Living Environment Deficiency
- Occupational Problems
- Readiness to Change
- Substance Use Disorders

SUGGESTIONS FOR PROCESSING THIS EXERCISE WITH THE CLIENT

The "What's Addiction Got to Do with My Problems?" activity helps clients focus on the connections between addictive behavior and legal or other problems. It is useful, when clients assess the outcomes of their actions, to point out ripple effects (e.g., going to jail is a primary consequence, which in turn interferes with holding a job, which makes it harder to earn income needed for bills). This exercise is useful as a group activity, with the group giving feedback and input. Follow-up may include "Analyzing Acting-Out Behavior" (28.A) and "Relapse Prevention Planning" (36.C) exercises contained in this manual.

WHAT'S ADDICTION GOT TO DO WITH MY PROBLEMS?

Addiction's consequences often include legal trouble. It's important to remember that legal problems (e.g., jail/prison, fines, probation) in turn cause problems in other areas, including work, finances, and relationships. It is also important to remember that taking responsibility for decisions that led to illegal acts, and the acts themselves, is necessary for recovery. Neither is easy. Sometimes we want to blame people, circumstances, or our addictions rather than be accountable. We may not want to admit that our illegal actions were related to our addictive behaviors. If we don't want to keep having legal problems, though, we have to do things differently. Until we accept responsibility, we can't take control and change the outcomes by choosing different actions.

This exercise will help you look at your legal problems, the consequences you've experienced, the patterns that have led to your breaking the law or not accepting responsibility, and strategies to avoid legal difficulties in recovery.

1. In the left-hand column, list your past and current legal issues. On the right, list how the illegal behavior was related to addictive behavior. Keep in mind that the relationship may be direct (e.g., got high and stole a car or stole money from work to gamble) or indirect (e.g., stole money to pay bills, which went unpaid due to gambling).

    Legal Problems   **Relationship to Addiction**

    _____   _____

    _____   _____

    _____   _____

    _____   _____

2. What consequences have you experienced as a result of legal difficulties? List the types of unpleasant results you've suffered due to the legal problem(s) listed in question 1. Include impact to self, relationships with others, finances, role success, value adherence, cultural factors, spirituality.

    _____

    _____

3. Have you tried to deny your actions or to blame something or someone else for your current or past legal problems? If so, how?

    _____

    _____

4. Identify three thoughts that helped you support or justify engaging in illegal activities.

    _____

    _____

5. How would continuing addictive behavior complicate your current legal difficulties or any legal difficulties that are still unresolved?

    _____

    _____

6. Following is a sample list of prosocial behaviors. Please list specific ways you can practice each in recovery. For example, for *honesty*, be more specific than "tell the truth." Describe how you will be honest in a situation where you have been dishonest in the past.

Prosocial Behaviors	What I Will Do
Honesty	_____
Helping others	_____
Reliability	_____
Consistency	_____
Dependability	_____
Acting responsibly	_____
Respecting rules even if I disagree with them	_____

7. What do you foresee as the biggest obstacle in preventing future legal problems?

    _____

    _____

8. List at least five strategies for meeting your social, emotional, and financial needs in recovery without criminal activity or addictive behavior.

    _____

    _____

    _____

9. List five ways prosocial behavior will help you maintain abstinence from all addictive behavior.

_____

_____

10. Identify three things you value most and how acting in a more prosocial way will affect each of them.

_____

_____

Be sure to bring this activity with you to your next therapy session, and be prepared to talk about any questions, thoughts, and feelings about the exercise.

ASSESSING MY ENVIRONMENT

GOALS OF THE EXERCISE

1. Maintain a program of recovery free from addiction and the negative impact of a deficient living environment.
2. Understand the negative impact of the current environment on recovery from addiction.
3. Identify connections between living environment deficiencies and addictive lifestyles.
4. Improve social, occupational, financial, and living situations sufficiently to increase the probability of successful recovery from addiction.
5. Prioritize needs for correcting environmental deficiencies and set goals to improve each.
6. Develop a peer group that is supportive of recovery and respectful of culture and identity.

ADDITIONAL PROBLEMS FOR WHICH THIS EXERCISE MAY BE USEFUL

- Adult-Child-of-an-Alcoholic (ACA) Traits
- Bipolar Disorder
- Depression–Unipolar
- Medical Issues
- Peer Group Negativity
- Self-Care Deficits—Primary
- Self-Care Deficits—Secondary

SUGGESTIONS FOR PROCESSING THIS EXERCISE WITH THE CLIENT

The "Assessing My Environment" activity encourages clients in early recovery to become more aware of their living environments and how those environments support or undermine their recovery, assess what they may need to change to reduce their risk of relapse, plan strategies for those changes, and get feedback. This exercise can be used as an individual or group activity. Follow-up with these clients could include sharing feedback received from program sponsors or others, tracking and reporting on progress made on plans, and other assignments such as "Personal Recovery Planning" (47.C) and "Relapse Prevention Planning" (36.C) contained in this manual. The therapist should take the lead in discussing social identities if there are any available support groups specific to them and any further treatment needs by other health care providers (e.g., trans-informed medical providers, LGBTQIA+ support groups, Spanish-speaking 12-step meetings).

ASSESSING MY ENVIRONMENT

Addictive behaviors and lifestyles may directly cause deficiencies in a person's living environment. These can include limited support from others for recovery efforts, the presence of triggers for relapse, social isolation, abuse or violence, financial problems, and/or inadequate food and shelter. Sometimes people are working their recovery programs in environments that undermine recovery or they do not feel safe being their authentic selves for fear of rejection, judgment, violence. They work very hard to succeed with these factors holding them back, when improving their living environments would make recovery less risky and difficult. A big step for many is asking for help before external stressors trigger a relapse. In this exercise you'll assess how your current environment may sabotage your recovery or cause other problems for you, decide what you want to work on first, and then develop a plan to work on each unmet need.

1. What, if any, are the problems in your living environment in the following areas?

    Family life:

    _____

    Social:

    _____

    Occupational:

    _____

    Financial:

    _____

    Spiritual/cultural:

    _____

    Recovery support that is affirming, inclusive, multiculturally sensitive:

    _____

    Necessities of daily life (food, shelter, clothing, etc.):

    _____

    Access to adequate health care:

    _____

2. List five ways your current living environment hinders your recovery efforts.

    _____

    _____

    _____

    _____

3. In what ways do your peers and family increase your risk of relapse (e.g., are they actively using, angry with you for past behaviors, unsupportive of your recovery and/or identities)?

    _____

    _____

4. What other problems do you experience in your current living environment (e.g., violence, emotional abuse, rejection, hiding authentic self out of fear, racism/oppression/discrimination, etc.)?

    _____

    _____

5. Pick the three most important deficiencies in your environment that you have control of and feel willing/able to address:

    _____

    _____

    _____

    _____

6. What five actions can you take to improve things in the areas you listed in question 5 as your most important deficiencies? The actions don't have to be dramatic—think of small steps. If you cannot think of five on your own, consult with your sponsor or someone in recovery or treatment you trust for other alternatives. How will taking the first step in a positive direction be helpful to you?

    _____

    _____

    _____

    _____

7. List three ways a recovery group could be/will continue to be beneficial in improving your living environment or supporting you as you make these changes.

    _____

    _____

Be sure to bring this handout with you to your next therapy session and be prepared to discuss your thoughts and feelings about the exercise with your therapist.

WHAT WOULD MY IDEAL LIFE LOOK LIKE?

GOALS OF THE EXERCISE

1. Maintain a program of recovery free from addiction and the negative impact of a deficient living environment.
2. Understand the negative impact of the current environment on recovery from addiction.
3. Develop a peer group that is supportive of recovery and affirming/inclusive.
4. Clarify and prioritize life values and goals.
5. Increase awareness of the effects of addictive behavior on achieving values and goals.

ADDITIONAL PROBLEMS FOR WHICH THIS EXERCISE MAY BE USEFUL

- Depression–Unipolar
- Readiness to Change
- Relapse Proneness
- Substance Use Disorders
- Suicidal Ideation

SUGGESTIONS FOR PROCESSING THIS EXERCISE WITH THE CLIENT

The "What Would My Ideal Life Look Like?" activity is written for clients who are having difficulty establishing concrete goals for a life in recovery. Its approach is to guide the client in establishing what their ideal would be in each of several life domains, then determining the difference between the current situation and that ideal and what action is necessary to achieve the ideal. The exercise then leads the client in thinking about whether addictive behaviors will help or hinder them in achieving these ideals and challenges rationalizations, working to increase cognitive dissonance and break down denial and minimization.

Follow-up could include establishing plans and timelines for some of the actions defined in this exercise and keeping a journal and sharing outcomes of those plans with the therapist and treatment group. *As this exercise is also recommended for clients experiencing suicidal ideation, it is vital to ask directly about urges or intent to harm self or others at each therapeutic contact and take whatever therapeutic action is needed to keep the client or others safe.*

WHAT WOULD MY IDEAL LIFE LOOK LIKE?

If you are working on establishing or maintaining recovery from an addiction, this activity will help you find the benefits of sobriety that mean the most to you personally. Whether sobriety or another goal is your greatest concern, it will help you set goals and focus on what changes in your life would make you happiest.

1. Do you have a clear vision of your ideal life? Please summarize that life in each area:

    a. Where would you live?

    _____

    b. What would your relationship/family situation be?

    _____

    c. What would your work be/educational pursuit?

    _____

    d. What would your proudest achievements be?

    _____

    e. What would your hobbies and leisure activities be?

    _____

    f. How would other people think of you?

    _____

    g. How would spirituality play a role?

    _____

2. What would it take to get from where you are today to where you want to be?

    a. Where would you live?

Situation Now	Ideal Situation	What Change Is Needed?

b. What would your relationship/family situation be?

Situation Now	Ideal Situation	What Change Is Needed?

c. What would your work/educational pursuits be?

Situation Now	Ideal Situation	What Change Is Needed?

d. What would your proudest achievements be?

Situation Now	Ideal Situation	What Change Is Needed?

e. What would your hobbies and leisure activities be?

Situation Now	Ideal Situation	What Change Is Needed?

f. How would other people think of you?

Situation Now	Ideal Situation	What Change Is Needed?

g. How would your spirituality be explored or contribute?

Situation Now	Ideal Situation	What Change Is Needed?

3. Let's look at the effects of sobriety on the following areas. Note how sobriety will help in each area.

a. Where you would live:

_____

_____

b. Relationship/family:

_____

_____

c. Work/education:

_____

_____

d. Hobbies/leisure:

_____

_____

e. What others think:

_____

_____

4. Some final questions:

a. If drinking, using, or other addictions sabotage your chances to achieve your dreams, but you keep practicing the addictive behaviors anyway, what message do you draw from this?

_____

_____

b. If someone you knew put an addictive behavior ahead of their dreams and ideals, what would you think it meant about their relationship with that behavior?

_____

_____

c. If this is happening in your life, do the people who know you think you have a problem? If they think you have a problem, but you feel you don't, how do you explain this?

_____

_____

Be sure to bring this handout back to your next therapy session and be prepared to talk about your thoughts and feelings about the exercise.

COPING WITH ADDICTION AND OTHER MEDICAL PROBLEMS

GOALS OF THE EXERCISE

1. Understand the relationship between medical issues and addiction.
2. Reduce the impact of medical problems on recovery and relapse potential.
3. Reduce the risk of relapse by using therapeutic strategies to cope with both addictive problems and other medical illnesses or injuries.
4. Participate proactively as an informed patient in the medical management of physical health problems.

ADDITIONAL PROBLEMS FOR WHICH THIS EXERCISE MAY BE USEFUL

- Chronic Pain
- Relapse Proneness
- Self-Care Deficits—Primary
- Substance-Induced Disorders
- Substance Use Disorders

SUGGESTIONS FOR PROCESSING THIS EXERCISE WITH THE CLIENT

The "Coping with Addiction and Other Medical Problems" activity is designed for clients with serious medical problems apart from their addictive issues. It addresses issues of the possible causal role of addictive behaviors in having suffered injuries or illnesses and coping strategies to achieve the best practicable quality of life for these clients. Follow-up could include referral to additional support groups that are focused on the specific medical problems that clients are experiencing. Another suggestion is bibliotherapy involving books such as *Kitchen Table Wisdom* by Rachel Naomi Remen, M.D., which addresses the interaction between spirituality and coping with physical trauma from the author's perspective as a therapist, physician, and a patient with a serious and chronic medical problem. Encouraging clients to establish consistent and regular mindfulness, relaxation, meditation, and stress management practices concurrently as part of treatment (approved by physicians for those with medical conditions that inhibit certain practices) will improve their overall health and should be consistently reinforced.

COPING WITH ADDICTION AND OTHER MEDICAL PROBLEMS

Some people suffer from both substance abuse problems and other medical problems that may be very serious, even life threatening. If you are working to recover from both an addiction and another serious or painful medical problem, this assignment will help you use the same tools for both tasks where possible and guide you in coping with some special challenges in this situation.

1. What's the connection between addiction and other medical problems? Sometimes there isn't one. It can be just coincidence or bad luck that the same person has a problem with addiction and is also badly hurt or sick. However, people who engage in addictive behaviors are more likely to get hurt or sick. Sometimes people's injuries or illnesses are directly caused by their drinking, drug use, or other high-risk behavior. This is not pointed out to blame anyone, but merely to acknowledge the role of cause and effect. This is empowering because it means that changing behaviors can lead to better outcomes. Please describe any ways your addictive behavior caused or contributed to your becoming injured or ill.

    _____

    _____

2. Sometimes the connection between addiction and medical issues works in the other direction. The medical problems come first, and people use substances for the pain or other symptoms, then they end up with addictions as well as the injuries or illnesses they started with. When people use drugs (street drugs or prescription medications) to try to cope with their medical symptoms, they may become addicted. Please describe how your medical problems may have led you to addictive behaviors in the search for relief.

    _____

    _____

3. Each issue alone, untreated, poses serious risks to health and living a life in recovery. For the best outcome of all health issues and recovery from addiction, the most

effective strategy is to treat all these issues at the same time. Describe any reasons you might have focused on one, the other, or neither at this time.

_____

_____

4. Many people find that some of the same methods they use to overcome substance use problems can also help them to deal with injuries or diseases that burden them with chronic pain and/or sharply limit their physical capabilities. These methods can be things like participating in support groups, learning new coping skills, and finding replacement methods and activities for things they can't do anymore. Identify five substance abuse recovery tools might help you deal with your own medical problems.

_____

_____

5. Some treatment approaches used for medical problems may not seem to fit into recovery from substance abuse, such as the use of narcotics for pain management. If your doctor has told you to take medications for your sickness or injury, have you talked with them about your substance abuse issues? If you have, what is the plan for avoiding problems with addiction? If not, what keeps you from sharing this information, and how might that affect your recovery from both issues?

_____

_____

6. What might happen to you and your recovery if you stopped taking those medications, or didn't take them as prescribed?

_____

_____

7. Have you also talked about this with people who are working with you on your addictive issues? If so, what did these people tell you?

_____

_____

If you are participating in a 12-step recovery program, are you aware of the policies your program has developed about the use of prescribed medications? Alcoholics Anonymous' official position is that if your doctor knows your history with addiction, is experienced working with people with addictions, and has prescribed medication with that knowledge, and you are taking it exactly as prescribed, then you are doing what you need to do to stay sober. Other 12-step programs have similar policies. If you have questions, check the official literature.

8. How will you manage medications and avoid misuse of them or have them result in a lapse?

    _____

    _____

9. Please use this space to describe the tools, methods, and resources you will use to cope with the combined challenges of an addiction and a serious injury or illness. If you haven't thought this far ahead yet, what questions and concerns do you have about this issue?

    _____

    _____

10. Identify a stress management plan approved by your physician and outline it here. Consider practicing daily strategies as you start to get in the habit. They do not need to be the same each day but something that interests and motivates you, so you have the best chance of making it a habit.

    _____

    _____

Be sure to bring this handout back to your next therapy session and be prepared to talk about your thoughts and feelings about the exercise.

PHYSICAL AND EMOTIONAL SELF-CARE

GOALS OF THE EXERCISE

1. Understand the connections among medical issues, self-care, and addiction.
2. Reduce the impact of medical problems on recovery and relapse potential.
3. Understand and participate proactively as an informed patient in the medical management of physical health problems.
4. Achieve and maintain the highest practicable level of function by maintaining recovery from addiction and effective management of medical problems.
5. Examine daily use of time and identify both healthy practices and areas for improvement.

ADDITIONAL PROBLEMS FOR WHICH THIS EXERCISE MAY BE USEFUL

- Borderline Traits
- Chronic Pain
- Depression–Unipolar
- Eating Disorders and Obesity
- Posttraumatic Stress Disorder (PTSD)
- Relapse Proneness
- Self-Care Deficits—Primary

SUGGESTIONS FOR PROCESSING THIS EXERCISE WITH THE CLIENT

The "Physical and Emotional Self-Care" activity is for clients with chronic or acute medical challenges who neglect this area and are at greater risk of relapse as a result. It focuses the client's attention on self-care and guides them in assessment of needs, habits, and resources, then in creating a structured self-care plan. Follow-up activities can include keeping a self-care log using the format in this exercise (clinicians may need to print additional pages for clients to use), reporting back to the therapist or group on progress, surveying role models on self-care practices, and completing the "Personal Recovery Planning" activity (Exercise 47.C).

PHYSICAL AND EMOTIONAL SELF-CARE

There's a link between poor self-care and relapse. When we abuse substances or practice other addictive patterns, we often neglect our needs, both physical (safety, nutrition, sleep, exercise) and emotional (competence, sense of value, acceptance, emotional support from healthy relationships, sense of control). This exercise will help you see what you're doing now to take care of yourself and where you can improve.

1. What five things are you doing today to take care of yourself physically?

    _____

    _____

    _____

    _____

2. This is a physical self-care tracking chart. Please keep a record for the next seven days. A well-rounded plan is best; include areas of proper nutrition, approved physical activities, adequate sleep, something calm/joyful:

Date	My Plan	What I Did	What Helped	Obstacles	How to Improve
Ex.	*Take a walk*	*No exercise*		*Procrastinated*	*Do first thing in a.m.*
Ex.	*Eat balanced meal*	*Ate breakfast*	*Planned meal*		
___	___	___	___	___	___
___	___	___	___	___	___
___	___	___	___	___	___
___	___	___	___	___	___

3. Looking back on the last week of self-monitoring and tracking, what insight did you gain from completing your tracking chart?

   _____

   _____

4. Emotional self-care is as important as physical self-care. It contributes to overall health and well-being. If neglected or not consistently attended to, it makes us prone to use of substances and poor mental health. Examples of emotional self-care include feeling safe, stable, and good about ourselves, managing stress/anxiety, feeling valued/seen/heard, being able to tolerate discomfort when the situation cannot be changed, and a sense of belongingness. Because substances and other addictive behaviors likely played a role in managing emotions, finding healthy replacements is vital to sustained recovery.

   Please answer these questions about your emotional self-care.

   a. What emotional needs do you have which are not being met today?

      _____

   b. What emotional needs did you try to meet with addictive behaviors in the past?

      _____

   c. Name five methods or resources you employ to help you provide for your emotional needs?

      _____

      _____

      _____

      _____

   d. What additional methods or resources do you need for emotional self-care, and where and how can you learn these methods or get these resources?

      _____

      _____

      _____

      _____

5. List five benefits that consistently addressing your physical and emotional health will have for you and your recovery.

   _____

   _____

   _____

   _____

6. Consider the added benefits of technology to allow ease of tracking, potential reminders, alarms, calendar of appointments/meetings/classes. Which would be most important for me to explore?

    _____

    _____

7. When feeling physically or emotionally unwell, what is one practice I can rely on to re-center my priority on self-care?

    _____

    _____

Be sure to bring this handout back to your next therapy session and be prepared to talk about your thoughts and feelings about the exercise.

BEING GENUINELY ALTRUISTIC

GOALS OF THE EXERCISE

1. Develop a realistic sense of self without narcissistic grandiosity, exaggeration, or excessive sense of entitlement.
2. Understand the relationship between narcissistic traits and addiction.
3. Develop empathy for other people, particularly victims of the client's narcissism.
4. Identify a healthy role model and examine that person's life for unselfish behavior.
5. Identify and plan ways to become less selfish in daily life.

ADDITIONAL PROBLEMS FOR WHICH THIS EXERCISE MAY BE USEFUL

*   Antisocial Behavior
*   Conduct Disorder/Delinquency
*   Oppositional Defiant Behavior
*   Partner Relational Conflicts
*   Peer Group Negativity

SUGGESTIONS FOR PROCESSING THIS EXERCISE WITH THE CLIENT

The "Being Genuinely Altruistic" activity targets self-centeredness, one of the core traits of both narcissism and addiction. It does so by examining the benefits of becoming unselfish in terms of enhanced self-esteem and improved relationships, guiding the client in identifying a role model and examining the ways that person models unselfish actions, and planning specific strategies to implement unselfish behavior in daily life. Follow-up could include videotherapy using films such as *Amélie* or others recommended in the book *Rent Two Films and Let's Talk in the Morning* by John W. Hesley and Jan G. Hesley, published by Wiley, as well as keeping a journal on the outcomes of actions planned in this exercise.

BEING GENUINELY ALTRUISTIC

What's the point of being altruistic? In a way, it seems like a contradiction to ask, "If I'm unselfish, what's in it for me?" However, it can be answered. For many reasons, being truly generous and unselfish helps people break addictive patterns and stay sober. So the answer to "What's in it for me?" may be "My health, my relationships, my job, my freedom, my sobriety, and ultimately my life." This exercise will help you to decide whether this is worthwhile for you and why, and if you decide you want to become a less selfish person, to find some ways to begin to work on it.

1. Why do you think it might help you live a happier life to become more unselfish?

   _____

   _____

   Some answers might include increased self-respect, better relationships with other people, less frustration and envy, and a better connection with your spiritual values.

2. What is something you value? What actions can you take to live in alignment with it?

   _____

   _____

3. Name a person whom you trust, admire, would go to for help with a problem, or want to be more like. Give a specific example of ways this person is unselfish or demonstrated unselfishness.

   _____

   _____

   What have you observed to be the ways this benefits them and those around them?

   _____

   _____

   _____

4. When you think about the value you stated in question 1, would any of those behaviors you witnessed help you live closer to your stated value? Outline three ways you could practice that behavior "in all your affairs."

   _____

5. The word *genuinely* in the title of this activity means that the unselfishness has to be real, not for show to impress people, solely to get recognized/credited, or to manipulate them. The best way to do this is to practice doing at least one generous thing a day and not letting anyone else know about it. What generous things could you do each day without anyone else knowing, including the people you do them for?

_____

_____

Pick one and practice it once a day for 2 weeks. Outline here your experience including how it made you feel, how easy/challenging it was.

6. How do you think your thoughts and feelings about yourself would change through your practicing generosity?

_____

_____

7. How would this make a difference in your ability to live the life you want to live, according to things that matter to you?

_____

_____

8. Name three ways unselfishness would support your ongoing sobriety/recovery from addictive behaviors.

_____

_____

9. Use this space to describe your plan to commit yourself to increasing behaviors that are unselfish in your daily life.

_____

_____

Be sure to bring this handout back to your next therapy session and be prepared to talk about your thoughts and feelings about the exercise.

GETTING OUTSIDE OF MYSELF

GOALS OF THE EXERCISE

1. Develop a realistic sense of self, without narcissistic grandiosity, exaggeration, or excessive sense of entitlement.
2. Understand the relationship between narcissistic traits and addiction.
3. Develop empathy for other people, particularly victims of the client's narcissism.
4. Identify past experiences of helping others and their positive effects.
5. List skills and abilities the client has that could be helpful to others.
6. Identify organizations or groups the client could help.
7. Create and carry out a plan to assist a group or organization of the client's choice.

ADDITIONAL PROBLEMS FOR WHICH THIS EXERCISE MAY BE USEFUL

- Antisocial Behavior
- Conduct Disorder/Delinquency
- Depression–Unipolar
- Oppositional Defiant Behavior
- Relapse Proneness
- Suicidal Ideation

SUGGESTIONS FOR PROCESSING THIS EXERCISE WITH THE CLIENT

The "Getting Outside of Myself" activity is based on the 12-step principle of service work. One tenet of Alcoholics Anonymous and other 12-step programs is that when nothing else works to help a person stay sober, helping another alcoholic/addict succeeds. This exercise presents this concept to the client, then guides the client in identifying benefits of past experiences of helping others. It guides the client in identifying special skills or abilities they have to offer and groups they might assist, then in creating a plan to engage in some form of formal or informal helping activity to reduce isolation, increase self-esteem, and get the client's emotional focus balanced between their own issues and those of others. This exercise is suitable for individual or group use, in session, or as homework. Follow-up can include keeping a journal about ongoing experiences with helping activities and discussing outcomes of these activities.

GETTING OUTSIDE OF MYSELF

Human connections have a healing power that helps us with many problems. Whether we are struggling with addictive patterns, depression, anxiety, grief, or physical illness, emotional isolation is often one of the sources of our problems and makes our suffering worse. Engagement in addictive behavior tends to increase self-centeredness, feeling as though you're the victim when things don't go as planned; it also increases feelings of isolation. Recovery offers the opportunity to move out of this self-centeredness and enjoy the benefits of meaningful social connection and find a sense of belonging with others. Connecting emotionally with others on a meaningful level, doing things that get our focus off our problems and pain, can help both us and others. It strengthens relationships and reduces our feelings of isolation, boosts our self-esteem, gives us the benefit of others' insights and experience, and lets us experience their interest in and regard for us. This exercise will guide you in connecting with other people in ways that will enhance your recovery.

1. Think back to a time when you got involved with helping others in some way: raising money for a good cause, helping friends move, helping a child do homework, helping an elderly person with day-to-day tasks. What prompted you to get involved? What did you do and how did you feel about it before and after?

    _____

    _____

2. Are you involved with any helping activities now, including service work in a 12-step program?

    _____

    If so, what are you doing, what led you to get involved with this activity, and how does it contribute to your sobriety today?

    _____

    _____

    _____

    _____

3. Use this space to list any special talents or training you have to offer (e.g., building or repairing things, teaching a skill, being multilingual, being artistic, being a good listener).

    _____

    _____

4. What organizations or groups of people could you volunteer to help? If you don't know of any, how could you find them?

    _____

    _____

5. Identify the benefits of getting involved and using your skills and talents to help someone else.

    _____

    _____

6. Use this space to plan to contact a group that could use your help, find something you can do to help them, and make a schedule for this activity, on a scheduled basis.

    _____

    _____

7. Identify any factors or fears, hesitations you have in initiating this. How will you work to push past them and engage in getting out of yourself?

    _____

    _____

   Be sure to bring this handout back to your next therapy session and be prepared to talk about your thoughts and feelings about this exercise. After you've been acting on your plan and helping in the way you've chosen for 2 weeks, talk with your therapist about how it's affecting your recovery.

ASSESSING READINESS AND PREPARING TO QUIT

GOALS OF THE EXERCISE

1. Accept chemical dependence on tobacco and begin to actively participate in a recovery program.
2. Establish and maintain total abstinence from nicotine products while increasing knowledge of the addiction and the process of recovery.
3. Develop personal reasons for working on a recovery plan for tobacco use disorders.
4. Withdraw from tobacco, stabilize physically and emotionally, and then establish a supportive recovery plan.

ADDITIONAL PROBLEMS FOR WHICH THIS EXERCISE MAY BE USEFUL

- Readiness to Change
- Relapse Proneness
- Substance Use Disorders

SUGGESTIONS FOR PROCESSING THIS EXERCISE WITH THE CLIENT

The "Assessing Readiness and Preparing to Quit" activity is designed to help the client plan for successful cessation of tobacco use. It is designed to be the client's creation. This exercise works well for individual therapy but can also be useful for groups. The larger tasks outlined in the exercise include assessing readiness and preparing to quit while assessing previous attempts at stopping. Psychoeducation about the risks of continuing use of tobacco products while also attempting to recover from other mental health or addiction issues will be vital to remove this as a relapse trigger itself. Follow-up could include "Addressing Relapse Triggers" (Exercise 24.B), "Relapse Prevention Planning" (Exercise 36.C), "Personal Recovery Planning" (Exercise 47.C), and "Use of Affirmations for Change" Exercise 24.C) in this manual.

ASSESSING READINESS AND PREPARING TO QUIT

No one starts using tobacco products because they want to get addicted. Some people don't think about it at all. Most people who use tobacco products become addicted very quickly, and many deny that they are addicted. Although everyone's experience is unique, common physical factors (i.e., physical pleasure and cravings, biological processes), as well as social (i.e., what your peers see as normal) and psychological factors (i.e., relaxation, pleasure), play important roles in maintaining the addiction. Giving up tobacco products requires taking a realistic look at this addiction and why it is so hard to quit. You can gain useful information from attempts you may have already made to quit (what worked, what didn't?).

This exercise (and the two following in this manual titled "Addressing Tobacco Relapse Triggers" and "Use of Affirmations for Change") will help you to plan the three basic components of a successful smoking/chewing cessation plan: (a) increasing your motivation, (b) finding and using supports, and (c) learning and using alternative coping skills.

PREPARATION/GETTING READY

1. What signs of addiction do you see in your use of tobacco products (e.g., increased use, multiple failed attempts to quit, tolerance, withdrawal, continued or resumed use despite negative consequences)?

   _____

   _____

2. What denial-oriented statements have you used to rationalize continuing to use (e.g., "My life is too stressful now," "I'm not mentally prepared to quit," "I'll probably fail if I try to quit now," "I'll quit the really bad stuff first and then take this on later")?

   _____

   _____

3. List five ways tobacco use has negatively affected your life and/or others' lives.

   _____

   _____

   _____

   _____

4. Many people make multiple attempts before successfully quitting. The benefit is that each time we learn something that can help us the next time. What are the top three reasons you want to give up tobacco use, as of today?

    _____

    _____

5. List 10 things that will result from establishing and maintaining total abstinence from tobacco products.

    _____

    _____

    _____

    _____

    _____

    _____

    _____

    _____

    _____

    _____

6. What family, social, and emotional challenges will you face in your recovery plan (think about environmental pressures, triggers, cues/cravings, withdrawal, fears)?

    _____

    _____

7. Part of a successful recovery plan is identifying your doubts and fears about quitting, to prevent setting yourself up for defeat even before you start. What are your doubts and fears about quitting?

    _____

    _____

8. If you've quit before, what worked for you, and what led to your return to using tobacco? Identify the feelings, sensations, cues that you'll need to get past this time to be successful.

    _____

    _____

9. Please set a start date to begin carrying out your plan.

    _____

10. How and when will you tell your family, friends, and coworkers about your plan? Are there any ways you can identify roles they can play to help you?

_____

_____

Be sure to bring this handout with you to your future therapy sessions and be prepared to discuss your thoughts and feelings about this exercise as you begin your recovery plan.

ADDRESSING RELAPSE TRIGGERS

GOALS OF THIS EXERCISE

1. Establish and maintain total abstinence from tobacco products while increasing knowledge of the addiction and the process of recovery.
2. Accept chemical dependence on tobacco and begin to actively participate in a recovery program.
3. Identify known triggers or cues for tobacco use relapse and develop strategies to maintain abstinence from tobacco.

ADDITIONAL PROBLEMS FOR WHICH THIS EXERCISE MAY BE USEFUL

- Readiness for Change
- Relapse Proneness
- Substance Use Disorders

SUGGESTIONS FOR PROCESSING THIS EXERCISE WITH THE CLIENT

The "Addressing Relapse Triggers" activity is designed to help the client plan for successful cessation of nicotine use. It is designed to be the client's creation. This exercise works well for individual therapy but can also be useful for groups. It is important to address the connection between tobacco addiction and other addictions and the significance of working on recovery from all addictions (including tobacco) and treatment of other mental health disorders concurrently.

ADDRESSING RELAPSE TRIGGERS

Establishing and maintaining total abstinence from tobacco products is similar to establishing abstinence and recovery from other addictions. Some of the same strategies you're using to address other addictive behavior or mental health issues will work with tobacco use recovery. This exercise is designed with the basic components of a successful tobacco use cessation plan in mind—specifically, planning for relapse, prevention, finding and using available supports, and learning/using alternative coping skills to replace the addiction(s).

1. Here is a partial list of common relapse triggers. Which of these triggers will you have to watch out for? Please *circle* all those that apply.

Negative emotions	Social pressures	Stress
Interpersonal conflict	Positive emotions	Boredom
Testing personal control	Anxiety	Self-defeating thoughts
Weakening motivation		Justifications for continued use
Specific situations	Times of the day	Specific events

   Paired association with other activities (i.e., morning coffee, driving, etc.)

Strong cravings	Other addictions

   List others specific to you that are not included:

   _____

   _____

2. Of these triggers, which can you avoid and how will you do that?

   _____

   _____

   _____

3. What is your specific plan to cope with each of the triggers you identified that you can't avoid?

   _____

   _____

4. Which of the following methods or sources of support will you use to deal with triggers and cues to smoke, chew, or snort tobacco products, and how will you use them?

   a. Self-help groups

   _____

   b. Acupuncture

   _____

   c. Medications

   _____

   d. Hypnosis

   _____

   e. Biofeedback

   _____

   f. Publications and reading materials

   _____

   g. Smoking cessation clinics and programs

   _____

   h. Online support

   _____

   i. Yoga/workout groups/clubs

   _____

   j. Other:

   _____

5. Believing it is possible and desirable takes us further in our motivation and efforts to discontinue use. What affirmations can you use to increase a positive attitude and hopeful outlook about this attempt?

   _____

   _____

6. Name five ways your family, friends, and coworkers can support you in your abstinence from tobacco products.

   _____

   _____

   _____

   _____

7. How will you handle cravings and other withdrawal symptoms? (Remember, they are temporary and will pass. The longer you abstain, the more your withdrawal symptoms will lessen in both frequency and intensity, the faster they will pass, and the better you will be at managing them.)

   _____

   _____

8. What other addictive behaviors need to be managed to keep your tobacco sobriety in check (e.g., eating disorders, alcohol use, gambling, etc.)? How do they work together to increase your relapse risk?

   _____

   _____

9. Managing emotions like stress or anxiety is vital to success. What strategy can you put in place for minimizing stressful situations or high-risk environments when you can and early on?

   _____

   _____

10. What rewards will you give yourself for abstinence, and when?

   _____

   _____

Be sure to bring this handout with you to your future therapy sessions and be prepared to discuss your thoughts and feelings about this exercise as you begin your recovery plan.

USE OF AFFIRMATIONS FOR CHANGE

GOALS OF THE EXERCISE

1. Learn how self-talk influences self-image, moods, and behavior.
2. Substitute positive self-talk for negative self-talk to improve self-perception and ability to cope with difficult situations.
3. Learn to use subject-specific affirmations to change behaviors and achieve or maintain abstinence from addictive patterns.

ADDITIONAL PROBLEMS FOR WHICH THIS EXERCISE MAY BE USEFUL

- Adult-Child-of-an-Alcoholic (ACA) Traits
- Borderline Traits
- Chronic Pain
- Depression–Unipolar
- Gambling
- Posttraumatic Stress Disorder (PTSD)
- Relapse Proneness
- Substance Intoxication/Withdrawal
- Substance Use Disorders

SUGGESTIONS FOR PROCESSING THIS EXERCISE WITH CLIENT

The "Use of Affirmations for Change" is an evidence-based activity, relying on two cognitive principles: (a) When people are presented with information repeatedly, they are likely to accept it as true, altering their cognitions more each time they're exposed to it; and (b) when people find their actions in conflict with their beliefs or values, it causes cognitive dissonance, which is usually resolved by modifying the behavior rather than the belief system, especially if the belief system continues to receive reinforcement. In this activity, this process is used to shift the client's cognition and behavior.

This exercise empowers the client, guiding them through a first use of a structured stress-management meditation, with the client choosing the goal and designing their own affirmation. Follow-up can include keeping a journal and reporting back to the therapist and treatment group, after 3 to 4 weeks, about changes experienced as a result of consistent daily use of affirmations.

USE OF AFFIRMATIONS FOR CHANGE

All of us have negative beliefs about ourselves because of painful experiences or things others have said to us. When we talk to ourselves, silently or aloud, what we say is often critical and negative. This negative self-talk molds our thoughts, feelings, and actions, and overcoming it takes work. However, when we do this work, we learn to think of ourselves in ways that are more balanced and realistic, that support our recovery efforts and feelings of self-worth, and that help us stop self-destructive behaviors. This exercise will help you identify the harmful messages you give yourself and increase your ability to replace them with more realistic and positive self-statements.

1. We all talk to ourselves as we go through the day, either aloud or silently in our thoughts. Over the next week, pay attention to the things you say to yourself, about yourself, and your actions. Also, notice when anyone else gives you messages about yourself (e.g., your boss, coworkers, family members, or friends). When you find yourself saying negative things in your self-talk, or when others are negative or critical to you, note here what negative messages you repeat to yourself or hear from others most often. Then rewrite them to express your desired situation and self-view in reasonable but positive terms and imagine what it would be like to hear these positive messages instead of the negative ones.

Negative Self-Statements	Positive Self-Statements (in Present Tense)
Ex.: I can't stay sober.	*I like being clean and sober.*
Ex.: I'm weak and this is too hard.	*I am learning new skills and getting better.*
_____	_____
_____	_____
_____	_____

2. Think about a situation in your life that bothers you. List the negative self-statements that accompany this situation, then describe your feelings when you think about these negative statements. Create positive self-statements to replace those negative messages.

Situation:

Negative Statement	Feelings Statement	Positive Replacement
_____	_____	_____
_____	_____	_____
_____	_____	_____
_____	_____	_____

3. In what ways do more positive self-statements change the experience?

   _____

   _____

4. Here's a specific way to use positive self-statements to solve a problem or make a change in your life, such as quitting smoking. This is based on two scientific principles. The first is that if we hear something over and over, we start to believe it: Why do you think negative messages have so much power? If this wasn't true, advertisers wouldn't spend their money to make sure we hear their messages repeatedly. The second principle is that when there is a mismatch between our actions and what we believe, it makes us uncomfortable, and we tend to change our actions to match our beliefs. This activity is designed to change your beliefs about a situation in your life so your actions will change to match the new beliefs. Name a problem or change you'd like to make here.

   _____

   _____

5. Now think about the way you want things to be in this situation and describe it in one short sentence. Use the present tense and use only positive terms: Talk about what *will be* going on, not what *won't be*. For our example of quitting smoking, the sentence could be something like "I love living smoke-free and breathing fresh air." Write your sentence here.

   _____

   _____

6. Now create a mental picture to go with that sentence, which is called an affirmation. For our example, you might picture yourself strolling along a beach taking deep breaths of clean salty air or walking in a pine forest in the mountains smelling the breeze through the trees. Close your eyes, picture this mental scene as clearly as you can for 10 or 15 seconds, and repeat your affirmation in a quiet voice. What is this like for you? What feelings and thoughts come up?

   _____

   _____

7. Now write your affirmation on small cards or pieces of paper and put them where you will see them several times a day, in places like your bathroom mirror, your wallet or purse, your car's dashboard, your desk, your refrigerator, an alarm that alerts you to read a message on your phone, and so on. For 1 month, make it part of your routine to stop what you're doing 10 times a day for 30 seconds to close your eyes, visualize your mental picture, and repeat your affirmation to yourself. You may even want to write it out before or after you do this. This will take only 5 minutes out of your day, and you can do it almost anywhere, so it won't be hard to do.

_____

8. Answer this question after a month of testing your affirmation: What changes do you see in your behavior from the time you started using this affirmation until now?

_____

_____

9. Has anything changed in how you feel about yourself, your perspective?

_____

_____

Be sure to bring this handout back to your next therapy session and be prepared to talk about your thoughts and feelings about the exercise.

INTERRUPTING COMPULSIVE THOUGHTS AND URGES*

GOALS OF THE EXERCISE

1. Develop and implement a daily ritual that interrupts the current pattern of compulsions.
2. Reduce time involved with or interference from obsessions and compulsions.
3. Function daily at a consistent level with minimal interference from obsessions and compulsions.

ADDITIONAL PROBLEMS FOR WHICH THIS EXERCISE MAY BE USEFUL

- Anxiety
- Bipolar Disorder
- Borderline Traits
- Depression–Unipolar
- Eating Disorders and Obesity
- Gambling
- Impulsivity
- Nicotine Use/Dependence
- Posttraumatic Stress Disorder (PTSD)
- Relapse Proneness
- Self-Harm
- Sexual Promiscuity
- Substance Use Disorders

SUGGESTIONS FOR PROCESSING THIS EXERCISE WITH THE CLIENT

"Interrupting Compulsive Thoughts and Urges" teaches clients to disrupt rumination and compulsive behavior by doing jobs or tasks they dislike when these thoughts arise. The exercise has three parts: First, the client lists three to five unpleasant tasks to perform

---

*Most of the content of this assignment (with slight revisions) originates from *The Adult Psychotherapy Homework Planner*, Sixth Edition, by A. E. Jongsma and T. E. Bruce (Wiley, 2021). Reprinted with permission.

when compulsive thoughts emerge. The list should include things they can do in varied settings (e.g., home, school, or workplace). Part Two asks the client to commit to trying this solution for 2 weeks. The final phase asks the client to assess changes resulting from the activity and consult with the therapist about possible modification(s). Follow-up can include reporting back to the therapist and/or group on outcomes and planning use of the technique for other behavior patterns the client wants to change.

INTERRUPTING COMPULSIVE THOUGHTS AND URGES

This intervention aims to reduce the frequency and intensity of compulsive thoughts and behaviors by having you perform a job or task you don't like when the thoughts come up. This method may seem unusual because most of us prefer not to do things we dislike. The idea is that by committing to perform these unpleasant tasks when compulsive cycles start, you'll be able to reduce the frequency of the compulsive thoughts or behaviors, which are also things you'd rather not be doing.

The assignment contains three parts. The first asks you to list unpleasant tasks you can perform in places where your compulsions arise, especially at home and work or school. Part Two is a commitment to try this approach for two weeks, then check how well it has worked. Part Three is talking with your therapist about any improvements you can think of in using this activity in your life.

CHOOSING SELF-INTERVENTION JOBS/TASKS

1. Think of three to five unpleasant jobs or tasks you can perform when compulsions emerge. The tasks should not be time consuming, but they should be unpleasant enough to disrupt your obsessions/compulsions. Examples: weeding for 10 minutes, scrubbing a toilet, or making small talk for a short time with an annoying person. You're asked to create a list of three to five unpleasant tasks because you can't always use the same task in different settings (e.g., you probably can't clean the bathroom at work unless it's part of your job). Some days will be better than others; you may have an increase in your compulsions on some days, but keep at it.

    What are three to five unpleasant tasks that you can perform to interrupt your obsessions/compulsions?

    a. _____

    b. _____

    c. _____

    d. _____

    e. _____

2. After reviewing the list, what job(s) or task(s) do you feel would be most effective at home?

_____

3. At school or work?

_____

4. In a public setting?

_____

EFFECTIVENESS ASSESSMENT

Please answer these questions after 2 weeks of performing the unpleasant job(s) or task(s):

1. When you began experiencing compulsive thoughts, how often did you use the tasks?

_____ 0–20%   _____ 20–40%   _____ 40–60%   _____ 60–80%   _____ 80–100%

2. If you didn't perform the jobs or tasks consistently (less than 60%), what interfered?

_____

_____

_____

3. Overall, how successful was this technique in interrupting or managing your compulsions?

1	2	3	4	5	6	7
Totally Unsuccessful			No Change			Highly Successful

4. Which jobs or tasks were most helpful interrupting your compulsions?

_____

_____

_____

5. Which ones, if any, were not effective in interrupting your compulsions?

_____

_____

_____

_____

6. If anything interfered with your use of this method and caused an increase in your symptoms, what happened?

    _____

    _____

MODIFICATIONS OF THE INTERVENTION

1. After evaluating your progress, what changes would you make with this method?

    _____

    _____

    _____

2. What other unpleasant jobs or tasks can you use to interrupt compulsive thoughts and actions?

    _____

    _____

    _____

Be sure to bring this handout back after you've done the 2 weeks of testing this method and talk over the results with your therapist and/or your therapy group.

REDUCING COMPULSIVE BEHAVIORS*

GOALS OF THE EXERCISE

1. Identify compulsive behaviors and their irrational basis.
2. Develop and implement realistic self-talk techniques to reduce the frequency of compulsive behaviors.
3. Develop and implement a daily ritual that interrupts the current pattern of compulsions.
4. Develop a greater sense of control over compulsive behavior rituals and reduce their frequency.

ADDITIONAL PROBLEMS FOR WHICH THIS EXERCISE MAY BE USEFUL

- Anxiety
- Bipolar Disorder
- Borderline Traits
- Depression–Unipolar
- Eating Disorders and Obesity
- Gambling
- Impulsivity
- Nicotine Use/Dependence
- Posttraumatic Stress Disorder (PTSD)
- Relapse Proneness
- Self-Harm
- Sexual Promiscuity
- Substance Use Disorders

SUGGESTIONS FOR PROCESSING THIS EXERCISE WITH THE CLIENT

The "Reducing Compulsive Behaviors" activity is for clients suffering from obsessive-compulsive disorder (OCD) who enter treatment believing that they have no control over their behavior patterns or thoughts. The exercise is designed to increase their sense of

---

*Most of the content of this assignment (with slight revisions) originates from *The Adult Psychotherapy Homework Planner,* Sixth Edition, by A. E. Jongsma and T. E. Bruce (Wiley, 2021). Reprinted with permission.

control and reduce the frequency of compulsive behaviors. You may want to review the main elements of this homework assignment with the client before it is given, helping them to understand positive self-talk and behavioral interruption principles. Review the client's success and make any adjustments in the technique as needed. Follow-up can include talking in individual or group therapy about ways to use this method in other areas of the client's life.

REDUCING COMPULSIVE BEHAVIORS

Compulsive behaviors are repetitive, intentional actions a person takes in response to obsessive thoughts or according to eccentric rules. They are done to relieve or prevent anxiety or discomfort, often about some dreaded possible event or situation. These ritualized actions either involve going to unnecessary extremes, such as relocking a door several times before leaving home, or aren't connected in a realistic way with what they are meant to relieve or prevent. This activity will help you examine your compulsive behavior rituals and provide you with techniques to increase your control over these behaviors and reduce the strength and frequency of the thoughts that drive them.

1.   Please list three compulsive actions you engage in on a frequent basis:

_____

_____

2.   Rate the degree of control you believe you have over these compulsive behaviors:

1	2	3	4	5
No Control				Total Control

3.   How do you believe these behaviors help (e.g., relaxing, less anxiety, stops my thinking about it)? What feelings, experiences are you attempting to avoid, modify?

_____

_____

4.   Rate how rational you believe your compulsive actions are (Do they make sense?):

1	2	3	4	5
Irrational and Unreasonable				Totally Rational and Reasonable

5. To what degree, if any, have you used alcohol/other drugs to reduce obsessions and/ or compulsive behaviors (distract yourself, decrease anxiety/tension, anesthetize)?

_____

_____

6. Positive realistic self-talk works well to counteract compulsive urges. Read the following self-talk messages, then write any additional messages you believe could be helpful for you.

   a. This behavior is not reasonable, and I will not do it.

   b. I can resist this urge, and it will go away eventually.

   c. Anxious feelings will return after I perform this action, so I'm not going to do it.

   d. I'm going to think of a pleasant, calm scene until this urge passes.

   e. I'm going to focus my attention on another task so that the urge passes.

   f. Others:

7. Select two of these messages you think would work best for you:

_____

_____

8. It also works to create and use rituals to interrupt compulsive patterns. The ritual is a substitute for a compulsive action, one that's more under your control. List some things you can use as substitute rituals when compulsive urges come up (e.g., clean house, take a walk, call a friend).

_____

_____

9. For 1 week, use positive self-talk and substitute rituals when you feel compulsive urges and rate how they work for you:

Day 1:

```
|-------|-------|-------|-------|
1       2       3       4       5
No                              Very
Success                   Successful
```

Day 2:

```
|-------|-------|-------|-------|
1       2       3       4       5
No                              Very
Success                   Successful
```

Day 3:

| 1 | 2 | 3 | 4 | 5 |

No
Success

Very
Successful

Day 4:

| 1 | 2 | 3 | 4 | 5 |

No
Success

Very
Successful

Day 5:

| 1 | 2 | 3 | 4 | 5 |

No
Success

Very
Successful

Day 6:

| 1 | 2 | 3 | 4 | 5 |

No
Success

Very
Successful

Day 7:

| 1 | 2 | 3 | 4 | 5 |

No
Success

Very
Successful

10. Using these techniques, please rate the degree of control you believe you have over your compulsive behaviors now:

| 1 | 2 | 3 | 4 | 5 |

No
Control

Total
Control

11. What work, if any, needs to be done to address your use of substances as they relate to your obsessions or compulsions?

_____

_____

Be sure to bring this handout back to your next session with your therapist and be prepared to talk about your thoughts and feelings about the exercise as well as any treatment issues related to addressing OCD and substance use.

INTEREST AND SKILL SELF-ASSESSMENT

GOALS OF THE EXERCISE

1. Assess personal interests and abilities and identify ways to apply existing personal skills in work situations.
2. Understand the relationship between the stress of occupational problems and addiction.
3. Plan ways to bring more meaning and fulfillment to work life.
4. Identify relapse risk factors in work situations and plan strategies to cope with them.

ADDITIONAL PROBLEMS FOR WHICH THIS EXERCISE MAY BE USEFUL

- Attention-Deficit/Hyperactivity Disorder (ADHD)—Adolescent
- Attention-Deficit/Hyperactivity Disorder (ADHD)—Adult
- Dependent Traits
- Depression–Unipolar
- Spiritual Confusion

SUGGESTIONS FOR PROCESSING THIS EXERCISE WITH THE CLIENT

The "Interest and Skill Self-Assessment" activity is designed to help clients gain clarity about their interests and priorities and identify things they do well. It provides encouragement to explore new ways to apply interests and skills in occupational pursuits. It guides the client through an interest self-assessment, a skill self-assessment, a recovery assessment, and a plan for implementing changes to their existing work situation or choosing what they may pursue in the future. It may be helpful for clients to visualize what their work lives would look like if they were truly fulfilling their lives' purposes.

If the new insights lead clients to decide to change their existing jobs or careers, it might be useful to have them work with career counselors. Follow-up could include bibliotherapy with the books *Do What You Are: Discover the Perfect Career for You Through the Secrets of Personality Type* by Paul Tieger and Barbara Barron-Tieger and/or *What Color Is Your Parachute? A Practical Manual for Job Hunters and Career Changers* by Richard Bolles.

INTEREST AND SKILL SELF-ASSESSMENT

If you're unsatisfied with your current job, if your work environment puts your recovery at risk, or if you have lost your job, it may help to analyze your interests and what you do well before you decide what to do about your future employment. When you do something that you enjoy and are good at, it improves the quality of your life. It's also vital to choose work that supports your recovery, or at least doesn't interfere with it. This exercise will guide you in determining your own interests and skills.

INTEREST SELF-ASSESSMENT

1. What parts of your current or most recent job are interesting and what parts do you like most? What do you dislike?

    _____

    _____

2. What work would you choose if you could do what you truly enjoyed? (For the purpose of this exercise, eliminate money, family, other responsibilities as factors.) And name three things that would contribute to your enjoyment of this work.

    _____

    _____

3. Of the items listed here, *circle* those that give your life the greatest meaning:

    Satisfaction with family life   Friendship/connection with others
    Good health   Spiritual awareness
    Helping others   Recognition
    Material success   Educational achievement
    Creative outlet/expression   Personal growth/awareness
    Career advancement   Integrity
    Sense of accomplishment
    Other(s):_____

SKILL SELF-ASSESSMENT

4.   What are your strongest skills or abilities?

_____

_____

5.   Do you use them in your current job? If so, how?

_____

_____

6.   If not, what work or employment would let you put those skills or qualities to good use? If not possible, where are there other opportunities to use your skills?

_____

_____

7.   What is the most important thing for you in choosing a profession and enjoying it (e.g., interest or skill, items in question 3)?

_____

_____

RECOVERY ASSESSMENT

8.   How does your current work environment, coworkers, work schedule, etc., support your recovery?

_____

_____

9.   How does your current work environment put your recovery in jeopardy (e.g., addictive actions encouraged, stressful work conditions, schedule prevents meeting and treatment attendance)?

_____

_____

_____

10.   How have you navigated these challenges, both successfully and not?

_____

_____

PUTTING-IT-ALL-TOGETHER PLAN

11. In reviewing your answers to the above questions, what parts of your current work situation are acceptable, and what things would you like to change?

    _____

    _____

12. What are you willing to do to work toward making these changes in:

    a. The next month?

    _____

    b. The next year?

    _____

13. What skills/resources may you have to develop/hone to increase your success in your current work environment (i.e., assertiveness, time management, realistic expectations of work performance/advancement opportunities, time needed for recovery obligations, etc.)?

    _____

    _____

14. If making a shift is not feasible at this time, what will you do to prevent work stress from affecting recovery or mood issues? What options are there for using your skills and strengths in meaningful ways where they can be appreciated?

    _____

    _____

Be sure to bring this handout to your future therapy sessions to discuss your questions, thoughts, and feelings with your therapist or group as you continue this activity.

WORKPLACE PROBLEMS AND SOLUTIONS

GOALS OF THIS EXERCISE

1. Maintain a program of recovery from addictive behaviors and cope constructively with workplace stressors that might be triggers for relapse.
2. Understand the relationship between the stress of occupational problems and addiction.
3. Identify connections between occupational problems and addictive behaviors.
4. Identify behavioral changes that would help resolve occupational problems.
5. Identify self-defeating thoughts and feelings associated with current and past work problems.

ADDITIONAL PROBLEMS FOR WHICH THIS EXERCISE MAY BE USEFUL

- Anger
- Antisocial Behavior
- Borderline Traits
- Impulsivity
- Legal Problems
- Living Environment Deficiency
- Narcissistic Traits

SUGGESTIONS FOR PROCESSING THIS EXERCISE WITH THE CLIENT

The "Workplace Problems and Solutions" activity is suited for clients who have consistently had behavioral problems at work. For those unable to see the connection between addictive behavior and work problems, this exercise will increase insight. For the client who can recognize a relationship between addiction and work problems but needs help identifying relapse risk factors, it will increase awareness and help with solutions. The activity helps clients identify feelings, thoughts, and behaviors that may be barriers to employment and helps them generate possible solutions. Awareness and personal responsibility for behavior are two critical aspects of recovery. Addressing workplace problems and their relationship to addictive behaviors requires dealing with the associated denial, minimization, or blaming. For clients who are not currently employed, it can be used to assess past difficulties so that future employment is geared toward success.

WORKPLACE PROBLEMS AND SOLUTIONS

Occupational problems can take many forms: problems with authority, conflict with coworkers, stressful work environments, addictive behavior being enabled or encouraged, abusive employers, difficult adjustment to retirement/layoff, underemployment/ unemployment due to performance or attendance problems, and so on. Cause-and-effect between addictions and problems at work can run both ways. Addictive behavior may cause work problems, and stressful work environments may contribute to addiction and relapse. This exercise will help you see connections between difficulties you've had with work and with addictive behavior, and create solutions.

1. List the last four jobs you've held and the problems you've had in each job:

    _____

    _____

    _____

2. Please list any common problems you have had in more than one work environment in the left-hand column. In the right-hand column, identify the connections to addictive behaviors or ways these problems are recovery issues. Following are some examples.

Problem	Relationship to Addiction/Recovery
Fired for insubordination	*Conflicts with authority figures*
Lack of meaning to life after leaving job	*Used addictive behaviors to cope*
_____	_____
_____	_____
_____	_____

    If you struggle to make the connection between addiction/recovery, talk at a meeting with your sponsor or in therapy for insights.

3.   If you are currently working, does your work environment place you at risk of relapse, and if so, how (e.g., coworker's addictions, job dissatisfaction, long work hours)?

_____

_____

4.   What is your plan to address each of the risks you identified in question 3?

_____

_____

5.   What discouraging thoughts or self-talk have you had, or do you have now, about your work situation (e.g., "I can't do this job," "I'll fail like the other times," "No one will hire me")?

_____

_____

6.   For each negative thought you identified in question 5, write a more realistic, positive replacement thought (e.g., "I'm as capable as the other people doing this job, if they can do it so can I," "I've learned from past mistakes and am better prepared").

_____

_____

7.   What behavior and/or attitude changes do you need to make to solve or avoid problems you've had at work in the past? It may help to ask others you trust to make suggestions.

_____

_____

8.   What will you do this week to address one of the problems you listed for question 3?

_____

_____

_____

9.   What will you do during the next month to address this problem?

_____

_____

10. After completing questions 7, 8, and 9 and carrying out the actions you said you would take, record your evaluation of how you did.

_____

_____

For successes, identify a positive affirmation to keep you encouraged.

For challenges, identify a positive affirmation to keep you engaged/motivated to keep trying.

Identify any areas where you might need additional support/assistance.

_____

_____

Be sure to bring this handout with you to future therapy sessions and talk over any questions or ideas you have and be prepared to talk about this assignment with your therapist or your group.

VALUES CLARIFICATION AND CONSISTENCY CHECK

GOALS OF THE EXERCISE

1. Accept the powerlessness over opioids and participate in a recovery-based program.
2. Establish a sustained recovery, free from use of all mood-altering substances other than prescribed medication.
3. Acquire skills necessary to address harms associated with addictive behaviors and lifestyle.

ADDITIONAL PROBLEMS FOR WHICH THIS EXERCISE MAY BE USEFUL

- Readiness to Change
- Relapse Proneness
- Substance Use Disorders

SUGGESTIONS FOR PROCESSING THIS EXERCISE WITH THE CLIENT

The "Values Clarification and Consistency Check" activity is for clients who may need their motivation enhanced for considering making changes to their substance use, bolstering their motivation to persist in treatment and identify how sobriety and recovery is more aligned with what is most important to them. Follow-up may consist of discussing answers further with the therapist or group, self-monitoring for ongoing negative consequences of addictive thinking, behaviors, and discussion of their significance. Consider assigning reading other materials related to Step 1 and Step 2 in the AA Big Book and the 12 Traditions between sessions and process this material in individual or group visits.

VALUES CLARIFICATION AND CONSISTENCY CHECK

This assignment will help you clarify your values. Our personal values start forming when we are very young. Over time, they are influenced by our caregivers, other family members, teachers and education, spiritual advisors, coaches, friends, mass media, and our lived experiences. Some of our values matter more than others. At times our values may conflict (e.g., being responsible and saving for our future vs. having fun). Values drive our choices and our behaviors. When our actions are in line with the things that are most important to us, we tend to feel good about ourselves and our decisions. When our values conflict with our choices and ultimate actions, we tend to feel guilty and ashamed and are left to resolve this conflict. An addictive lifestyle is riddled with conflicts in values and behavior, where behaviors we engage in are not consistent with what we believe and value. They may also negatively affect important relationships and how we feel about ourselves. When we continue to engage in addictive behaviors, we can also rationalize to make ourselves feel OK. Many people consider changing their behavior(s) when their behavior conflicts with their personal goals/values or things that are very valuable to them. They find when they explore this further, they work to commit themselves, albeit challenging, to make decisions and align their behaviors with those goals/values. This activity is designed to get you to explore this further.

1. Identify at least three personal values (e.g., freedom, honesty, job/career success, financial independence, physical appearance, having love/being loved, family). Write them here.

   _____

   _____

2. Over the past 6–12 months, what percentage of your time, money, effort was spent on each of these values?

   _____

   _____

3. Over the past 6–12 months, how many incidents have taken place in which your actions conflicted with one or more of the top 3 values you listed above?

   _____

   _____

4. How have your addictive behavior patterns and identified consequences put you in conflict with things that matter most to you?

_____

_____

5. Describe how this makes you feel.

_____

_____

6. What attempts have you made to reconcile the discrepancy or address how you've felt about it?

_____

_____

7. Reflect what brought you to seek help or get sober at this time. Describe how it is related to finding another way of living a life free of addictive behaviors and increasing patterns to live a more value-based life.

_____

_____

8. By comparison, identify an event or incident where your actions were more aligned with your stated values. What was the outcome and how did you feel about yourself?

_____

_____

9. It is a simple concept, yet hard to do. If we remember our values and take actions that support them, we tend to experience less discomfort and more satisfaction in life and how we feel about ourselves. Recovery and treatment give us the opportunity to explore and practice this in all areas of our lives, not just the decision related to addictive behavior. This works in one of two ways:

   a. Taking planned, committed action each day to engage in behavior that aligns with our values as we work toward goals in recovery.

      i. Identify three activities you can do each day that are consistent with your values. Write about what you can do and how you will do it.

      _____

      _____

      ii. What obstacles or barriers might exist and what might you consider doing to overcome them?

      _____

      _____

b. When faced with a dilemma, stop, think it through, and identify which decision/choice/action is consistent with what you stated was important to you at this time.

i. Think of a past incident where a values conflict may have occurred.

ii. How did your actions contradict your stated values? (Which value did it contradict?)

iii. What happened to you and others as a result?

iv. What were your feelings at the time of the incident and after making your decision?

v. What action would have been more consistent with your stated values?

vi. What might you do now should this incident reoccur and what would you envision the outcome would be?

_____

_____

10. Identify how addiction, relapse, and recovery tasks are related. What actions are you willing to commit to in each of the areas to foster more consistency between values and behaviors?

_____

_____

11. Identify support people who can keep you consistently assessing, keep you accountable, and support you.

_____

_____

Be sure to bring this handout back to your next session with your therapist and be prepared to talk about your thoughts and feelings about the exercise.

STARTING AGAIN, NOT OVER

GOALS OF THE EXERCISE

1. Accept powerlessness over opioid use and participate in a recovery program.
2. Acquire the necessary skills to maintain long-term abstinence from opioids, any other substances, and other addictive behaviors.
3. Gain an understanding of compulsive behaviors not involving use of alcohol or other drugs.
4. Reduce the risk of relapse by applying techniques that work for substance use disorders to other addictive behaviors.

ADDITIONAL PROBLEMS FOR WHICH THIS EXERCISE MAY BE USEFUL

- Readiness to Change
- Relapse Proneness
- Substance Use Disorders

SUGGESTIONS FOR PROCESSING THIS EXERCISE WITH THE CLIENT

The "Starting Again, Not Over" activity is designed for clients whose primary addiction is to opioids but could be helpful for all substance use disorders and nonchemical addictions. It is also meant for any folks in recovery who are at risk for switching addictions. The primary focus is on relapsing and lapsing and how to use that information to build upon for another attempt. Follow-up may include participation in appropriate 12-step programs, keeping a journal to self-monitor for signs of building lapses/relapses, and reporting back on insights and progress. Additionally, relapse prevention planning and recovery planning should occur simultaneously once motivation matches that commitment. Consider any activities, reading material, or podcasts that help reinforce the "how come" one should try again and that long-term, sustained recovery from a substance use disorder is possible.

STARTING AGAIN, NOT OVER

Folks in recovery from addictive behaviors must address lapses and relapses. Each is an opportunity for growth. Not everyone makes it back. You have, and harvesting the insights from lapses/relapses is another opportunity to work toward a sustained life in recovery. The goal of this assignment is to use what you've learned from previous attempts at sobriety, to reevaluate what worked before, identify what obstacles and barriers were present and/or not addressed, consider alternatives and how they might work for you this time, and use the information to develop a revised plan to sustain longer term recovery from opioid use disorder.

1. What motivated you to enter treatment or seek help this time?

    _____

    _____

2. What do you believe contributed to your last lapse or relapse? For consistency, a lapse is defined as a temporary and reversible use of an addictive substance and a relapse is a decision to return to a repeated pattern of abuse. Which do you believe best describes your last experience?

    _____

    _____

3. As you evaluate it, what do you believe contributed to the last lapse or relapse? Consider any, all, or other of the options listed here: untreated other mental or physical health disorders? Discontinued replacement treatment? Avoided treatment/recovery program options? Stayed engaged in high-risk environments, people? Experienced overwhelming suffering, loss, shame, and did not know how to address it? List your insight about this below:

    _____

    _____

4. Some critical components of a successful recovery plan/program ingredients include:

    a. Medication adherence: taking what is prescribed to you as it is prescribed

    b. Avoiding use of all other mood/mind-altering substances not prescribed to you

   c. Attending all recommended treatments

   d. Having alternative activities for pleasure that support sobriety

   e. Utilizing assistance and support from a sober support network

   f. Feeling accomplished in tasks that are meaningful to you (work, school)

   g. Addressing other health or co-occurring issues—depression, anxiety, chronic pain, trauma, etc.

   h. Having basic needs met—safe housing, access to adequate health care, food security and proper nutrition, etc.

   i. Managing cravings and cues

   j. Avoiding high-risk relationships, environments, and activities

Of those listed here, where did the breakdowns occur?

_____

_____

5. Assess motivation moving forward. What am I willing to consider currently to incorporate my own wisdom and that of others for a different outcome?

_____

_____

6. Recovery is a process. It is active, evolving, nonlinear, and as complicated as you are. It requires attending to all things about yourself that you are aware of and willing currently to address. This might include negotiating relationships/a social life built around your addictive behavior and in a culture obsessed with substance use.

_____

_____

7. The only way to live in recovery is by incorporating recovery behaviors "in all your affairs" (AA Big Book). Identify how you will use the substance abuse recovery tools listed in question 4 differently this time to make the most of what a program of recovery has to offer; identify those that would be new for you this time and those you will need some assistance locating or developing.

   a. Sources of support (sober, 12-step, recovery-oriented, faith traditions, identity/culture affirming)

_____

   b. Coping skills to handle triggers, cues, and cravings without returning to any substance use or compulsive behavior (e.g., stress management, relaxation training, anger management, financial management, conflict resolution, problem solving)

_____

   c. Medication adherence

_____

   d. Replacement activities for socializing and pleasure; managing down time and boredom

_____

   e. Skills for handling relationship issues

_____

   f. Addressing interactions with former "using" friends without being lured or pressured into old behaviors, environmental considerations

_____

   g. Activities that bring a sense of purpose and accomplishment

_____

   h. Other areas that are known challenges from previous lapses/relapses:

_____

8. Sobriety and recovery can hold everything and more that a substance use disorder promised to deliver, without the added pain and misery, but it is hard work. What ways can you challenge yourself to keep a mindset that is recovery affirming?

_____

_____

9. What concerns, skepticism, ambivalence do you have this time that you might be willing to explore further in therapy?

_____

_____

10. What additional insights and/or questions do you have about this attempt at sobriety that feel important to note? List them here.

_____

_____

    Be sure to bring this handout back to your next session with your therapist and be prepared to talk about your thoughts and feelings about the exercise.

ANALYZING ACTING-OUT BEHAVIOR

GOALS OF THE EXERCISE

1. Decrease the frequency of occurrence of angry thoughts, feelings, and behaviors.
2. Gain insight into patterns of self-defeating impulsivity.
3. Learn to recognize patterns leading to impulsive self-sabotage and stop them before they lead to serious consequences.

ADDITIONAL PROBLEMS FOR WHICH THIS EXERCISE MAY BE USEFUL

- Anger
- Antisocial Behavior
- Attention-Deficit/Hyperactivity Disorder (ADHD)—Adolescent
- Attention-Deficit/Hyperactivity Disorder (ADHD)—Adult
- Dangerousness/Lethality
- Impulsivity
- Peer Group Negativity
- Sexual Promiscuity

SUGGESTIONS FOR PROCESSING THIS EXERCISE WITH THE CLIENT

The "Analyzing Acting-Out Behavior" activity is written primarily for clients with patterns of impulsively engaging in oppositional, antisocial, and/or self-defeating behavior with little thought of the consequences. It works to heighten motivation for change by focusing the client on emotional discomfort at not understanding their own behavior, then offers a guided analysis of the client's mental and emotional state just before the behavior, the trigger, and the acting-out process. It further prompts the client to engage in self-monitoring in future acting-out situations. Finally, it asks the client to list strategies to stop impulsive acting-out upon realizing that they are doing it again. This is intended to break the cycle of unthinking acting out by triggering awareness of consequences and the fact that the behavior is self-defeating and diverting the client to an alternative strategy they have chosen.

This exercise is useful for individual or group homework and discussion. Follow-up can include having significant others involved. In the case of adults, getting feedback from family or partners, and in the case of adolescents, involving parents, teachers, coaches, ministers, etc. Have the client get feedback from them and share it with the therapist or group.

ANALYZING ACTING-OUT BEHAVIOR

Do you ever find, when someone asks you why you did something that led to trouble, that the only honest answer you can give is, "I don't know"? If so, you know that response doesn't satisfy people. You may have asked yourself the same question before they did. Impulsive and self-destructive actions, ones we later regret, are part of addiction. So is blaming others for acting-out behavior rather than taking responsibility for it. Not knowing may be valid, but recovery requires us to keep working at it so we might understand ourselves better. It helps to get a better understanding of our own thoughts and feelings when we're doing those things, so we can cut the process short when it starts and increase our personal accountability for our behavior. This exercise will help you learn to do that.

1. Think about the last time you did something impulsive that got you into serious trouble or caused you to feel strong regrets later. Briefly describe that situation (including the triggering event(s) if known) and the resulting consequences.

   Situation: _____

   Your actions: _____

   Outcome/consequences: _____

2. Carefully study what was going on inside you at the time. What were you thinking just before you took the action that caused you problems? (Try to avoid judging as good/bad and just note the thoughts.)

   _____

   _____

3. What emotions were you feeling? (Try to avoid justifying or rationalizing and just note the feelings.)

   _____

   _____

4. One of the best ways to analyze this kind of impulsive behavior is to carefully teach someone else how to do it. This may sound strange, but it often helps people gain greater understanding. Explain in detail how you act out impulsively. If you are

unable to do this currently, the next time you find yourself starting to act on a thought or feeling that's likely to result in problems, pay close attention to what you're thinking, feeling, and doing. If you forget to do this until after you've acted impulsively, write down the details as soon as you can, while they're fresh in your mind. Try to capture as clear a set of "instructions" as you can on how to do what you do when you act out. Write those instructions here.

_____

_____

_____

_____

5. If you realize that you're starting to have the same kinds of thoughts and feelings that have led you to act self-destructively before, what can you do to stop the process before you get in trouble or end up doing something you later wish you hadn't? Thoughts and feelings can come on pretty fast, strong, and intense and sometimes they are a result of something that comes from before. List at least five strategies you will implement to interrupt, halt, pause the process. Once paused, how can you slow down? Calm down? Name five actions to calm yourself.

_____

_____

_____

_____

6. Identify five benefits that will result in learning to reduce impulsive acting out behavior and taking more responsibility for your actions.

_____

_____

_____

_____

Be sure to bring this handout back to your next therapy session and be prepared to talk about your thoughts and feelings about the exercise.

LEARNING TO ASK INSTEAD OF DEMAND

GOALS OF THE EXERCISE

1. Understand the effects on others of different forms of expression.
2. Decrease the frequency of angry or overbearing thoughts, feelings, and behaviors.
3. Practice asking for things instead of demanding them in one relationship and evaluate the results.
4. Create a plan to adopt a respectful style of communication.

ADDITIONAL PROBLEMS FOR WHICH THIS EXERCISE MAY BE USEFUL

- Attention-Deficit/Hyperactivity Disorder (ADHD)—Adolescent
- Attention-Deficit/Hyperactivity Disorder (ADHD)—Adult
- Family Conflicts
- Narcissistic Traits
- Partner Relational Conflicts

SUGGESTIONS FOR PROCESSING THIS EXERCISE WITH THE CLIENT

The "Learning to Ask Instead of Demand" activity is designed for clients whose communication and relationship styles frequently present as disrespectful or inconsiderate. Its approach is to examine reasons why people may resist asking for what they want rather than demanding it, then shift to a pragmatic view with the aim of finding the communication style that will work best. It then asks the client to select a relationship on which to conduct a 1-week experiment with a more respectful style and report on the outcome. Follow-up for this exercise could include ongoing discussion with the therapist or treatment group on the impacts of communication styles in other relationships. For adolescents, ask parents or teachers to monitor behavior and provide feedback. Encourage the client to run experiments on several different relationships and note the differences.

LEARNING TO ASK INSTEAD OF DEMAND

Why should you work at learning to ask people for what you want instead of demanding it? One reason is that it works better. Think about your own reactions. How do you feel when someone asks you for something, compared to when they demand it? Most of us prefer to be asked. Substance/addictive disorders are not terribly polite conditions; the relationship with them is very demanding. We can relate to how it feels. Learning to communicate in different ways is a skill to be learned and developed.

1. List several negative consequences of speaking with others in a way that is demanding, aggressive, argumentative, blaming, and angry (think about relationships, your substance use, and the ways you feel about yourself).

    _____

    _____

2. Identify several possible benefits in learning to communicate with others in a way that is more respectful, polite, and considerate.

    _____

    _____

3. One reason why many people try to tell others what to do, rather than requesting, is that they don't feel right asking, especially if they feel others owe them respect. They may feel they would look weak or unsure of themselves if they asked others for things rather than telling them what to do. This may be due to family or cultural traditions or other reasons. When you picture yourself asking someone to do something rather than telling them, what feelings does this bring up for you?

    _____

    _____

    _____

    _____

4. Some of the most powerful people in history have also been very polite to those around them. Great leaders like Abraham Lincoln have been known for being respectful to everyone they talked with. Many people believe that truly strong people are more likely to be gentle because they don't need to prove their strength by pushing people around. Think of a strong person who is polite and considerate to others. What is your general impression of that person?

_____

_____

5. No matter how we feel about being respectful, to get cooperation in a relationship we need to put ourselves in the other person's place. Think about situations where others order you around—parents or other family members, bosses, partners, or teachers. Now imagine how you'd feel if they asked you politely rather than telling you what to do. What's the difference, based on how that person approached you?

_____

_____

6. There is always more than one message in everything we say—one message in our words, and at least one message in the way we speak those words. When we ask others for things (e.g., simply saying "please" and "thank you," saying "Would you . . ."), we're also saying, *I respect your feelings and your dignity, you matter, and I care how you feel.* When we leave these things out and simply order people around, the unspoken message is, *Your feelings and dignity aren't important, I don't have to be polite to you,* and *I don't care how you feel.* You may care very much about that other person's feelings, but your delivery and word choice doesn't communicate this.

Let's run an experiment. In a current relationship in which you're used to simply telling the other person what to do, try switching the way you do things for a week, asking this person for what you want instead of demanding it. You might tell them you're doing this experiment. You can explain that you're practicing a new way of communication to show that they're important to you, and that you're going to try asking for things instead of demanding them. You may slip into the old way during the week. You can *ask* them to remind you, and they can do that by *asking* you to rephrase what you've said. How does it feel to imagine doing this? What challenges do you envision?

_____

_____

_____

7. In session with your therapist or in your group, practice/rehearse/role-play some examples of what this experiment would sound like and write examples here.

_____

_____

8. After trying this experiment for 1 week, please describe the results here. How did you feel doing it this way? What were others' reactions to your behavior? How many reminders did you need?

_____

_____

9. If you feel this experiment was worthwhile, please use this space to describe a plan to practice this more respectful approach to dealing with people in all your relationships.

_____

_____

Be sure to bring this handout back to your next therapy session and be prepared to talk about your thoughts and feelings about the exercise.

PERSISTENCE IN SPITE OF PANIC

GOALS OF THE EXERCISE

1. Reduce the frequency, intensity, and duration of panic attacks.
2. Reduce the fear that panic symptoms will recur without the ability to manage them.
3. Learn to accept occasional panic symptoms and fearful thoughts without use of substances or other addictive behaviors.

ADDITIONAL PROBLEMS FOR WHICH THIS EXERCISE MAY BE USEFUL

- Anxiety
- Childhood Trauma
- Eating Disorders and Obesity
- Posttraumatic Stress Disorder (PTSD)
- Relapse Proneness
- Sleep Disturbance
- Social Anxiety

SUGGESTIONS FOR PROCESSING THIS EXERCISE WITH THE CLIENT

The "Persistence in Spite of Panic" activity is for clients who experience panic but feel helpless to change it, and it is affecting engagement in daily and/or recovery activities. Educating clients about anxiety and panic and normalizing healthy levels of each is important in getting clients motivated to address this issue. Some psychoeducation about the fearful but benign nature of the fight or flight response can also be helpful. Educating about how to extinguish a fear response may also build motivation to do the work that terrifies them. Clients with complex trauma history or an acute stress response may benefit from addressing this issue concurrently with trauma treatment. Understanding how substance use/addictive behaviors was an attempt at avoiding a negative affect state also helps them see that they can learn new behaviors to control panic. Follow-up can consist of teaching relaxation, imagery, mindfulness, and biofeedback techniques to deal with all levels of anxiety, fear, and panic.

PERSISTENCE IN SPITE OF PANIC

Managing panic is multifaceted, and managing panic in recovery comes with its own set of challenges. Feelings of panic are intense and uncomfortable and the fear of them recurring along with feeling like you'll lose control, have a heart attack, or that you're "going crazy" is enough to cause people to do whatever it takes to avoid having another one. Many times, people feel so certain they are going to die or that something is medically wrong, causing them to seek emergency medical treatment. Feelings of panic can occur in the context of other things like stress, depression, substance use disorders, withdrawal, or other medical issues. Often people will avoid circumstances in which they have experienced panic; this invariably backfires as more situations are avoided, substance reliance to numb (avoid) them increases, leading to significant changes in activities, relationships, routines, and, at its most severe, isolation. The good news is that they are treatable by changing our perceptions, thoughts, and behaviors. The willingness and ability needed to face the fears and discomfort keep people from seeking adequate treatment; the skepticism that anything could treat them or that someone could feel comfortable enough tolerating some degree of anxiety/panic also keeps people from getting well. For those with addictive behaviors, it poses a risk to relapse and sustained recovery free of panic/agoraphobia. This exercise will get you started on gaining knowledge, awareness, and insight into panic and challenge you to increase your willingness to treat it.

1. Identify when your panic began. Consider if it was before or after your substance use/addictive behaviors, related to another mental or physical health condition, or seemed to come out of the blue. Write about your insights here.

   _____

   _____

2. What fears do you have associated with your panic?

   _____

   _____

3. What happens when you feel panic? Describe the physical, emotional, thinking experiences.

   _____

   _____

4. To what degree is your substance use/addictive behavior associated or related to it?

    _____

    _____

5. What efforts have you taken to keep panic to a minimum? To what extent have these worked to decrease or eliminate your feelings of anxiety and panic?

    _____

    _____

6. What have you modified or given up to prevent panic attacks from recurring? Additionally, how do you feel about these changes?

    _____

    _____

7. Identify five benefits of learning to manage panic differently, tolerate it, or eliminate it completely?

    _____

    _____

8. Are there any other challenging situations you've had to address in your lifetime that you believe you handled successfully? If so, what did you do to address it? Are there any conclusions to be drawn about your ability to manage challenging experiences? What were the behaviors, actions, choices, supports you relied on or had to employ to manage this other challenging situation?

    _____

    _____

9. What are your thoughts about beginning a process of using known strategies described in this exercise to work on your panic disorder?

    _____

    _____

10. Before engaging in any behaviors to actively address panic and the fears associated with panic, you will have to practice relaxation strategies. Identify what you generally do to manage anxiety that works to calm you. Practice this strategy in various places and at various times during the day, before and after you return from an outing, meeting, work/school, or family function. The purpose of this practice is to get so good at it that it becomes second nature to you when you really need it. Write the results of this focused practice here and talk with your therapist about your confidence in doing it before moving on to exposure experiments.

    _____

    _____

11. Imagination exercise: You may want to practice this exercise for the first time in therapy or with your therapist so you can focus on following the instructions while your therapist provides gentle guidance and helps you monitor. Begin by engaging in deep, measured, calm breathing. Create an affirmation you can repeat to yourself while breathing that affirms your ability to be calm and do this exercise. Imagine yourself doing something or going somewhere that brings your anxiety up to a low level that you can manage and tolerate. Create an affirmation you can repeat to yourself as you gently imagine yourself doing something/going somewhere slightly more anxiety provoking. Remind yourself that you are just imagining it and there is nothing to be feared; continue to breathe in a calm and measured way until you feel your anxiety and fears lessen.

_____

_____

12. Identify three additional situations, people, events, places, actions that would increase anxiety slightly and at least one that you've feared having panic. Work up to these in your imagination. The purpose is that once you feel confident, you've been able to back your anxiety down and tolerate some of it, you can begin to do the same thing outside your imagination.

_____

13. Identify sober support people who can continue to encourage you. What do you want them to know and how would you like them to encourage you to face your fears? Provide them with the affirmations you are using that work, and they can remind you of them if needed.

_____

Be sure to bring this handout back to your next session with your therapist and be prepared to talk about your thoughts and feelings about the exercise.

MASTERING POSITIVE FEEDBACK TO FACE FEARS

GOALS OF THE EXERCISE

1. Reduce the frequency, intensity, and duration of panic attacks.
2. Reduce the fear that panic symptoms will recur without the ability to manage them.
3. Learn to accept occasional panic symptoms and fearful thoughts without use of substances or other addictive behaviors.

ADDITIONAL PROBLEMS FOR WHICH THIS EXERCISE MAY BE USEFUL

- Anxiety
- Eating Disorders and Obesity
- Posttraumatic Stress Disorder (PTSD)
- Relapse Proneness
- Social Anxiety

SUGGESTIONS FOR PROCESSING THIS EXERCISE WITH THE CLIENT

The "Mastering Positive Feedback to Face Fears" activity examines the client's thoughts, beliefs, perceptions, and fears that fuel panic and a range of avoidance behaviors, including use of addictive behaviors or substances. Skills training in progressive muscle relaxation, guided imagery, mindfulness, and deep breathing are foundational. Psychoeducation and skills training in cognitive-behavioral therapy, reality testing, distraction, acceptance and commitment therapy skills, distress tolerance is also encouraged while working with those with panic disorder. A range of strategies should be employed, and motivation needs to be relatively high for clients to be willing to expose themselves to things that create fear. As feelings of confidence and self-efficacy build, motivation and willingness to engage in these interventions are likely to increase. Attending to relapse prevention cues is critical and managing panic should be included on their plan if it is a co-occurring focus of treatment. Working concurrently with a physician to rule out any biological concerns or consider a medication assessment to assist in successful treatment of panic is advised.

This activity and the previous one may take several sessions to work through; as clients have more success in facing and managing their fears and, as confidence builds, they may be able to do more work in between sessions on their own. It is important to assess the environmental safety of clients who feel anxious and panicky. If a living environment remains unsafe, understanding anxiety and panic in that context is different; it may exist because it's needed. Safety planning and talking about places and people they can feel safe with is warranted.

MASTERING POSITIVE FEEDBACK TO FACE FEARS

Each attempt we make toward doing something positive and different increases our confidence and motivates us to continue. Additionally, as we increase positive coping and get more positive results even around complex and challenging things, more positive things come our way. That doesn't mean that we don't continue to have challenges. At times we tell ourselves we will do something different when we feel better or when something changes. Recovery is an action-oriented process so we must not wait for things to get better or easier before we start healing. Sobriety is living fully in the present moment with all the past stuff, the memories, the fears, and the struggles. Addictive lifestyle brings with it difficult experiences and emotions, negative thoughts about ourselves and the world, unpleasant memories and losses, unwanted urges and sensations, traumatic experiences, and struggles that sometimes take a while to clean up. We will worry about all this stuff, resent it, feel defeated and overwhelmed by it at times, and it all puts us at risk to return to use unless we do something else. Recovery is about hope, courage, compassion, and the ability to act and move forward, heal, change, find joy, create optimism even with all of that. Being able to identify the challenges, accept them for what they are and believe and commit to doing something differently in a positive direction will help us transform and master our biggest challenges.

Avoidance is a coping strategy well known to anyone who has struggled with addiction. The same ways we learned to avoid, we can learn to feel safe, confident, and competent. Avoidance is a negative feedback loop—we feel anxious and we avoid, which brings relief; this pattern continues. In this process we generate beliefs and hypotheses about our abilities to manage our emotions or how safe/dangerous something may be, which increases anxiety the next time it shows up. The other issue is we decrease our ability to learn how to tolerate discomfort, we feel anxious/fearful more often about more things, and we continue to avoid it. Learning to face our fears is critical for recovery. It restores our confidence, improves our mood, and allows us to be fully present in the moment.

Changing our pattern of response involves tolerating the discomfort, accurately assessing threats, calming ourselves, and addressing our thoughts differently. This in turn builds our confidence and we don't have to rely on avoidance to feel relief.

1. Imagine yourself feeling confident in a situation that makes you feel anxious or panicky, even one that you've consistently avoided. What is it like for you to imagine this? Identify any doubts or self-criticism or fears that accompany this and write those here.

    _____

    _____

2. In situations where you've felt anxious and panicky, what have you done to address the discomfort in the moment? What do you suppose might happen instead if you utilized a self-statement that could keep you present and situated to solve the problem at hand? What might that self-statement sound like? Identify a low anxiety provoking situation in which you'd be willing to run this experiment and return to therapy to report the results.

    _____

    _____

3. Panic and anxiety flood our system with alarms even when there is no actual threat. For those with significant trauma this was necessary for your survival. Once we are in safe spaces, our bodies and minds continue to feel flooded with fear and anxiety when triggered or uncomfortable. We overly attend to the internal cues, overestimating danger, and our inability to tolerate it.

    Learning to notice how you feel in the moment, quickly assess for any real danger, and work to negotiate the situation without fleeing/avoiding it is important, and we get better as we expose ourself to it and practice. What thoughts come up for you when thinking about exposing yourself to situations that cause anxiety and panic (those where there is no actual danger)? What do you think you might need to begin to consider acting on this in a positive direction?

    _____

    _____

4. What conclusions have you drawn about what is likely to happen, if you will be able to cope with it, what you must do to survive it? Think about noting the situation from an objective perspective and attending to the external cues to successfully solve the problem or address the situation. Think about interrupting any fear-driven internal dialogue or scanning, engaging in a calming strategy to calm your body and get your logical brain back online. What will you do to calm yourself and refocus on the situation, not your fears?

    _____

    _____

5. In this same situation, what alternative thoughts could you use that are self-affirming, more realistic rather than fearful, to either reduce panic or worries that you will panic? Write some examples here:

    _____

    _____

6. With your therapist, select a handful of specific fears about panic and what you believe may happen. Map out feedback loops that address alternate thoughts that are more realistic; strategies for distracting or not attending to those thoughts; ways to calm your anxiety, self-statement that affirms your ability to manage and tolerate, your automatic fear-based self-statements and counterstatements to change those, and self-soothing strategies. After outlining the plan, work through testing this map in real-life situations and use therapy to process the successes and challenges.

    Each attempt you make toward defusing the fear and doing something that keeps you present and engaged, building confidence in your ability to control your thoughts and emotions, will reduce your fear. As you increase positive actions, more positive things will come. You will learn to diffuse fear-based reactions to things that are not dangerous. This work is challenging. Continue to process in therapy or in support groups any ways this challenges your sobriety.

Be sure to bring this handout back to your next session with your therapist and be prepared to talk about your thoughts and feelings about the exercise.

AM I TEACHING MY CHILD ADDICTIVE PATTERNS?

GOALS OF THE EXERCISE

1. Terminate addictive behavior and resolve parent–child relationship conflicts.
2. Understand the relationship between addictive behavior and parent–child conflicts.
3. Understand how parental behaviors contribute to multigenerational cycles of addiction.
4. Improve parenting skills by learning to role-model healthy and nonaddictive behaviors.

ADDITIONAL PROBLEMS FOR WHICH THIS EXERCISE MAY BE USEFUL

- Adult-Child-of-an-Alcoholic (ACA) Traits
- Borderline Traits
- Childhood Trauma
- Dependent Traits
- Family Conflicts
- Partner Relational Conflicts
- Readiness to Change

SUGGESTIONS FOR PROCESSING THIS EXERCISE WITH THE CLIENT

The "Am I Teaching My Child Addictive Patterns?" activity is intended for clients who are at risk of transmitting addictive behavior patterns to their children. It aims to increase motivation for recovery by helping clients see how these behaviors increase the risk of the next generation falling into similar patterns. It lists patterns of addictive thinking and behavior and asks clients to provide examples and then think of ways to model healthy alternatives.

This activity is suitable for use as an individual or group exercise, in session, or as homework. Follow-up can include tracking strategies for change identified in the exercise.

AM I TEACHING MY CHILD ADDICTIVE PATTERNS?

For nearly all parents, one of our greatest hopes is to give our children good childhoods. Many of us who grew up in troubled families promised ourselves we'd do better than our parents. One of the worst things about addictive patterns is that they tend to be passed on, generation after generation. Think about your family's history. How far back do the patterns go? Those before you probably felt as you do, not wanting to pass the issues on to their children. Why did it happen despite their hopes? Wanting to do better isn't enough. First, we can't teach what we never learned. Second, the connections between addiction and these patterns of thinking, feeling, and behavior may not be obvious, so we may set our children up to repeat our problems without knowing we're doing it. In this exercise we'll look at attitudes and patterns that are built into addictive lifestyles, so you can work to break the generational cycle. Please look at these patterns, list ways you may have been role-modeling them for your children, and decide what you will do to change each one.

1. *Dishonesty*. Lying to ourselves and others, stealing, putting on a front, and playing mind games (e.g., denial, blaming, rationalizing, focusing on looking good over inner qualities).

    Ways I've modeled or taught dishonesty to my children:

    _____

    Ways I'll model and teach honesty:

    _____

2. *Self-centeredness and using people*. Putting our wants above others' well-being; manipulation, controlling, objectifying others; conning, bullying, etc.

    Ways I've modeled or taught self-centeredness and using people to my children:

    _____

    Ways I'll model and teach consideration and respect for others:

    _____

3. *All-or-nothing thinking*. Seeing ourselves, others, and situations in extremes; perfectionism; feeling we are better or worse than everyone else; seeing normal problems as disasters.

   Ways I've modeled or taught all-or-nothing thinking to my children:

   _____

   Ways I'll model and teach realistic, shades-of-gray thinking:

   _____

4. *Doing things to excess*. Going overboard with using, drinking, eating, spending, work, greed, or any activity, often leading to painful consequences.

   Ways I've modeled or taught going to excess to my children:

   _____

   Ways I'll model and teach moderation:

   _____

5. *Impulsiveness*. Lack of self-control, not attending to consequences of our actions.

   Ways I've modeled or taught impulsiveness to my children:

   _____

   Ways I'll model and teach maturity and self-control:

   _____

6. *Impatience and unrealistic expectations*. Expecting instant gratification, intolerance for frustration or delays, wishful thinking, perfectionism.

   Ways I've modeled or taught impatience to my children:

   _____

   Ways I'll model and teach patience:

   _____

7. *Isolation from others*. Lack of trust, poor communication, loneliness, judging ourselves by different standards (usually harsher) than we apply to everyone else, refusal to ask for help.

   Ways I've modeled or taught isolation to my children:

   _____

   Ways I'll model and teach connection to others:

   _____

8. *Shame.* Low self-esteem, feeling that we are defective/stupid/ugly/crazy/bad, feeling that if we fail at something or do bad things, we're bad people.

Ways I've modeled or taught shame to my children:

_____

Ways I'll model and teach self-respect:

_____

9. What are ways I will manage negative self-talk about my worries related to the negative impact on my kids, setting them up for a lifestyle of hardship, shame, guilt or other destructive behaviors?

_____

_____

10. What are three things I can say to myself that will foster a desire to persist in recovery when I feel discouraged or overwhelmed?

_____

_____

Be sure to bring this handout back to your next therapy session and be prepared to talk about your thoughts and feelings about the exercise.

WHAT DO I WANT FOR MY CHILDREN?

GOALS OF THE EXERCISE

1. Identify impacts of the client's addictive behaviors on their children.
2. Compare client's childhood experiences to those they are passing on to the next generation.
3. Decrease parent–child conflict and increase mutually supportive interaction.

ADDITIONAL PROBLEMS FOR WHICH THIS EXERCISE MAY BE USEFUL

- Adult-Child-of-an-Alcoholic (ACA) Traits
- Anger
- Borderline Traits
- Childhood Trauma
- Family Conflicts
- Impulsivity
- Partner Relational Conflicts
- Substance Use Disorders

SUGGESTIONS FOR PROCESSING THIS EXERCISE WITH THE CLIENT

The "What Do I Want for My Children?" activity is aimed at clients whose children are adversely affected by the client's addictive patterns. It aims to refresh and reinforce the client's ideals as a parent and increase cognitive dissonance between those ideals and addictive behavior. Follow-up can include bibliotherapy with books such as *My Daddy Was a Pistol and I'm a Son of a Gun* by Lewis Grizzard and videotherapy using films such as *When a Man Loves a Woman, The Great Santini*, or others as recommended in the book *Rent Two Films and Let's Talk in the Morning* by John W. Hesley and Jan G. Hesley, also published by Wiley.

WHAT DO I WANT FOR MY CHILDREN?

This assignment will help you strengthen your motivation for sobriety and recovery by focusing on how your actions affect your children's lives, both positively and negatively.

1. Think back to your childhood. All of us looked at some of the things our parents (or whoever raised us) did and told ourselves, "I want to do the same thing with my children someday." All of us also looked at some of their actions and promised ourselves, "I would **never** do that with my kids." List the top five items you said to yourself in each category growing up:

   a. "I will do the same thing for my children someday."

   _____

   _____

   _____

   _____

   b. "I will never do that to my kids."

   _____

   _____

   _____

   _____

2. If you were strongly affected as a child by the addictive behavior of one or both of your parents, caregivers, or of some other adult who played an important role in your life, please write briefly about what happened and how you felt about it then:

   _____

   _____

   _____

3. Please list any ways you intended or intend to do better as a parent, present or future, than you have done up to now because of your drinking, drug use, or other addictive behavior:

    _____

    _____

4. Now list parental goals you have that drinking or using might interfere with:

    _____

    _____

5. If you see that your addictive behavior interferes with your ability to give your children the kind of childhood you want for them, but you keep drinking or using anyway, what justification or rationalizing have you done to avoid taking a closer look at this?

    _____

    _____

6. If someone you knew put an addiction ahead of their ability to do their best as a parent, what would you want to say to them based on how you felt as a child?

    _____

    _____

7. If your children believe you have a problem and you believe you don't, how will you explain this conflict between your values and your actions to them when they ask? How do you/will you reconcile the discrepancy?

    _____

    _____

    _____

8. In what ways has your addictive behavior(s) caused conflicts between you and your children?

    _____

9. List five positive aspects and five negative aspects of your relationship with your children.

_____

_____

_____

_____

_____

_____

_____

_____

10. What are the ways you would like your relationship to be different?

_____

11. How might a program of recovery, a period of abstinence, or going to treatment benefit you and your relationship with your children? Consider the potential impact on them and your current and ongoing relationship with them.

_____

_____

12. What next steps are you willing to take to work toward creating the childhood you imagined for your children, increase the positive aspects of your relationship, and minimize/eliminate the negatives?

_____

_____

Be sure to bring this handout back to your next therapy session and be prepared to talk about your thoughts and feelings about the exercise.

COMMUNICATION SKILLS

GOALS OF THE EXERCISE

1. Understand the relationship between addiction and partner relational conflicts.
2. Develop and maintain effective communication and sexual intimacy with a partner.
3. Identify ways the client succeeds and fails in communicating with important others.
4. Identify better ways to communicate and learn to use those skills.
5. Learn to teach and use effective communication strategies with others in the client's life.

ADDITIONAL PROBLEMS FOR WHICH THIS EXERCISE MAY BE USEFUL

- Adult-Child-of-an-Alcoholic (ACA) Traits
- Anger
- Borderline Traits
- Family Conflicts
- Narcissistic Traits
- Occupational Problems
- Oppositional Defiant Behavior
- Parent–Child Relational Problem
- Social Anxiety

SUGGESTIONS FOR PROCESSING THIS EXERCISE WITH THE CLIENT

The "Communication Skills" activity is intended for clients whose relationships are troubled due to poor communication skills, on the part of the clients themselves or others. This is critical to relapse prevention, as a common relapse trigger is relationship conflict, and the most common source of relationship problems is poor communication. Follow-up for this exercise could include guided practice in group, couples, or family therapy; keeping a journal about the outcomes of this assignment; and reporting back to the therapist and treatment group on outcomes.

COMMUNICATION SKILLS

Saying what we mean clearly, in a way that is respectful to ourselves and others, is a learned skill. So is hearing what others are telling us. Communication takes two skills: expressing ourselves clearly and listening actively. This exercise will help you communicate more effectively.

1. Please name the person with whom you have the most trouble communicating, and why you think this happens. Then do the same for the person with whom it's easiest for you to communicate.

   Person   **Why It's Challenging**
   _____   _____

   Person   **Why It's Easier**
   _____   _____

2. We all have communication styles we use most. The following are a number of styles. *Circle* those that you believe describe how you generally communicate:

   a. *Aggressive.* Expressing ourselves with little regard for others' rights, thoughts, or feelings. Aggressive communication can be abusive and judgmental. It may include name-calling, yelling, sarcasm, ridicule, and hostile body language.

   b. *Passive-aggressive.* Not expressing ourselves openly. Hinting; talking behind others' backs; sarcasm; constant complaining; expecting others to know what we think, feel, or want without telling them; refusing to talk even when others can see we're upset.

   c. *Passive.* Not expressing ourselves in ways we fear might upset others, or possibly any way at all. Giving short, uninformative answers; agreeing with whatever others say.

   d. *Assertive.* Expressing our thoughts, feelings, and wishes clearly without ignoring those of others; being able to say "no" in a way that respects both others and ourselves.

Which best describes your style? Please give an example of how you use this style in two of your closest relationships.

_____

_____

_____

3. Let's look at specific elements of communication and identify alternative actions that generally have better outcomes. As you read the following list, where do you see yourself?

    a. *Mind-reading*. We try to infer what someone else is thinking or feeling without asking for them to clarify or we assume that we know without asking. Most people resent it when others do this to them—it often triggers arguments. Think of a time someone put words in your mouth. Describe how you felt, the reaction you had, and whether it helped the communication:

    _____

    _____

    If you find yourself mind reading with others, interrupt yourself, then ask the person you are talking to how they are feeling or what they are thinking. Note what happens here.

    _____

    _____

    b. *Name-calling*. We get upset with others because of their words and actions. Calling people names isn't referring to their actions, it's labeling who and what they are—things they can't change. It's hurtful. Name-calling is one of the surest ways to turn a conversation into an argument. Think of a time when someone called you names. Describe the situation, how you felt, the reaction you had, and the impact it had on communication:

    _____

    _____

    If you find yourself name calling, stop immediately, apologize. Describe what you think happened.

    _____

    _____

    c. *Interrupting or long speeches*. These two go together. If we cut others off or finish their sentences for them, the message is, "What you have to say isn't important enough for any more of my time." Also, we're often wrong about what people were about to say when we finish their sentences. It works better to listen until they finish expressing their messages. Of course, for one person to let another talk uninterrupted, both must know they'll have a chance to speak too. Think of a time someone went on and on or kept interrupting you. Describe how you felt, the impact it had, on you, and whether it helped the communication:

_____

_____

If you find yourself interrupting, interjecting, or going on and on, catch yourself and stop talking. Ask them to continue what they were saying.

_____

_____

d. *Be specific.* If we say, "You always ____" or "You never _____," we aren't describing a specific action; we're labeling that person. We're also mistaken. Even if they *often* or *seldom* do something, it's unlikely that they *always* or *never* do it. If we tell others they always or never do things, they'll immediately think of exceptions. They'll probably feel hurt that we don't recognize those exceptions. Think of a time someone did this to you. Describe how you felt, and whether it helped the communication:

_____

_____

If you find yourself engaging in you always/you never language, stop yourself and clarify what you heard them say.

_____

e. *"Kitchen sinking."* We may have many problems to work out with someone, but if we bring them all up at once, then they will feel overwhelmed. It's sometimes called "kitchen-sinking," because it feels to the other person that we're throwing everything at them including the kitchen sink. Think of a time someone "kitchen-sinked" you. Describe how you felt, and how it affected the communication:

_____

_____

If you tend to do this when communicating with others, slow down and consider one thing at a time.

_____

f. *Blaming.* A near-guaranteed way to pick a fight is to blame someone for your own feelings or actions by saying "You made me feel" or "You made me do _____." Other people can't *make* us do anything unless they use physical force. They can't make us feel or think a certain way. Do *you* want to be blamed for someone else's actions and feelings? To solve a problem instead of starting a fight, it works better to say, "When you did (*action*), (*result*) this happened, and I felt (*emotion*)." (See h.) Think of a time someone blamed you for their feelings or actions. Describe the situation, how you felt, and whether it helped the communication:

_____

_____

If you tend to blame others for how you feel or what you did, stop and consider how you can accept responsibility for your own behavior and feelings. How might this benefit you and the relationship?

_____

g. *Respond to both the spoken and unspoken parts of the message.* We need to listen to other people's words and respond to the emotions we sense in their facial expressions, body language, and tone after we check to be sure we understand them accurately. It helps when people see that we're paying attention and trying to understand them. Think of a time someone acknowledged your feelings as well as your words. How did they let you know? How did you feel about it?

_____

_____

h. *Use a structured communication method.*

i. Agree to talk about the issue at a specific time soon and at a place that is practical for both people and as free of distractions as possible.

ii. Agree on who will talk and who will listen first (you'll trade places often).

iii. The first person makes a short statement using the following format:

Event/Result/Emotion
"When (*an event*) happened/you did (*action*), it caused (*result*), and I felt (*emotion(s)*)."

Think of a time you were upset with someone. How would you have expressed your viewpoint in this format?

_____

4. The listener then checks for understanding by paraphrasing the message, expressing it in their own words: "If I understand what you're telling me, it is (*paraphrased message*)." This is key because the same words may mean different things to two people.

_____

5. The first person agrees that the second person got the message right, restates any part that was left out or mixed up, or deletes anything that got added.

6. Trade places and repeat the process. After the first time, you can switch to telling one another "I would like you to _____." The feedback works the same as before.

7. If you are not willing or able to do what the other person wants, tell them so in plain English: "I'm not willing to_____/I can't _____because _____." If you can, offer a compromise. Think of a time someone wanted you to do something you were unable or unwilling to do. How could you have expressed this to the other person?

8. Keep repeating this process until you both feel you clearly understand each other's perceptions, feelings, wants, and what you are willing to do for each other.

9. These techniques can seem awkward, but they get easier with practice. To complete the exercise, talk with two important people in your life and practice these skills with them. Imagine times you've felt most understood, heard, and work to recreate this. With intense emotions, conflicts, we may have to stop, slow down, get our brains and bodies calm and try again.

Be sure to bring this handout back to your next therapy session and talk with your therapist about the results and any questions or problems you have about communication skills.

RELATIONSHIP ASSESSMENT

GOALS OF THE EXERCISE

1. Understand the relationship between addiction and partner relational conflicts.
2. Develop the skills necessary to maintain open, effective communication, sexual intimacy, and enjoyable time with a partner.
3. Terminate addiction and resolve the relationship conflicts that increase the risk of relapse.
4. Reframe both addiction and conflict as problems to be solved, having much in common with other problems already solved in the past.
5. Maintain a program of recovery, free of addiction and partner relational conflicts.

ADDITIONAL PROBLEMS FOR WHICH THIS EXERCISE MAY BE USEFUL

- Adult-Child-of-an-Alcoholic (ACA) Traits
- Borderline Traits
- Dependent Traits
- Family Conflicts
- Parent–Child Relational Problem
- Suicidal Ideation

SUGGESTIONS FOR PROCESSING THIS EXERCISE WITH THE CLIENT

The "Relationship Assessment" activity guides clients in a systematic self-assessment to identify what issues exist in their primary relationship from their perspective and to imagine how their partner may feel. Follow-up can include keeping a journal and reporting back on successes and lessons learned. This exercise could be adapted for use in a couples session to gain actual feedback from the partner and to work on communication, problem solving, conflict resolution, and recovery issues together.

RELATIONSHIP ASSESSMENT

Looking at all our relationships in recovery is important. Learning to identify our role in conflict in our relationships, as well as being able to see our partner's perspective, is necessary to improve relationships. Our relationships may have been damaged by our addictive behavior, and the ways we relate (or didn't relate) in our relationships can result in stress and subsequently relapse if they are not changed. Building our primary relationships into supportive ones requires being able to evaluate what's happened and find ways to begin to shape different interactions. This exercise will help you begin this process. Remember that we can only do our own work. By continuing to work on ourselves, those closest to us may begin to trust us enough to try too. It's important to remember that you benefit from working on yourself, and this facilitates sustained recovery.

1. From your perspective, what are the nature and causes of conflicts in your relationship with your partner (i.e., communication, finances, children, dishonesty, negativity, sexual issues, etc.)?

   _____

   _____

2. What would you imagine your partner's perspective would be?

   _____

   _____

3. How has addictive behavior contributed to conflicts? List three instances.

   _____

   _____

4. If your relationship existed prior to addictive behavior, were the conflicts the same or different? If different, in what ways and what do you believe contributed to the change?

   _____

   _____

5. How have you chosen addictive behavior as a reaction to conflicts?

    _____

    _____

6. What are the positive aspects of your relationship from your perspective?

    _____

    _____

7. What would you imagine your partner would say?

    _____

    _____

8. How would these positives be enhanced by your abstinence/recovery?

    _____

    _____

9. What behavior changes do you believe you need to make to improve the relationship?

    _____

    _____

10. From your perspective, what changes do you believe your partner needs to make?

    _____

    _____

11. Now that you've gathered the data about both negatives and positives, what are the benefits you see in working to resolve the issues you and your partner identified?

    _____

    _____

12. What's the preliminary plan to do this work?

    _____

    _____

13. After completing the exercise, consider going back and asking your partner about their perceptions. Record them on the same form next to your answers. Compare them to yours. What shared perceptions and differences do you notice?

    _____

    _____

14. As you begin to make changes, how will you address impasses? Frustrations? Relapse/lapse triggers? Strong emotions? Guilt? Shame? Anger?

_____

_____

Be sure to bring this handout back to your next therapy session and be prepared to talk about your thoughts and feelings about the exercise.

CREATING RECOVERY PEER SUPPORT

GOALS OF THE EXERCISE

1. Maintain a program of recovery free of addiction and negative influences from peers.
2. Learn the skills necessary to develop a new peer group that is addiction free and supportive of working a program of recovery.
3. Become more aware of positive changes and progress in treatment by getting feedback from other people.
4. Increase emotional support from others.

ADDITIONAL PROBLEMS FOR WHICH THIS EXERCISE MAY BE USEFUL

- Attention-Deficit/Hyperactivity Disorder (ADHD)—Adolescent
- Attention-Deficit/Hyperactivity Disorder (ADHD)—Adult
- Conduct Disorder/Delinquency
- Dependent Traits
- Legal Problems
- Living Environment Deficiency
- Opioid Use Disorder
- Oppositional Defiant Behavior
- Relapse Proneness

SUGGESTIONS FOR PROCESSING THIS EXERCISE WITH THE CLIENT

The "Creating Recovery Peer Support" activity is intended for clients who may not feel ready to cut ties with old peer groups. They may not believe that peer associations affect recovery negatively. Multiple efforts may be needed to work through the resistance, ambivalence, fear, and grief related to ending peer relationships, even if the client understands that their influence is negative. Motivational enhancement strategies will be critical to have them reduce defensiveness, ambivalence, fear, and increase readiness to consider changes to support recovery. It may help to role-play ways to distance or end unhealthy relationships and initiate healthy new ones. It may also be useful to help the client educate their family and supportive friends about addiction and the recovery process. Helping clients reconcile the discrepancy between what they know they need to do and what they want and feel ready to do is necessary to make change happen in this area.

CREATING RECOVERY PEER SUPPORT

When actively engaged in addictive behavior, you likely heard a lot of negative feedback about your peers. In the early phases of sobriety and recovery, you might hear a lot about "people, places, and things" and the need to dissociate from "using peers." Of course, this is easier said than done. In a first treatment attempt or early in our sobriety, it is common to believe that the only thing that needs to change is the negative behavior itself (i.e., stop using drugs, gambling, acting impulsively). It is also common to believe that we can continue to associate with the people we have used with and just not use ourselves. We believe we will be able to easily refuse or that our "friends" will understand our situation and not offer or pressure us.

This theory has been tested by many people who have found recovery, most often with negative results. Continuing to believe it's possible and putting yourself in that situation places you, like all others with addictive behaviors before you, at high risk of relapse and the negative consequences associated with it. The time-tested way to succeed in getting sober and sustaining sobriety and recovery is developing relationships and a peer group that supports recovery. There are many reasons why 12-step programs exist, and there are many reasons why these programs work. One is being helped by and subsequently helping others with whom you have a shared experience.

1. To increase the likelihood of staying in recovery, each of us needs to develop a new peer group that is free of addictive behaviors and supports working a program of recovery. Describe your thoughts about establishing relationships with those not engaged in addictive behavior.

   _____

   _____

2. What are the benefits to you and your recovery in increasing opportunities for fellowship with positive peers?

   _____

   _____

3. What do you foresee as potential barriers given your current feelings, attitudes, perceptions of doing this?

_____

_____

4. What skills do you need to develop new friends?

_____

_____

5. List five negative thoughts/attitudes/perceptions you tell yourself about a new group of peers that will argue against trying to work on this (i.e., "They won't understand me like my old peers," "They'll all be boring").

_____

_____

6. What alternative positive thoughts will you use to challenge these thoughts to increase your chances of taking the initiative, putting in the time, and persisting in making new friends?

_____

_____

7. How will you address the loss of old peers, some of whom you may have known a long time or have felt very close to or have been through a lot with?

_____

_____

8. Which members of your family can become a positive support and help you in your recovery?

_____

_____

9. Write a brief plan to start identifying and making new social contacts, finding places you belong, creating experiences and opportunities you are not actively working to escape/numb/avoid.

_____

_____

_____

Be sure to bring this handout back to your next therapy session and be prepared to talk about your thoughts and feelings about the exercise. Consider talking about this topic in a 12-step meeting to hear what others have to say about their experience with this situation.

WHAT DO I NEED AND HOW DO I GET IT?

GOALS OF THE EXERCISE

1. Maintain a program of recovery free of addiction and negative influences from peers.
2. Understand that continued association with a negative peer group increases the risk of relapse.
3. Develop a new peer group that supports working in a recovery program.
4. Address fears related to giving up the former peer group.
5. Find healthier ways to meet needs that old peer relationships fulfilled.

ADDITIONAL PROBLEMS FOR WHICH THIS EXERCISE MAY BE USEFUL

- Attention-Deficit/Hyperactivity Disorder (ADHD)—Adolescent
- Attention-Deficit/Hyperactivity Disorder (ADHD)—Adult
- Conduct Disorder/Delinquency
- Dependent Traits
- Legal Problems
- Living Environment Deficiency
- Oppositional Defiant Behavior
- Relapse Proneness

SUGGESTIONS FOR PROCESSING THIS EXERCISE WITH THE CLIENT

The "What Do I Need and How Do I Get It?" activity is for clients whose recovery efforts are undermined by peer interactions. It guides clients to assess this for themselves and draw conclusions based on data they collect. Clients may not feel ready to cut ties with old peer groups. They may not believe that peer associations affect recovery negatively. Multiple efforts may be needed to work through the resistance, ambivalence, fear, and grief related to ending peer relationships, even if the client understands that their influence is negative. It may help to role-play ways to distance or end unhealthy relationships and initiate healthy new ones. Helping clients reconcile the discrepancy between what they know they need to do, what they hear repeatedly from others in recovery or treatment, and what they want and feel ready and able to do is necessary to make change happen in this area. These may be relationships that have existed for a long time and that are as strong as family ties. Provide space and time to process the closure of these relationships; even though they are negative influences, they are losses. Allowing them to hope for something better for old friends who still use but knowing they must distance themselves is a process.

WHAT DO I NEED AND HOW DO I GET IT?

Some of the hardest challenges people face in early recovery are relationships with family members, significant others, and friends who continue to engage in addictive behavior or illegal activities, don't understand or support recovery, mock, undermine, ignore treatment and recovery, and encourage addictive behaviors. As you get healthier physically, emotionally, and spiritually, you may find you have less and less in common with some of the people who were closest to you before you got into recovery. Each of us has the right and the responsibility to choose with whom we will associate. We deserve to have the people in our lives support our recovery and respect our decision to live free of addiction. We need to eliminate risks that lead back toward addictive lifestyles and behaviors, and this may include people with whom we've shared important parts of our lives. To maintain recovery, we need to increase our contact with positive people who support nonaddictive lifestyles. This exercise will help you assess your peer group for risks, identify the benefits of being around people who support your recovery, and begin identifying what you are willing to do for yourself to create a more recovery-oriented support system.

1. Please list five situations when peers/family encouraged you to engage in addictive behavior or illegal activity.

   _____

   _____

   _____

   _____

2. We are responsible for our own choices, but the people we associate with can be a powerful influence. Does your current peer group support addictive behavior (e.g., do they encourage use, use around you, act unsupportive, or make fun of your recovery)? What influence do they have on you?

   _____

   _____

3. What are some things you've said, done, or heard others say, to deny that peers, influence has on thinking or behavior? What do you think about those statements?

_____

_____

4. Does continued involvement with your peer group increase your risk of relapse? If so, how do your peers undermine your success in treatment? List up to five ways.

_____

_____

_____

_____

5. What worries do you have about breaking off your connections with current peers and making new contacts?

_____

_____

6. What are the main advantages and disadvantages of changing your peer group from one that increases your risk of relapse to one that encourages a nonaddictive lifestyle?

Advantages   **Disadvantages**

_____   _____

_____   _____

_____   _____

7. What needs has your addictive peer group fulfilled for you (e.g., fun, excitement, second family, sense of belonging, etc.)?

_____

_____

8. Imagine explaining to your peer group your need to distance or end your relationship for your own well-being. What would you want them to know?

_____

_____

9. If a friend told you that they needed to stop spending time with you for their own good, would you respect your friend's decision? If so, what are your thoughts about making the same decision for yourself?

_____

_____

10. Write a brief preliminary plan to start identifying and making new social contacts. Consider where you might look to start and what interests/activities/experiences might lead to a potential connection.

_____

_____

After completing this exercise, consider working on the exercise also contained in this manual titled "Creating Recovery Peer Support" (Exercise 32.A). It will assist you more specifically in the considerations of creating a peer group supportive of recovery and meeting all the needs of your old group.

Be sure to bring this handout back to your next therapy session and be prepared to talk over your thoughts and feelings about this topic with your therapist or with your group.

COPING WITH ADDICTION AND PTSD

GOALS OF THE EXERCISE

1. Understand the connections between posttraumatic stress symptoms and addiction.
2. Learn coping skills to bring posttraumatic stress symptoms and addiction under control.
3. Promote healing and acceptance and reduce relapse risk by using coping strategies for both addictions and problems related to anxiety disorders.

ADDITIONAL PROBLEMS FOR WHICH THIS EXERCISE MAY BE USEFUL

- Adult-Child-of-an-Alcoholic (ACA) Traits
- Anger
- Anxiety
- Borderline Traits
- Childhood Trauma
- Depression–Unipolar
- Grief/Loss Unresolved
- Panic Disorder
- Self-Harm
- Sexual Abuse
- Social Anxiety
- Suicidal Ideation

SUGGESTIONS FOR PROCESSING THIS EXERCISE WITH THE CLIENT

The "Coping with Addiction and PTSD" activity is for clients who are suffering from unresolved trauma, panic attacks, and related disorders. It addresses self-medication and risky behaviors as factors in trauma and offers healthier ways to cope with the combined challenge of trauma and addiction. Follow-up can include referral to support or therapy groups for PTSD or other anxiety disorders, assignments to try alternative coping strategies, and reporting back to the therapist and/or treatment group on outcomes. Attend to the pace and triggers associated with this exercise. Clients should have some time in sobriety and some skill in managing negative emotional states and intense emotions and be working well in therapy.

COPING WITH ADDICTION AND PTSD

Many people suffer from both substance abuse problems and trauma and stress-related disorders, posttraumatic stress disorder (PTSD) being one of them. What are the connections between addiction and trauma- and stress-related disorders? People who abuse alcohol or other drugs are more likely than others to find themselves in risky and stressful situations and suffer trauma, and people with trauma-related disorders are at a higher risk to become addicted to alcohol or other drugs if they self-medicate to relieve their symptoms. If they encounter another traumatic experience in recovery or old ones resurface, some don't believe they can cope without alcohol or other drugs. It's important to recognize that childhood trauma can be associated with and absence of what was needed to feel safe, attached, nurtured; childhood and later trauma can be a byproduct of something extraordinary and destructive, like sexual assault, domestic violence, being a victim of a crime, as examples. Certainly not everyone is affected the same way and it doesn't take the same healing path. This exercise will help you begin to plan to overcome issues of this kind when you're ready and for the benefit of improved quality of life and sobriety.

1. In some cases, people experience traumatic events because of their drinking, drug use, or other high-risk addictive behaviors. Please describe any ways you feel your addictive patterns have led to you suffering traumatic experiences:

    _____

    _____

2. Sometimes the connection between addiction and anxiety works in the other direction: The traumatic experiences or other anxiety problems come first, and when people use chemicals (or intense experiences) to temporarily block the pain, they develop an addiction. Have painful experiences led you to drink, use, or otherwise act out addictively? If so, how?

    _____

    _____

3. List five ways managing your PTSD symptoms will be important for your sobriety from addictive or other self-destructive behaviors.

_____

_____

_____

_____

4. Many people find that methods they use to overcome addictions, such as participating in recovery programs, learning coping skills, and finding replacement activities for substance use also help them deal with trauma-related disorders. What recovery tools might help you deal with PTSD, panic attacks, or related disorders?

_____

_____

5. On the other hand, some techniques that are often used with anxiety disorders may not seem to fit into recovery from substance abuse, such as the use of anti-anxiety drugs and other prescribed mood-altering medications. If your doctor instructs you to take medications for a trauma-related disorder, have you talked about your substance abuse issues with that doctor? If so, what was the feedback? If not, what keeps you from talking to your doctor about this recovery issue, and how might withholding affect your treatment and your risk of relapse?

_____

_____

6. If you are working a 12-step program, do you know your program's policy about the use of prescribed mood-altering medications? Alcoholics Anonymous takes the position that if your doctor knows your history of addiction, is experienced in working with people with addictions, has prescribed your medication with that knowledge, and you are taking it exactly as prescribed, then you're doing what you need to do to stay sober. Other programs have similar policies. If you have questions, check the official literature.

_____

7. Please describe the tools you will use to cope with the combined problems of substance abuse and symptoms of stressor related disorders (intrusive memories, sleep struggles, avoidance behavior, intense arousal, depersonalization):

_____

_____

_____

8. Identify ways to make your living environment, your relationships, your social support, your body a safe place to exist. Talk with your therapist about when and if additional, specific trauma treatment would be of benefit.

_____

_____

Consider working through the exercises "Relapse Prevention Planning" (Exercise 36.C) and "Personal Recovery Planning" (Exercise 47.C) in this manual to assist you in both addressing the complexity of symptoms in healing from PTSD and incorporating your PTSD symptoms into the plan for recovery from alcohol, other drugs, and/or other addictive behaviors. Be sure to bring this handout back to your next therapy session and be prepared to talk about your thoughts and feelings about the exercise.

SAFE AND PEACEFUL PLACE MEDITATION

GOALS OF THE EXERCISE

1. Learn coping skills useful for bringing posttraumatic stress disorder symptoms and addiction under control.
2. Learn and practice a healthy method to achieve deep relaxation in many situations.
3. Improve ability to cope with stress in a healthy way.
4. Learn to achieve relief from posttraumatic stress symptoms.
5. Recognize the first signs of anger and use behavioral techniques to control it.

ADDITIONAL PROBLEMS FOR WHICH THIS EXERCISE MAY BE USEFUL

- Anxiety
- Attention-Deficit/Hyperactivity Disorder (ADHD)—Adolescent
- Attention-Deficit/Hyperactivity Disorder (ADHD)—Adult
- Borderline Traits
- Childhood Trauma
- Chronic Pain
- Grief/Loss Unresolved
- Medical Issues
- Obsessive-Compulsive Disorder (OCD)
- Self-Harm
- Sexual Abuse
- Sleep Disturbance
- Substance Intoxication/Withdrawal

SUGGESTIONS FOR PROCESSING THIS EXERCISE WITH THE CLIENT

The "Safe and Peaceful Place Meditation" activity is useful for managing stress and anxiety, particularly if these are chronic. It is also useful for pain management and insomnia. This exercise guides the client in a personalized multisensory imagery exercise in which they create a mental construct of a safe and peaceful place and practice temporarily withdrawing from engagement with stressors. With practice, this exercise can become a very effective method of achieving quick relaxation. This exercise can be used in individual or group therapy and as an opening routine for treatment groups. Follow-up can include practice at home and teaching the exercise to someone else.

SAFE AND PEACEFUL PLACE MEDITATION

Do you sometimes wish you could just get away from the situation you're in or from what you're thinking and feeling? This is normal and healthy, but it may not be practical to leave a situation right away, and it's hard to leave our thoughts and feelings behind even when we do go somewhere else.

This exercise will teach you how to get away even when you can't go anywhere, without using substances to do so. It will guide you in creating a mental picture of a safe and peaceful place where you can temporarily relax, so that you can come back to your situation calm and refreshed. Practice is important. The more you practice, the better it will work for you. With enough repetition, this tool can be used to quickly achieve calm and inner peace even during great pain, anger, and anxiety.

For many people, it works best to do this with their eyes closed, so you may want to have someone you trust and feel safe with read this to you while you follow the instructions or record it in your own voice to play back and listen. If you cannot close your eyes, you can affix your gaze down toward the floor in front of your feet.

1. *Image*. What is a place that makes you feel calm, peaceful, and safe to think about? Please think of the place that best fits this description for you and form a mental picture of this place. It may be a real place you've been—anything from a favorite beach to your grandparents' kitchen, a place you've heard about and would like to go, or an imaginary place. Whatever is relaxing for you is right for you. Briefly describe this safe and peaceful place.

    _____

    _____

2. *Emotions and sensations*. Focus on this image or mental picture. Relax your muscles and breathe deeply and slowly, from your belly. What emotions do you feel? What pleasant physical sensations do you feel, and where are they located in your body?

    _____

    _____

3. *Enhancement*. Explore this imagery in more detail. Savor it with all your senses and enjoy the idea of being in this safe and peaceful place. When you look around in this

place in your mind's eye, what do you see happening? What do you hear? Is it warm or cool? What does the air feel like against your face? Is there a distinctive aroma? Please describe whatever sensory details you can think of:

_____

_____

4. *Cue or keyword.* Please think of a word to represent this place. Keep this word in mind while you keep exploring the mental picture, the sights, the sounds, and all the sensations of peace and safety and pleasure of this place. Focus on whatever pleasant things come to each of your senses in turn, keeping this keyword in mind. Now let your mind dwell on those pleasant sensations and repeat the keyword to yourself over and over. Try blanking out the pleasant place you have been thinking of, then thinking of the keyword, and let the image come back to you quickly and vividly. Notice how your body is feeling more relaxed. Repeat this a few times.

_____

5. *Coping with mild stress.* Test this to relax and overcome negative feelings. Blank out your safe and peaceful place again. Now think of a minor annoyance, a situation or person that isn't a big problem but gets on your nerves. What kinds of negative physical sensations are coming to you when you think of this annoyance? Where are they located in your body?

_____

_____

Now think of your keyword. Again, think of the safe and peaceful place in your mind's eye that goes with the keyword. Think of the visual image, the scenery, the sounds, and the pleasant physical sensations. Focus on deep and deliberate breathing as you do this. As you think of this, how does your body feel? What is happening to the negative sensations you felt in your body?

_____

_____

6. *Practice.* For the next 2 weeks, practice this at least twice a day. Use it if you find yourself getting irritated or anxious. You can also use it when you are feeling physical pain or discomfort, or if you have trouble sleeping. As you practice, keep noticing anything about your mental image of the peaceful and safe place that makes it more vivid and more relaxing for you, and keep those details in mind for future times when you do this exercise. As an added help to learning to use it, try teaching it to someone else and see how it works for them.

Use this space to record anything you notice or learn about using this meditation exercise.

_____

_____

Be sure to bring this handout back to your next therapy session and be prepared to talk about your thoughts and feelings about the exercise. If there are challenges in the next 2 weeks as you practice, be sure to talk about this in therapy and work through them. Challenge any skepticism you may have that this could work. Increase thoughts of openness to possibility and see if this helps.

COPING WITH ADDICTION AND SCHIZOPHRENIA SPECTRUM DISORDERS

GOALS OF THE EXERCISE

1. Gain an understanding of the interaction between addictions and psychosis.
2. Develop adaptive methods to cope with symptoms of psychosis and seek treatment when necessary while maintaining abstinence from substance abuse.
3. Stabilize cognitive functioning adequately to allow treatment in an outpatient setting.

ADDITIONAL PROBLEMS FOR WHICH THIS EXERCISE MAY BE USEFUL

- Bipolar Disorder
- Depression–Unipolar
- Self-Care Deficits—Primary
- Self-Care Deficits—Secondary
- Substance-Induced Disorders
- Substance Use Disorders

SUGGESTIONS FOR PROCESSING THIS EXERCISE WITH THE CLIENT

The "Coping with Addiction and Schizophrenia Spectrum Disorders" activity is designed to help the client with symptoms of psychosis cope with the challenges of this dual diagnosis. Its approach is to examine issues of self-medication and the possible role of substance abuse in the development of thought disorders and to offer strategies for integrating recovery work on both problems. Follow-up may include referral to a Double Trouble 12-step group, to another dual-diagnosis recovery/support program, or to a support group specifically focused on thought disorders.

Another suggestion is to give homework assignments to use coping strategies identified through this exercise in a structured way and report back on the outcomes. It may be helpful to involve family members to increase treatment compliance, to send consistent messages to the client, and to help them create a "rescue plan" when symptoms of one or both disorders necessitate a higher level of care.

COPING WITH ADDICTION AND SCHIZOPHRENIA SPECTRUM DISORDERS

Some people suffer from both substance abuse problems and what are called *psychoses* or *thought disorders*, most often schizophrenia. If you are working to overcome both problems, the purpose of this assignment is to help you use the same tools for both tasks where possible and to guide you in handling the special challenges of this type of mental health issue.

How are substance use and thought disorders connected? People who abuse alcohol or other drugs can suffer from thought disorders as a result, and people with thought disorders are at a higher risk to have problems with substance abuse because they are more likely to self-medicate in efforts to find relief from the symptoms of their mental illness.

1. In some cases, people find the beginnings of their thought disorder seem to be connected to their substance use. Please describe any ways you feel your substance use has led to your thinking becoming distorted.

   _____

   _____

2. Sometimes the connection between addiction and thought disorders works in the other direction: The hallucinations, false beliefs, or other symptoms of psychosis come first, and when people use drugs (street drugs, alcohol, psychoactive prescription medications other than those prescribed for them by a psychiatrist, or nicotine) to try to control or cope with these symptoms, they become dependent on those substances. Please describe how your thought disorder's symptoms may have led you to drink or use other drugs in the search for relief from symptoms.

   _____

   _____

   _____

3. Many people find that some methods they use to overcome addictions, such as participating in recovery programs, learning new coping skills, following a recommended treatment plan, and finding replacement activities for substance use, also help them

deal with thought disorders. What recovery tools might help you deal with your thought disorder symptoms?

_____

_____

4. On the other hand, some techniques that are used with thought disorders may not seem to fit into recovery from substance abuse, such as the use of antipsychotic drugs and other prescribed medications. If a doctor has instructed you to take medications for a thought disorder, have you talked with that doctor about your substance abuse issues? If so, what did they tell you about this? If not, what keeps you from talking to your doctor about this?

_____

_____

5. What did your doctor tell you might happen if you stopped taking your medications or didn't take them as prescribed?

_____

_____

If you are working a 12-step program, do you know your program's policy about the use of prescribed mind-altering medications? Alcoholics Anonymous takes the following position: If your doctor knows your history of addiction and is experienced in working with people with addictions, and you are taking the prescribed medications exactly as prescribed and not using any nonprescribed mind-altering substances, then you are doing what you need to do to stay sober. Other programs have similar policies. If you have questions, check the official literature.

_____

6. How will consistently taking your prescribed medications improve your recovery efforts for both problems?

_____

_____

_____

_____

7. What other self-care behaviors will you need to attend to? Identify those you may need assistance with?

_____

_____

8. Identify three people who support you in your recovery efforts from both problems. How can each help you stay sober and address necessary medical treatment for your thought disorder? Identify the benefit of staying sober and following your individualized treatment plan.

_____

_____

Be sure to bring this handout back to your next therapy session and be prepared to talk about your thoughts and feelings about the exercise.

PLANNING A STABLE LIFE

GOALS OF THE EXERCISE

1. Identify early warning symptoms of decompensation to get help as quickly as possible.
2. Stabilize cognitive functioning adequately to allow treatment in an outpatient setting.
3. Develop adaptive methods to cope with symptoms without relapse into addiction and seek treatment when necessary.

ADDITIONAL PROBLEMS FOR WHICH THIS EXERCISE MAY BE USEFUL

- Bipolar Disorder
- Depression–Unipolar
- Impulsivity
- Posttraumatic Stress Disorder (PTSD)
- Substance-Induced Disorders

SUGGESTIONS FOR PROCESSING THIS EXERCISE WITH THE CLIENT

The "Planning a Stable Life" activity is for the client who experiences psychotic symptoms as a result of mental illness, a co-occurring disorder, or chemical addiction and who is working toward developing a comprehensive recovery plan. The clinician must work from the client's perspective. It may require that, of the various things the client suggests as components of the plan, the clinician will need to clarify with which components they can assist and support. Recovery is both defined and carried out by the client. Essential elements include instilling hope, educating, receiving support, personal responsibility, and learning to advocate for oneself.

It may be useful to have supportive family members attend a session so the client can share the plan with them and educate them regarding their roles in the plan. You can also include family members as active participants in the planning process. Family and others often have information that is useful and information of which the client may or may not be aware. Assessing for psychotic symptoms and ability to engage in appropriate treatment and self-care will guide the degree to which others may be involved.

PLANNING A STABLE LIFE

The relationship between thought-disordered symptoms and addiction can vary. Thought-disordered symptoms may be a direct result of chemical use or abuse; the use of substances may make existing symptoms worse; or people may use chemicals to self-medicate already-present negative symptoms. In any case, most people want troublesome symptoms to go away, and they want to feel better and live independent lives. In addition to managing symptoms, you will need to find ways to cope with the feelings associated with symptoms of psychosis, such as a feeling of inadequacy, fear of dependence on others, and/or fear of being intruded upon. Recovery means working toward having more to life than coping with symptoms of the illness itself. This exercise will help you design a safety and recovery plan so that you can reach your goals and plan to avoid problems or cope with them if they arise.

With your therapist, caseworker, sponsor, or another trusted supportive person, write out your stability plan. When your plan is complete, keep one copy at home, one with you when you're away from home, and give copies to your therapist or caseworker and to any family members or friends you are asking to help you follow your plan. Please make sure to include each of the following in your stability plan:

1.   Your daily routine (what your day-to-day schedule will look like)

_____

2.   Your medications (what they are, the dosages, and when they are to be taken)

_____

3.   Your diet (what it will include and things to avoid or limit)

_____

4.   Your sleep plan (include a bedtime ritual describing how you will get ready for bed; a consistent sleep/wake schedule is the ideal)

_____

5. Activities for fun that don't involve addictive behavior or substances

6. Supportive people (non-family members) and how to contact them

7. Supportive family members and how they can be helpful to you

8. Your personal goals (what you'd like to accomplish, both short and longer term)

9. Topics about which you and/or your family members and other supporters need more information

10. Barriers that could get in the way of maintaining stability (feelings related to taking medications, dealing with side effects of medications, fears, limited support, etc.), with simple strategies to avoid or overcome each barrier

11. A list of thoughts, feelings, and behaviors that indicate your symptoms are getting worse, including critical symptoms that indicate a need to respond urgently

12. For each warning sign you listed for question 11, please write instructions for yourself about what to do, including names and phone numbers of people you will contact. Also, please write instructions about what those supportive people you've identified in questions 6 and 7 can do to help you.

13. A list of techniques and resources that have worked before to help you stabilize your symptoms, your moods, or your urges to return to addictive behaviors

14. A crisis intervention plan should be developed before a crisis takes place, when you are calm and able to plan and think clearly. Include strategies that you already know work, who you'd like to be involved, what is *not* helpful, and other suggestions for the people who will help you when a crisis occurs.

Use the space here to outline your plan:

_____
_____
_____
_____
_____
_____
_____
_____
_____
_____

Be sure to bring this handout to your next therapy session and be prepared to ask for assistance when needed and talk over your thoughts and feelings about this exercise with your therapist.

ADDRESSING READINESS AND MOTIVATION

GOALS OF THE EXERCISE

1. Establish a sustained recovery that is free of addictive behaviors.
2. Increase awareness of personal losses and problems associated with addictive behaviors.
3. Collect objective facts about the impact of alcohol, other drug use, or addictive behaviors.
4. Increase motivation for change to avoid further problems brought on by or made worse by addictions.

ADDITIONAL PROBLEMS FOR WHICH THIS EXERCISE MAY BE USEFUL

- Eating Disorders and Obesity
- Gambling
- Nicotine Use/Dependence
- Sexual Promiscuity
- Substance Use Disorders

SUGGESTIONS FOR PROCESSING THIS EXERCISE WITH THE CLIENT

The "Addressing Readiness and Motivation" activity is suited for individual or group use. This is, in a way, the opposite of the "Consequences of Continuing Addictive Lifestyles" exercise. Whereas the latter guides the client in creating a *yet list* of negative consequences, this activity walks them through systematically listing at one time in one place the negative things that have already happened—in a way, conducting a self-intervention. Follow-up to this exercise might include writing reflections; sharing responses with the therapist, treatment group, and program sponsor; and moving on to the "Personal Recovery Planning" activity (Exercise 47.C).

ADDRESSING READINESS AND MOTIVATION

People don't usually get treatment or help until they find themselves in crisis. Crises are good motivators to enter recovery. However, to stay in recovery, we need to look at our addictive behaviors over the long run, beyond the crises. If you wonder whether you have a problem with alcohol, drugs, or other addictive behaviors or how serious your problem is, compare the events in your life with each of these categories.

What brought you to treatment this time:

1. Following is a brief, partial list of common experiences that encourage people who are practicing addictive lifestyles to decide that they should change these patterns, that their addictions are causing them problems, and that they want help. Please *check* all those that apply to you.

    ### Loss of Important Relationships
    _____ Divorce or equivalent
    _____ Children, parents, siblings alienated
    _____ Loss of close friendships
    _____ Loss of respect from coworkers
    _____ Death of close friend/companion from overdose

    ### Practical Difficulties
    _____ Unpaid debts
    _____ Loss of employment
    _____ Loss of a vehicle
    _____ Loss of a home
    _____ Loss of professional status
    _____ Bankruptcy
    _____ Legal problems (e.g., arrest, jail, probation, loss of driver's license)

Dangerous/Harmful Situations

_____ Health problems

_____ Recreational accidents

_____ DUIs, DWIs, or car wrecks

_____ Work injuries, falls, or other accidents

_____ Fights while under the influence or coming down

_____ Harm to others as a result of one's own actions under the influence

_____ Suicidal ideation, attempts

_____ Self-injury

_____ Violence

_____ Withdrawal when quitting

_____ Psychosis

_____ Chronic health condition(s)

Things We Thought We Would Never Do

_____ Disappoint friends

_____ Repeatedly breaking promises

_____ Lying to partners/families

_____ Stealing from partners/families/work

_____ Disappoint employers

_____ Abusing family members

_____ Selling drugs

_____ Endangering others, especially children

_____ Exchanging sex for alcohol or other drugs

_____ Committing crimes to support addiction

_____ Continuing to use despite mounting negatives

2. What other ways has addiction negatively affected your life? Look back at the list. What are the items you endorsed that have the most impact on how you feel about yourself?

_____

_____

3. When you think about your life without alcohol, other drugs, or other addictive behavior, how do you feel?

_____

_____

4. On a scale of 1 to 10 (1 = not at all and 10 = extremely important), how important is it for you to stop your use of alcohol, other drugs, or other addictive behavior? Explain your rating.

_____

_____

5. On a scale of 1 to 10 (1 = not at all and 10 = extremely confident), how confident are you that you could begin to make changes to your alcohol, other drug, or other addictive behavior if you wanted to? Explain your rating.

_____

_____

What else might you need to increase your confidence that you could change if it were important enough?

_____

_____

6. On a scale of 1 to 10 (1 = not at all and 10 = extremely), how willing are you to take the first steps and address the problems you identified above? Explain your rating.

_____

_____

Name that first step here if you're willing:

_____

_____

_____

Be sure to bring this handout back to your next therapy session and be prepared to talk about your thoughts and feelings about the exercise.

PROBLEM IDENTIFICATION: IS IT ADDICTION?

GOALS OF THE EXERCISE

1. Cooperate with addiction assessments and accept the diagnosis and treatment plan.
2. Accept responsibility for the problems caused by addiction and accept the need for treatment.
3. Establish and maintain total abstinence from addictive behaviors while increasing knowledge of how addiction has affected the client's life and the process of recovery.
4. Increase client ownership of the issues by creating a personal definition of the problem of substance use and/or other addictive behaviors.

ADDITIONAL PROBLEMS FOR WHICH THIS EXERCISE MAY BE USEFUL

- Gambling
- Nicotine Use/Dependence
- Substance-Induced Disorders
- Substance Use Disorders

SUGGESTIONS FOR PROCESSING THIS EXERCISE WITH THE CLIENT

The "Problem Identification: Is It Addiction?" activity is designed for the client who is resistant to accepting a diagnosis of a substance use disorder (previously abuse or dependence) due to mistaken ideas about what the term means. It explains the *DSM-5* criteria, in terms the client is familiar with, and analyzes how they fit their situation. It is a useful exercise at the time of entry into treatment as a vehicle to get the client to consider additional treatment. Follow-up can include reviewing the client's findings from this exercise with the therapist, treatment group, and program sponsor.

PROBLEM IDENTIFICATION: IS IT ADDICTION?

1. Describe what led you to treatment this time.

   _____

   _____

2. Identify what contributes to your ambivalence about treatment currently? *Circle* all that apply and identify others if they are not included on the list below.

   a. I'm not ready.

   b. I do not believe it is necessary now.

   c. There are too many gains/positives to substance use/behavior.

   d. I believe it is too difficult to get sober.

   e. I question if it's worth it or if it will work.

   f. There are too many barriers (e.g., transportation, money, childcare, etc.). Please list them.

   g. Others (list): _____

3. Think about what the most important things are in your life.

   a. What are your personal goals?

      _____

      _____

   b. What would you like to have happen considering what's most important in your life?

      _____

      _____

4. What treatment and recovery recommendations have been made for you by treatment staff, other people in treatment, family, and/or friends? Please write these recommendations here.

   _____

   _____

   _____

5. What evidence helps explain the recommendation?

    _____

    _____

6. What are your own thoughts, feelings, and impressions about this recommendation? What evidence backs it up?

    _____

    _____

7. How do you reconcile your ambivalence/resistance to the recommendation with what others are saying?

    _____

    _____

8. To identify the benefit of treatment and get the most out of it, it's important to identify your own patterns of addictive/abusive use of alcohol, other drugs, or other behaviors. For each of the following patterns, please write about whether it happened and the specific evidence that it did or did not happen during your use/engaging in the behavior.

    a. Needing more of the substance/engaging in the behavior more (or going to greater extremes) to get the desired effect or getting less effect with continued use of the same amount:

        _____

        _____

    b. Having negative physical symptoms in the absence of the substance or continuing to use to avoid the negative symptoms (e.g., withdrawal):

        _____

        _____

    c. Using a substance/engaging in a behavior in larger amounts or longer than intended:

        _____

        _____

    d. Persistent desire to cut down or control your use of the substance or engaging in the behavior but being unsuccessful:

        _____

    e. Increasing the time spent thinking about, acquiring, or using a substance/engaging in a behavior and recovering from the effects:

        _____

f. Having cravings or strong desires to use or engage in the behavior:

_____

g. Failure to fulfill major responsibilities or role obligations because of your use of the substance or practicing the behavior:

_____

h. Continued use or practicing the behavior despite persistent, recurrent social, interpersonal, psychological, and physical problems:

_____

i. Reducing involvement or giving up important social, occupational, recreational, and family activities because they conflict with using the substance or the behavior:

_____

j. Recurrent use or practicing of the behavior in ways that are physically hazardous:

_____

9. In addition to the signs/symptoms of problematic use of substances or other behaviors, there is generally a progression from first use to addiction. Most people start using/engaging in a behavior, like how it makes them feel, and do not anticipate problems. Then tolerance and withdrawal appear. With ongoing use, people deliberately and routinely use alcohol/other drugs or other behaviors to cope, and "normal" life is disrupted. At this point, people may make efforts to cut down or quit. With additional use, people can no longer decide to use or not use sometimes despite the recognition of the importance to quit. Please write about where you believe you are in this progression, providing the evidence. Share this information with your therapist, group, or sponsor and include this feedback.

_____

_____

10. After working through this exercise, do you believe your current behavior will get you closer to what you really want out of life? What would be the hindrance? And what would you be willing to do to make some positive changes that get you closer to those goals? How would substance use need to be modified or changed?

_____

_____

Be sure to bring this handout back to your next therapy session and be prepared to talk about your thoughts and feelings about the exercise.

EARLY WARNING SIGNS OF RELAPSE

GOALS OF THE EXERCISE

1. Develop coping skills to use when experiencing high-risk situations and/or cravings.
2. Increase awareness of personal early warning signs of relapse.
3. Learn that relapse is a process and how a person can prevent that process from continuing to its completion in their life.

ADDITIONAL PROBLEMS FOR WHICH THIS EXERCISE MAY BE USEFUL

- Eating Disorders and Obesity
- Gambling
- Nicotine Use/Dependence
- Readiness for Change
- Self-Harm
- Substance Use Disorders
- Suicidal Ideation

SUGGESTIONS FOR PROCESSING THIS EXERCISE WITH THE CLIENT

The "Early Warning Signs of Relapse" activity is intended to help clients in early recovery learn about cognitive, emotional, and behavioral changes that are often seen in the early stages of relapse (before an actual return to active addiction) and plan strategies to counter these changes if and when they see them. This exercise is also useful to prepare for the "Relapse Prevention Planning" activity (Exercise 36.C). Follow-up can include sharing the information gathered with a program sponsor and keeping a journal to track and record "red flag" symptoms. Combining this activity with "Taking a Daily Inventory" (Exercise 47.C) provides additional information to prevent relapse.

EARLY WARNING SIGNS OF RELAPSE

In addition to external pressures to use, our attitudes, thoughts, and behaviors play a key role in relapse. Learning about early warning signs can help you avoid going back to drinking, using, or other addictive patterns. This exercise will help you identify your personal warning signs, stop the relapse process, and turn it around before you pick up a drink or drug or return to another addictive behavior.

When a person picks up a substance, walks into a casino, that is part of a lapse; if they otherwise return to an addiction, that's the completion of the relapse process, not its beginning. Before that happens, there are many warning signs. Knowing the warning signs can help you interrupt the process and avoid lapses and relapse.

1. Relapse-related changes in thinking may include persuading yourself that some new method of controlled drinking, drug use, gambling, etc., will work; remembering the good times and overlooking the problems; thinking of addictive actions as a reward for success or a way to celebrate; or believing that one cannot succeed in recovery. List five specific examples of how your thinking changed before your last relapse, or similar changes you've seen in others.

    _____

    _____

    _____

2. Emotions and attitudes also change as a person drifts toward lapse or relapse. Determination, optimism, teamwork, and motivation may be replaced by forms of negativity such as apathy, selfishness, and a feeling that being unable to drink, use, gamble, or so on is an undeserved punishment. Please list specific examples of how your attitudes changed before your last relapse, or similar changes you've seen in others.

    _____

    _____

    _____

3. Another area where there are clear differences between an actively addicted person's lifestyle and that of a recovering person is in how they relate to others. Before returning to active addiction, our behavior slips back into patterns such as self-isolation, manipulation, dishonesty, secretiveness, and being demanding and resentful. Please list specific examples of how your ways of relating to other people changed before your last relapse, or similar changes you've seen in others.

_____

_____

4. You have probably also seen common behavior patterns in yourself and others who were abusing alcohol or other drugs or practicing other addictions and seen very different patterns in recovering people. When a person is sliding back toward active use, their behaviors start looking more like they did before recovery. Some typical addictive behavior patterns include irregular eating and sleep habits, neglect of health, irresponsibility, recklessness, procrastination, impulsivity, and other patterns showing a loss of self-control and the growth of chaos in one's life. Please list specific examples of how your behavior changed before your last relapse or similar changes you've seen in others.

_____

_____

5. Together with the other changes described in this exercise, the feelings and moods of actively addicted people tend to be different from those they experience in recovery. Common addictive patterns of feelings and mood include irritability, anxiety, depression, hopelessness, indifference, self-pity, anger, and self-centeredness. Please list specific examples of how your feelings and moods changed before your last relapse, or similar changes you've seen in others.

_____

_____

6. Now think back, check with others if possible, and identify whatever warning signs from all the areas that you or others saw in you before your last relapse. If you've never tried to quit before and have no experience of relapse, list the main patterns that were normal for you when you were drinking or using. Either way, please write these red flags down. If possible, identify in order or which ones happen earliest and how they might progress.

_____

_____

_____

Continuing to assess and self-monitor, keeping your eyes wide open is necessary in early sobriety/recovery. Continue to remind yourself of your motivation for getting into treatment and what you hope will be the outcome to keep motivation high. Talk in group, at recovery meetings, or with your therapist any time motivation dips and what you believe contributes to it.

Once you've completed this exercise, you've gathered the information to be used to complete Exercise 36.C, "Relapse Prevention Planning" in this manual. Be sure to bring this handout back to your next therapy session and be prepared to talk about your thoughts and feelings about the exercise.

IDENTIFYING RELAPSE TRIGGERS AND CUES

GOALS OF THE EXERCISE

1. Increase awareness of personal situational triggers and cues to relapse.
2. Recognize high-risk situations involving increased risk of relapse.
3. Develop coping skills to use when experiencing high-risk situations and/or cravings.
4. Learn refusal skills to use when tempted to relapse into addictive behavior.

ADDITIONAL PROBLEMS FOR WHICH THIS EXERCISE MAY BE USEFUL

- Eating Disorders and Obesity
- Gambling
- Nicotine Use/Dependence
- Posttraumatic Stress Disorder (PTSD)
- Readiness to Change
- Sexual Promiscuity
- Substance Use Disorders

SUGGESTIONS FOR PROCESSING THIS EXERCISE WITH THE CLIENT

The "Identifying Relapse Triggers and Cues" activity is designed to help the newly recovering client identify environmental and internal relapse triggers and plan strategies to cope with those triggers. Follow-up may include the "Relapse Prevention Planning" activity (Exercise 36.C) or "Personal Recovery Planning" (Exercise 47.C) in this manual, keeping a journal, and reporting back on outcomes of strategies identified. Provide psychoeducation about the process of recovery and normalize it as nonlinear and an evolving and active process that changes as they change; they will need different things at different times. Strategies that they may need and rely on hourly/daily in early recovery may be unnecessary in later stages.

IDENTIFYING RELAPSE TRIGGERS AND CUES

Relapse is common and preventable. To avoid it, you have to stay aware of things that can trigger us to behave addictively and be ready to react effectively to such triggers. This exercise will help you identify relapse triggers and plan to cope with them.

RISKY SITUATIONS

1. Relapse is often triggered by sights, sounds, and situations that have gone together with addictive behaviors in your past. Many of us find that unless we stay on guard, our thoughts automatically turn back to old behavior patterns when we are around people with whom we drank, used, gambled, etc. Please describe the people with whom you usually practiced addictive behaviors in the past. Where and when did you typically have contact? How do they have access to you now and how do you have access to them?

   _____

   _____

2. Addictive behaviors are often part of social activities. You may know people who expect you to continue to do the old things with them. They may not care about your recovery, and they may use persuasion, teasing, or argument to try to get you to relapse. Who are the people most likely to pressure you to relapse?

   _____

   _____

3. Many recovering people find that family members, friends, or coworkers have enabled their addictions by helping them avoid the consequences, making it easier for them to keep doing the same things. Identify five ways others have enabled your addictive behaviors.

   _____

   _____

   _____

   _____

4. For each of the groups listed, describe how you will avoid relapse triggered by their actions.

   a. Drinking/using/gambling, etc. companions:

   _____

   b. People pressuring you to relapse:

   _____

   c. Enablers:

   _____

5. What social situations do you think will place you at greatest risk to relapse?

   _____

   _____

6. Many people also used addictions to cope with stress, and sometimes relationship issues can be extremely stressful. When you think about your future, how could relationship difficulties put you at risk for returning to addictive patterns?

   _____

   _____

7. For many of us, our addictions had also become a daily routine, something we did at certain times (e.g., just after work). In your daily routine, when are you most vulnerable to relapse?

   _____

   _____

8. Many people feel the urge to "test" their recovery in challenging situations (e.g., being with drinking friends and going to old hangouts). This is an unnecessary risk that often leads to relapse. Describe any ways in which you've tested your ability to stay in recovery.

   _____

   _____

   _____

   _____

   _____

9. To guard against stress-induced relapse, please think about current situations and future life events that you need to be ready to handle without escaping into addictions. What are they, and what's your plan to handle these situations? What changes are you willing and able to make to handle the pressures and temptations you may face?

_____

_____

Think about your current motivation and commitment to recovery. What can you do to keep focused on this?

INTERNAL TRIGGERS

10. When you experience urges or cravings to act out addictively, how does your body feel? List them in the space provided.

_____

_____

11. When you experience urges to act out addictively, what emotions do you usually feel?

_____

_____

12. As mentioned earlier, we've often used addictions to cope with stress (i.e., to change, avoid, numb feelings we dislike to ones that are more comfortable). What feelings will place you at greatest risk for relapse?

_____

_____

13. Following are some common feelings for which people have used chemicals to cope. It's important not only to be determined to avoid addictive behaviors, but also to know what you will do instead. If you don't have an alternative to replace substance abuse, your risk of relapse is high despite your willpower, logic, and good intentions. Next to each feeling, describe what you will do instead of acting out addictively to cope with that feeling.

Feeling	What You Will Do to Cope
a. Anger	_____
b. Anxiety	_____
c. Boredom	_____
d. Sadness	_____
e. Fatigue	_____
f. Fear	_____

g. Frustration _____

h. Loneliness _____

i. Indifference _____

j. Self-pity _____

k. Shame _____

l. Depression _____

m. Self-loathing _____

n. Other feelings: _____

14. Failure to act on known triggers and cues will most often result in a lapse or relapse. What warning signs can you watch for (e.g., discontinuing meeting attendance, not managing interpersonal conflicts, resuming relationships with using friends, etc.) that will cue you early?

_____

_____

Be sure to bring this handout back to your next session with your therapist and be prepared to talk about your thoughts and feelings about the exercise.

RELAPSE PREVENTION PLANNING

GOALS OF THE EXERCISE

1. Practice a program of recovery that includes regular participation in recovery group meetings, working with a sponsor, and helping others in recovery.
2. Develop a relapse prevention plan of action using information gathered in previous exercises.
3. Develop coping skills to use when experiencing high-risk situations and/or cravings.
4. Take greater responsibility for recovery and increase chances of success through planning.

ADDITIONAL PROBLEMS FOR WHICH THIS EXERCISE MAY BE USEFUL

*   Eating Disorders and Obesity
*   Gambling
*   Nicotine Use/Dependence
*   Peer Group Negativity
*   Self-Harm
*   Sexual Promiscuity
*   Substance Use Disorders

SUGGESTIONS FOR PROCESSING THIS EXERCISE WITH THE CLIENT

The "Relapse Prevention Planning" activity is for clients beginning in recovery or experiencing stresses that raise the risk of relapse. It provides a structured framework drawing on earlier exercises to anticipate relapse triggers and cues, plan coping or avoidance strategies, spot early warning signs of relapse, and identify resources and strategies to use to maintain recovery. For best results, have the client complete "Identifying Relapse Triggers and Cues" (Exercise 36.B) and "Early Warning Signs of Relapse" (Exercise 36.A) before this activity.

Follow-up may include having the client present the plan to the therapist, attend a treatment group, meet with a sponsor to get feedback, keep a journal, and report on outcomes. "Relapse Prevention Planning" should be revisited frequently in those early months of sobriety to not only address known risks but also address those issues and situations that the client couldn't reasonably predict and any lapses that do occur before they result in a significant return to use. Assess for suicidal ideation in those with history of suicidal ideation and nonsuicidal self-injury, and relapse proneness. Have them develop a safety plan so if risk increases due to feeling helpless and hopeless, particularly after a relapse following a sustained sober period, it is available as a resource.

RELAPSE PREVENTION PLANNING

If you have identified your own personal relapse triggers and relapse warning signs, you have a good understanding of your relapse process and how to spot it early, before it leads you to an actual return to your addiction. Now it's time to take this information and plan specific strategies to put it to use. The more work you do on this plan and the more specific you are, the more prepared you will be to deal with day-to-day living and unexpected stressful events without reliance on alcohol, other drugs, or addictive behavior patterns. Revisiting this plan is also important as recovery needs will change as you make changes.

1. First, consider your thoughts and feelings about sobriety. What brought you to treatment at this time? Are you ready to take any action needed, to go to any lengths, and to live your life without using mind-altering chemicals or addictive behaviors to block painful feelings or seek pleasure? Describe your attitude about this and what will help you sustain this motivation.

    _____

    _____

2. What consequences are likely if you relapse? What gains do you hope for?

    _____

    _____

3. Refer to the exercises on relapse triggers and warning signs or draw on whatever information you have about the process of relapse (particularly if you've relapsed before). List what you consider your five most important relapse triggers and warning signs at this time and what you will do to cope with each of them.

Triggers/Warning Signs	**Specific Plan to Avoid Drinking or Using**
Ex.: Feeling hopeless	*Review progress, ask others what growth they see*
_____	_____
_____	_____
_____	_____
_____	_____
_____	_____
_____	_____

Work with your therapist, your group, or others to rehearse how you'll handle these situations.

4. Recovery is not a solo process, which is why people who try to quit without help from others usually relapse. There is no need or reason to try and do it alone. Who will you contact for support and assistance? Identify as many as you can in the order in which you would contact them.

    Name   **Phone Number**

    _____   _____
    _____   _____
    _____   _____
    _____   _____
    _____   _____
    _____   _____
    _____   _____
    _____   _____

    _____
    _____
    _____
    _____

5. *Emergency planning.* Your relapse prevention plan should include what you will do if you encounter a crisis—a stressful situation that triggers a strong urge to use or drink. If you encounter an unexpected event that puts you at risk, your plan of action will be:

    _____
    _____

6. You should also have some general-purpose strategies ready for use if you encounter relapse triggers or warning signs you hadn't specifically planned for. List three general-purpose strategies to stay clean and sober.

    _____
    _____

7. Changing your routine is important in staying sober. How will you begin and end each day in a way that supports sobriety and recovery?

    _____
    _____

8. Your plan should include support groups, such as Alcoholics Anonymous, Narcotics Anonymous, Gamblers Anonymous, and so on. Do your research and talk to others about specific groups that may be beneficial to you, particularly if there is a particular identity or group it would feel easier to engage with. List meetings you will commit yourself to attend regularly.

Name of Group	Day and Time	Location
_____	_____	_____
_____	_____	_____
_____	_____	_____
_____	_____	_____
_____	_____	_____

9. Do you foresee any obstacles/barriers to implementing this plan? If so, what are they and what will you do to address them?

_____

_____

10. What will you do about these roadblocks to your recovery or any others you experience?

_____

_____

11. If your plan isn't enough, and you lapse or relapse, what will you do to get back on track in your recovery as quickly as you can? Remind yourself that success is built on learning from our lapses, and we get better each time we do it.

_____

_____

12. What other issues will I be addressing and how? If active in therapy, what goals do I have for this part of my work?

_____

_____

Be sure to bring this handout back to your next therapy session and be prepared to talk about your success and challenges in working your plan. It is helpful to note what other group members and recovery acquaintances have found helpful. You can modify and revise your plan as needed.

ASSESSING SELF-CARE DEFICITS

GOALS OF THE EXERCISE

1. Understand the relationship between addictions and problems with self-care.
2. Learn basic skills for maintaining a clean, sanitary living space.
3. Understand and verbalize the need for good hygiene and implement healthy personal hygiene practices.
4. Regularly shower or bathe, shave, brush teeth, care for hair, use deodorant, and wear clean clothing.
5. Improve self-care and learn about community resources available for assistance.
6. Experience increased social acceptance via improved appearance and/or self-care.

ADDITIONAL PROBLEMS FOR WHICH THIS EXERCISE MAY BE USEFUL

- Bipolar Disorder
- Chronic Pain
- Depression–Unipolar
- Living Environment Deficiency
- Opioid Use Disorder
- Psychosis
- Self-Care Deficits—Secondary
- Substance-Induced Disorders

SUGGESTIONS FOR PROCESSING THIS EXERCISE WITH THE CLIENT

The "Assessing Self-Care Deficits" exercise is suited for use with clients, concerned family members, case workers, or guardians. It may be used to identify which self-care deficits are related to addiction and which are related to other mental health or developmental concerns. After identifying the most serious deficits and resolving them, follow-up may consist of using the information generated in this exercise as a basis for a discussion of secondary gains associated with not taking care of oneself and/or as part of a relapse/aftercare plan.

ASSESSING SELF-CARE DEFICITS

Self-care involves many things. Some of it involves taking care of our bodies (e.g., hygiene, grooming, seeking proper medical/dental care, taking medications as prescribed, eating a balanced diet), and some of it involves taking care of our environments (e.g., keeping our living environments sanitary and safe, responding to crisis situations appropriately). Addiction can seriously interfere with our motivation, self-discipline, desire, and available time to do these things. At times, we may have relied on others to do some of these things for us. Part of beginning the recovery process is to assess the areas of self-care we've neglected and the impact of that neglect so that we can begin to take better care of ourselves. As we act, we feel better about ourselves, and ultimately our interactions with others improve. This exercise will help you begin this process. This may be an embarrassing topic to work through, but it's one many people have dealt with; we can't solve problems of which we aren't aware and those we aren't willing to face, and our recovery depends on it.

1. Please use this space to create an inventory of your functioning in these areas of self-care.

    a. Positive aspects of self-care (what you currently do to promote healthy self-care):

    _____

    _____

    b. Negative aspects of self-care (positive actions you avoid or neglect or negative things you do that interfere with healthy self-care):

    _____

    _____

2. What are the personal, social, occupational, health, and relational impacts of not taking care of yourself?

    _____

    _____

    _____

3. What feedback have people given you about times you've neglected self-care?

   _____

   _____

4. Imagine for a moment the positive changes that can result when you give more attention to your appearance, hygiene, medical care, and a sanitary living environment. Please describe what this will look and feel like for you:

   _____

   _____

5. It is useful to prioritize which self-care areas you will focus on first. What is the first thing you'll do differently?

   _____

   _____

6. Please briefly outline a specific plan for daily self-care (i.e., doing the same things in the same order each day) and taking care of your self-care priorities (e.g., making an appointment for a full physical and dental checkup):

   _____

   _____

   Research apps, props, technology to help. As our brains heal, we may need to incorporate several external supports to prompt or remind us.

7. What help do you need to begin to carry out your plan? What resources are available in your community to help you?

   _____

   _____

8. Who can you ask for help? What do you need from each of them?

   _____

   _____

9. What are the perceived barriers (i.e., time, motivation, money, significance to you, motivation, etc.)?

   _____

   _____

10. As you work to incorporate these activities into your daily routine, it may be helpful to create a daily chart of what activities need to be accomplished each day and check them off as you go. Be as specific as possible and, to start off, include even small tasks like eating breakfast, taking a shower, brushing teeth, going to a meeting. Include times of the day as reminders if it's an activity that is scheduled at a particular time (i.e., doctor's appointment, taking a medicine). It will allow you to self-monitor your success as well as areas for continued growth. Use the following template on a separate piece of paper.

Day	Tasks to Complete
Monday	_____
Tuesday	_____
Wednesday	_____
Thursday	_____
Friday	_____
Saturday	_____
Sunday	_____

Post this in places you will see often. Take a picture on your smartphone so you have easy access to it. Avoid overscheduling each day; stick to the basics and then add priorities. As you gain skill and confidence and start to feel better, you can add additional things.

Be sure to bring this handout to your next therapy session, and be prepared to talk about your thoughts, feelings, successes, and challenges related to the exercise.

RELATING SELF-CARE DEFICITS TO MY ADDICTION

GOALS OF THE EXERCISE

1. Understand the relationship between addiction and self-care deficits.
2. Learn the benefit of addressing self-care and how it relates to recovery.
3. Learn basic skills for maintaining a clean, sanitary living space.
4. Understand and explain the need for good hygiene and practice healthy personal hygiene.
5. Regularly shower or bathe, shave, brush teeth, care for hair, use deodorant, and wear clean clothing.
6. Experience increased social acceptance because of improved appearance and/or functioning around self-care.

ADDITIONAL PROBLEMS FOR WHICH THIS EXERCISE MAY BE USEFUL

- Bipolar Disorder
- Depression–Unipolar
- Opioid Use Disorder
- Psychosis
- Self-Care Deficits—Secondary
- Substance-Induced Disorders

SUGGESTIONS FOR PROCESSING THIS EXERCISE WITH THE CLIENT

The "Relating Self-Care Deficits to My Addiction" exercise is designed as a follow-up exercise to the first exercise in this section, "Assessing Self-Care Deficits." It can be assigned and processed as a motivational activity. For clients with severe deficits, it is important that they begin to make behavioral changes to their self-care habits and that measurable progress is noted before attempting to achieve further insight into its relationship to their addictive lifestyles. This exercise can also be used to facilitate discussions related to relapse prevention planning (see exercise 36.C).

RELATING SELF-CARE DEFICITS TO MY ADDICTION

Primary self-care activities include behaviors related to hygiene, grooming, proper nutrition, interpersonal social and communication skills, keeping a safe/clean living environment, and responding to crises appropriately. Addictive lifestyles interfere with functions like these in many ways. This exercise will help you learn more about how addiction has affected your ability to take care of yourself and improve your quality of life by correcting deficits. An addictive lifestyle was organized around different priorities; establishing a schedule for positive self-care creates focus, direction, predictability, structure, and organization to support a healthy lifestyle.

1. If you have neglected your primary self-care activities, what role do you think your addictive behaviors have played in that neglect?

    _____

    _____

2. Secondary gains are benefits we obtain without their being obvious reasons for doing things. What secondary gains have you experienced when you neglected your self-care (e.g., getting others to do things for you, avoiding intimacy or uncomfortable situations, avoiding responsibilities)?

    _____

    _____

3. What negative consequences have come from continued neglect of primary self-care activities?

    _____

    _____

4. If you've done Exercise 37.A, "Assessing Self-Care Deficits," you've identified some areas in which you feel you need to make improvements in your self-care. Please refer to your responses from that exercise to help answer these questions:

    a. What benefit(s) will come, or have already come, from improving your self-care in these areas?

        _____

        _____

b. How does paying attention to these self-care activities support your recovery? Your confidence? Your self-esteem?

_____

_____

c. What progress have you made so far in improving your self-care? What are your next three steps?

_____

_____

Be sure to bring this handout with you to your next therapy session and be prepared to discuss your thoughts and feelings about the exercise.

FILLING IN SELF-CARE GAPS

GOALS OF THE EXERCISE

1. Demonstrate increased organization of, and attention to, daily routines resulting in personal responsibilities being fulfilled.
2. Increase proficiency in independent daily living skills and knowledge of available community resources.
3. Consistently use available addiction recovery and/or mental health community resources.
4. Prioritize independent activities of daily living (IADLs) upon which to focus efforts and improve functioning.
5. Take responsibility for own IADLs up to the level of the client's potential and develop resources for obtaining help from others.
6. Plan and implement timely, appropriate, and safe responses to emergency situations.

ADDITIONAL PROBLEMS FOR WHICH THIS EXERCISE MAY BE USEFUL

- Living Environment Deficiency
- Opioid Use Disorder
- Self-Care Deficits—Primary

SUGGESTIONS FOR PROCESSING THIS EXERCISE WITH THE CLIENT

The "Filling in Self-Care Gaps" exercise is for clients with secondary self-care skill deficits. As with the exercise "Assessing Self-Care Deficits," this activity may be done with a client, family, caseworker, or guardian, depending on the client's level of functioning. It may be necessary to consider literacy, educational level, cultural differences, family values, gender differences, environmental barriers, and other mental health issues when assessing deficits and working toward solutions. Role-playing can help clients practice skills individually or in a group. Follow-up can include discussion of perceived versus actual barriers and ways to work through each. Knowledge of available community resources will be necessary.

FILLING IN SELF-CARE GAPS

Sometimes in our daily lives we have to do things we aren't good at or interested in. If we neglect our responsibilities, though, it creates stress and puts our stability and independence at risk. We can't always rely on others to do these things for us. As a result of addiction, we may have managed our responsibilities poorly and/or created additional problems that have become as important as the original responsibilities; we have to include these daily tasks in our recovery plans too. This exercise will help you see what areas you need to address and how you can begin.

1. Following is a sample list of independent activities of daily living and examples of each:

    a. *Financial responsibilities* (e.g., opening accounts, preparing and following a budget, paying bills, addressing debt, paying taxes)

    b. *Medical responsibilities for self and/or children* (e.g., scheduling and attending appointments, filling prescriptions)

    c. *Educational/occupational responsibilities* (e.g., being on time, interacting with coworkers, performing assigned tasks, using study skills, managing time)

    d. *Legal responsibilities* (e.g., keeping court dates, finding counsel, attending required appointments, informing work supervisors about these responsibilities and limitations)

    e. *Using community resources* (e.g., dealing with transportation, daycare, financial assistance, church/spiritual activities, planning for emergencies)

    f. *Using treatment and recovery resources* (e.g., recovery meetings, treatment resources)

2. Review this list. Please *circle* any areas in which you currently see deficits in your life.

3. For the deficits you circled, please decide what barriers keep you from succeeding in those responsibilities (e.g., lack of organization, attention issues, lack of motivation, dependence on other people, physical health issues, withdrawal, lack of knowledge, need for skills training, or anxiety issues).

_____

_____

4. Prioritize, from most important to least, the problem areas from question 2 that you would like to address.

   _____

   _____

5. Who are the people you will need help from, and what do you need from each of them? Identify the role they may play, and practice/role-play in therapy or group how you will ask them for help.

   _____

   _____

6. Create a weekly and a monthly calendar (including all days of the week) including treatment sessions, support group meetings, all medical appointments, meetings/ times to call your sponsor, work hours, children's appointments, when bills are due, when prescriptions need to be filled, payday, when you will grocery shop, and all other activities and deadlines you need to meet. Calendar templates are easily found online for free, can be created from scratch, or synced on a phone or handheld device. Pick what is easiest and most likely to be used consistently.

   _____

7. Begin your plan the day after you create it. You will continue to add items to your calendar. Make a habit of checking your schedule at the beginning and end of each day. Check in with your therapist, caseworker, or group members frequently about your progress and challenges. Remember, some of these skills take practice to master, but they do get easier over time, and each skill you learn makes it easier to learn more skills and tackle additional problems. After 2 weeks, write about how this plan is working.

   _____

   _____

8. What is the plan for responding to urgent situations, particularly if you neglect to address a commitment or obligation?

   _____

   _____

9. How will you avoid procrastination when motivation is low?

   _____

   _____

10. What benefits (i.e., to your recovery, your self-esteem) might result from increasing success at addressing self-care responsibilities?

_____

_____

Be sure to bring this handout with you to your future therapy sessions and be prepared to discuss your thoughts and feelings about the exercise.

WORKING TOWARD INTERDEPENDENCE

GOALS OF THE EXERCISE

1. Develop a program of recovery and increase knowledge of community resources.
2. Demonstrate increased organization of and attention to daily routines, resulting in personal responsibilities being fulfilled.
3. Consistently use available addiction recovery and/or mental health community resources.
4. Identify relevant community resources and ways to access them for help with independent activities of daily living (IADLs).
5. Take responsibility for own IADLs up to the level of the client's potential and develop resources for obtaining help from others.
6. Plan and implement timely, appropriate, and safe responses to emergency situations.

ADDITIONAL PROBLEMS FOR WHICH THIS EXERCISE MAY BE USEFUL

- Attention-Deficit/Hyperactivity Disorder (ADHD)—Adult
- Dependent Traits
- Peer Group Negativity
- Psychosis
- Self-Care Deficits—Primary

SUGGESTIONS FOR PROCESSING THIS EXERCISE WITH THE CLIENT

The "Working Toward Interdependence" exercise is designed to help clients who may not be accustomed to seeking help or know how to find and use healthy community resources. Follow-up may include making appropriate referrals and/or guiding the client in investigating resources in their community and practicing specific skills in gaining access to them.

WORKING TOWARD INTERDEPENDENCE

Addictive lifestyles negatively affect personal independence. Continuing in an addictive lifestyle can interfere with effectively carrying out independent activities of daily living (e.g., banking, shopping, interacting with others, responding to crisis, organizational skills, using community resources) and can ultimately undermine an individual's ability to live independently. This exercise asks you to take an inventory of your independent daily living skills and will help you make some decisions about areas on which you can begin to work and when you can rely on others for support and assistance.

1. What positive and negative experiences have you had with your day-to-day activities of independent living while you've been engaging in your addiction?

    _____

    _____

2. What are three ways in which your addiction threatens your independence?

    _____

    _____

3. What problems have you had because you neglected or avoided daily living tasks or relied on others to do them for you while you were actively engaged in an addictive lifestyle?

    _____

    _____

4. What do you see as the benefits of personally taking responsibility for carrying out daily living tasks in healthy and adaptive ways?

    _____

    _____

5. If you've done Exercise 38.A, "Filling in Self-Care Gaps," you identified areas of your life where you believe there are deficits. Do you know what resources in your community could provide you with some help in these areas? With which are you familiar, how will they help you, and which ones do you need help locating?

    _____

    _____

6. Of the resources you know, do you use them consistently and when you need them? If not, what interferes (e.g., finances, transportation, day care)?

    _____

    _____

7. After identifying your deficits and some resources that could help you with them, think about what personal barriers reduce your desire or ability to follow through (e.g., communication skills, confidence, fear, motivation). Please list them here.

    _____

    _____

8. Who could help you in addressing these deficits? What do you need from each person you identified, and how will you ask for it?

    _____

    _____

9. Choose one of the barriers you've identified. With the help of your therapist, develop a step-by-step plan to begin to face and overcome that barrier. Briefly describe your plan here.

    _____

    _____

    Especially in early recovery, the details of managing day-to-day living, personally healing, and resolving the difficulties created by your past addictive behavior can seem overwhelming. It is important to prioritize things, take challenges a step at a time, and ask for help when you need it.

    _____

    _____

10. What evidence will you see to know that you're making improvements in independent daily living skills?

    _____

    _____

11. Others will know your plan is working and things are improving if they see what evidence?

    _____

    _____

    Be sure to bring this handout back to your next therapy session and be prepared to talk about your thoughts and feelings about the exercise.

UNDERSTANDING SELF-HARM AND ADDICTION

GOALS OF THE EXERCISE

1. Learn to identify the emotional and psychological short-term rewards provided by self-harm.
2. Identify common patterns shared by self-harm and addiction.
3. Understand the ways that continued self-harm increases the risk of relapse into addiction.
4. Identify and list at least two nonharmful alternative strategies for meeting the same emotional needs that self-harm has fulfilled in the past.

ADDITIONAL PROBLEMS FOR WHICH THIS EXERCISE MAY BE USEFUL

- Adult-Child-of-an-Alcoholic (ACA) Traits
- Anxiety
- Borderline Traits
- Depression–Unipolar
- Partner Relational Conflicts
- Sexual Promiscuity

SUGGESTIONS FOR PROCESSING THIS EXERCISE WITH THE CLIENT

The "Understanding Self-Harm and Addiction" activity is intended to help clients understand the reasons for self-harm, see the connections between self-harm and addiction and the ways self-injury can increase the risk of relapse, and find replacement activities to meet the same needs that they have used self-injury for in the past. Follow-up may include discussing the issue with the therapist and group, support group referrals, bibliotherapy, and videotherapy.

UNDERSTANDING SELF-HARM AND ADDICTION

Sometimes, people who become addicted to substances also find themselves addicted to other dangerous or self-destructive behavior patterns. One of these is self-harm. This can be confusing and frightening to both the people who are hurting themselves and those around them; in the short term, self-harm meets valid psychological and emotional needs, but in the longer term the medical risks outweigh the benefits. It can also jeopardize a person's recovery by increasing the chances that they will relapse into abusing alcohol and/or other drugs. Like addressing addictive behaviors, recovery is a process that encourages development and use of strategies to cope that nurture, heal, are compassionate and gentle rather than harmful and self-defeating. As part of your recovery, this activity will help you understand all of these aspects of self-harm and find safe and nonharmful ways to meet the same needs self-harm may have helped you meet in the past.

1. There are four core emotional needs that many people meet by hurting themselves, although there may be others. For any of these payoffs you've experienced by hurting yourself, please write a sentence about what you did and how it changed your feelings or thoughts in a way that felt good to you.

    Feeling alive. Self-harm can break through emotional numbing with a jolt of intensity. Your experience:

    _____

    Empowerment. Self-harm can help people who feel powerless over what happens in their lives to feel that they do have control of what they do to their bodies. Your experience:

    _____

    Communication. A wound can speak louder than words to tell the world, "This is how I feel." Your experience:

    _____

    Bliss. The body responds to injury by releasing endorphins, natural opioids, in the brain, which can produce a high like that of an opiate. Your experience:

    _____

2. Beyond the medical problems that self-injury can cause directly, self-harm increases the risk of relapse with alcohol and other drugs. Please *check* off any of these consequences of self-harm that you've experienced or that you believe would be a threat to your recovery if you did experience them:

_____ Many people who hurt themselves to reach the goals listed here find that when the good feelings wear off, they're left feeling shame and self-hate.

_____ Many folks who self-injure feel a need to keep this part of their lives a secret. Secrets like this create distance and emotional barriers, isolating them from loved ones and friends.

_____ When others do find out a person is hurting themselves, they often don't understand and react with negative judgments, anger, or fear, and they may distance themselves.

_____ Like any mood-altering drug or behavior, self-injury itself can become an addiction.

What negatives are associated with your own self-harm behaviors? What relationship exists between self-harm and addictive behavior for you personally (one precipitates the other, one prevents the other, more often co-occur)?

3. At this point it may seem you have to choose between the danger of self-harm and the misery of enduring the feelings you could temporarily block by hurting yourself. A third solution is to find replacements—other ways to get those payoffs without the negatives that come with self-injury. For each of the following, think of other activities that interest you and that you think might work for you:

Feeling alive: _____

Empowerment: _____

Communication: _____

Bliss: _____

What are three benefits of engaging in alternative behaviors while working to abstain from self-injurious behavior?

_____

_____

4. Finally, make a plan. What healthy ways to meet your needs will you try, and when? If there are times when and where you're most vulnerable to self-injury, it might be good to try new ideas shortly before those times. Name one activity for each reward and write when you'll try it:

    Feeling alive: _____

    Empowerment: _____

    Communication: _____

    Bliss: _____

5. Describe your attachment to self-harm behavior. What would it mean to you to abstain from it?

    _____

    _____

Be sure to bring this handout back to your next session with your therapist and be prepared to talk about your thoughts and feelings about the exercise.

SELF-HARM RISK FACTORS, TRIGGERS, AND EARLY WARNING SIGNS

GOALS OF THE EXERCISE

1. Learn to identify the emotional and psychological conditions that create greater risk of using self-injury as a coping mechanism, in general and for the individual client.
2. Identify the specific kinds of situations that are self-harm triggers for the client so that they can learn to be vigilant and avoid those situations if possible or be prepared with healthy alternative coping techniques if the situations are unavoidable.
3. Discover personal early warning signs indicating the client is slipping into addictive patterns of thought, emotion, and behavior that have led to self-harm in the past.

ADDITIONAL PROBLEMS FOR WHICH THIS EXERCISE MAY BE USEFUL

- Anxiety
- Depression–Unipolar
- Borderline Traits
- Dependent Traits
- Impulsivity
- Relapse Proneness
- Suicidal Ideation

SUGGESTIONS FOR PROCESSING THIS EXERCISE WITH THE CLIENT

The "Self-Harm Risk Factors, Triggers, and Early Warning Signs" activity is designed to help clients learn about and become vigilant for the patterns of internal risk factors that raise their risk of self-injury, to do the same with external/situational triggers, and to detect any slipping into a self-injury-prone state of mind as early as possible and take action to prevent the completion of that process. Follow-up may include discussing the issue with the therapist and group, support group referrals, and bibliotherapy.

SELF-HARM RISK FACTORS, TRIGGERS, AND EARLY WARNING SIGNS

If you've worked through Exercise 39.A, "Understanding Self-Harm and Addiction," then you've looked at how self-injury can be an addiction and at how people who intentionally hurt themselves are usually trying to achieve reasonable goals but using a method that often creates more pain than it relieves. Do you find that you always feel equally tempted to reach for a chemical or behavioral fix—are you always in the same amount of emotional pain? If you're like most people, you see that sometimes, some situations, and some emotional conditions make you more vulnerable than others.

From that, it follows that we can anticipate when our internal thoughts and feelings put us at greater risk, what external situations are likely to push us toward self-harm, and what changes in our thoughts, emotions, and actions are signals that we're slipping.

This activity will help you identify those internal and external dangers and those early signs that you may be heading for trouble, so you can learn to catch and reverse the process as early as possible.

1. *Internal dangers*: Which mental and emotional states put us at greatest risk of self-harm? We can look at the payoffs it provides, then see when we're most likely to crave those payoffs. In the previous activity, we saw four common ways self-harm makes people feel better in the short term: *feeling alive, empowerment, communication,* and *bliss*. When do we want those most? When we feel the opposite. To see when this is going on for you, please answer these questions:

   a. When do you feel the most unalive (i.e., people have described this as feeling numb, mechanical, dead inside)? What thoughts and feelings are parts of that experience?

   _____

   _____

   b. When do you feel the most powerless over what's going on in your life, and what thoughts are going through your mind at those times? What does it feel like inside for you?

   _____

   _____

c. When do you feel the most invisible and unheard, as if others don't understand you or what you want them to know about your life? What thoughts and feelings do you have at those times?

_____

_____

d. When do you feel the most unblissful, whether that means you're in pain, depressed, angry, or fearful? What are you likely to be thinking, and what emotions do you feel at those times?

_____

_____

e. When are you most susceptible to engaging in self-harming behaviors? Identify known triggers, urges, and temptations?

_____

_____

f. What have you done to delay or avoid self-injury even when you felt the urge to do it?

_____

_____

2. *External dangers*: For you, what situations trigger the thoughts and emotions you just listed, where you feel the most unalive, powerless, unheard, and/or unhappy? Please list your top four situations, the people that contribute to those feelings, and thoughts you have in those situations.

_____

_____

3. Now what may be the most important part: learning to recognize the changes in our thoughts and emotions far enough in advance of the actual self-injury to change course and meet the need to change how we feel in a healthier way. As with other addictive behaviors, the return to destructive behavior is the completion of the relapse, not the beginning—relapse begins long before that point. If you can recall specific ways your thinking, moods, and actions changed during that transition from recovery to self-injury, then you will know some things to watch for.

It can also help to talk with other people in recovery with similar challenges and ask them about early warning signs, so you can watch for those patterns in yourself. Write down any specific changes you've seen in yourself when you were headed for a relapse into self-harm, especially if you didn't realize then what the changes meant.

4. What is the motivation and benefit to you to discontinue or abstain from self-harming behaviors currently?

    _____

    _____

Be sure to bring this handout back to your next session with your therapist and be prepared to talk about your thoughts and feelings about the exercise.

IT WASN'T MY FAULT

GOALS OF THE EXERCISE

1. Identify and address feelings of guilt, shame, and/or not deserving healthy sexual, emotional, and spiritual relationships as a result of having experienced sexual abuse.
2. Work through issues resulting from sexual abuse by understanding what happened and learning how to manage the associated feelings.
3. Resolve issues of having been sexually abused and increase ability to attain healthy intimacy.
4. Achieve acceptance of having been sexually abused without feeling that this condones what the abuser(s) did or entails accepting further sexual, other physical, or emotional abuse.
5. Move away from seeing oneself as a victim and establish an identity as a survivor.

ADDITIONAL PROBLEMS FOR WHICH THIS EXERCISE MAY BE USEFUL

*   Adult-Child-of-an-Alcoholic (ACA) Traits
*   Borderline Traits
*   Childhood Trauma
*   Eating Disorders and Obesity
*   Family Conflicts
*   Grief/Loss Unresolved
*   Parent–Child Relational Problem
*   Partner Relational Conflicts
*   Posttraumatic Stress Disorder (PTSD)
*   Self-Harm

SUGGESTIONS FOR PROCESSING THIS EXERCISE WITH THE CLIENT

The "It Wasn't My Fault" activity is meant for clients suffering from sequelae of having been sexually abused. It addresses problems of distorted thinking about the nature of, and responsibility for, the abuse. Follow-up could include assignment of "Internal and External Resources for Safety" (Exercise 40.B) and "Corresponding with My Childhood Self" (Exercise 9.A); bibliotherapy related to the process of recovery from sexual abuse;

homework assignments to engage in healthy relationship-building activities and report back to the therapist and/or a treatment group on the results; and assignment to a treatment/support group for sexual abuse survivors. Preparation for this exercise should include making a safety plan for clients to use if they become emotionally overwhelmed while doing the exercise. This is a consent-based activity so the client is aware of the potential triggers and can participate in as much or as little as they feel able each time. Ongoing assessment for the need for specialized trauma treatment should be monitored and discussed with the client.

IT WASN'T MY FAULT

People who survive sexual abuse include all genders and gender identities, economic classes, and ages from small children to seniors, all ethnicities, and religions. Their abusers, likewise, may be as diverse as victims and come from all backgrounds. The abuse may be obviously violent or more subtle. It can be a one-time event or go on for years.

Despite all these outward differences, all these situations have four things in common. First, like other forms of abuse, sexual abuse is always wrong. Nothing anyone can do makes it right for someone to violate anyone else's rights and attack them sexually, in other physical ways, emotionally, or psychologically. Second, it is always an act of aggression—there is always a power differential, with the abuser having more power than the abused, whether by armed or unarmed violence, threatened or carried out, or because of the perpetrator being in some position of authority. Third, it is never about who the abused person is as a person—the person being abused is being used as an object for someone else's gratification, and it's about the abuser, not the abused. Fourth, sexual abuse is never the fault of the person who is abused. There is no way anyone can make someone else abuse them in any way, including sexually—if the abuser did not want to commit the offense, they wouldn't.

Survivors sometimes have trouble believing these things, because they may have been taught that what was done to them was somehow their own fault, or that the offenders couldn't control themselves, or that it wasn't wrong. None of these statements are true. Still, survivors may struggle for many years with feelings of guilt and shame connected with the idea that they were targeted because of something they did or didn't do, or the belief that having been abused makes them somehow less-than, not as deserving as other people of love, peace of mind, and a happy and fulfilling life. It doesn't help that many subcultures perpetuate these judgments. This exercise will help you begin to identify and address these issues.

1. Have you blamed yourself for any abuse you experienced? If so, what makes you believe it was your fault? Did you reach this belief on your own, or did someone else teach it to you?

    _____

    _____

2. Would you expect anyone else to feel guilty or ashamed because of something another person did against their will? If not, why should a higher standard of responsibility apply to you than to anyone else?

_____

_____

3. As for self-worth: Do you believe that being abused by someone else can make someone deserve more abuse afterward, whether by themselves or others? If you know other people who have suffered abuse of any kind, do you look down on them because someone else hurt them? If not, again, what makes you believe you have to meet a different standard than anyone else?

_____

_____

4. Self-judgments live in the heart. Many people know intellectually that things other people did weren't their fault but still feel responsible, guilty, ashamed, and less-than. You may easily see that others don't deserve to feel that way but still struggle with the feelings yourself. If you were talking to another person who had the same experience as you, what would you tell them?

_____

_____

5. What does your answer to question 4 tell you about your own capacity for compassion, understanding, and empathy? In other words, about a key part of your own character.

_____

_____

6. Here is an activity that might be helpful when feelings of shame, guilt, or low self-worth related to being a survivor of sexual abuse arise *(**Important: If you find yourself becoming overwhelmed with painful feelings, stop immediately, and contact your therapist or follow whatever safety plan you've worked out with them.**)* It may be beneficial to do this exercise in therapy. First, if you can, find a picture of yourself taken around the time your abuse happened. Find a comfortable place to sit where you'll have privacy and won't be interrupted or distracted. Sit with the picture, some paper, and a pen or pencil. Think back to what it was like when your abuse happened, not the specific details of the abuse(s). Imagine that you could visit your early self and offer some reassurance, clarity, and hope. Write what you would say to your younger self.

_____

_____

7. Now imagine what it would have been like for you, then, to be visited by a supportive adult—your future self—and to have that future self say the things to you that you just wrote. How would that have made you feel, and what would you have wanted to say in response?

_____

_____

8. What benefit would come from increasing self-compassion, less self-blame and shame, giving yourself permission to heal from an extraordinary set of circumstances?

_____

_____

Once you've answered those questions, sit, rest, and meditate about whatever came up for you. If it has changed any part of how you think and feel about yourself, journal about that change and be prepared to discuss this in your next individual or group therapy session.

INTERNAL AND EXTERNAL RESOURCES FOR SAFETY

GOALS OF THE EXERCISE

1. Work through issues resulting from sexual abuse by understanding what happened and learning to manage the associated feelings.
2. Resolve issues of having been sexually abused and increase ability to attain healthy intimacy.
3. Overcome learned helplessness and unrealistic feelings of being unable to avoid being victimized and become more proactive and assertive in matters of personal safety.
4. Move away from seeing oneself as a victim and establish an identity as a survivor.

ADDITIONAL PROBLEMS FOR WHICH THIS EXERCISE MAY BE USEFUL

- Adult-Child-of-an-Alcoholic (ACA) Traits
- Borderline Traits
- Childhood Trauma
- Eating Disorders and Obesity
- Family Conflicts
- Grief/Loss Unresolved
- Posttraumatic Stress Disorder (PTSD)

SUGGESTIONS FOR PROCESSING THIS EXERCISE WITH THE CLIENT

The "Internal and External Resources for Safety" activity is meant for clients who experienced sexual abuse in settings in which they were powerless or overpowered (e.g., childhood, incarceration, coercion with violence, power differentials). It guides clients in reframing their current circumstances, seeing resources for maintaining safety that were unavailable before but can be used now, and taking concrete action to empower themselves and minimize the risk of further abuse. Follow-up could include assignment of "It Wasn't My Fault" (Exercise 40.A), bibliotherapy related to sexual abuse recovery, and exploring possible treatment/support groups for sexual abuse survivors. Working through this exercise in therapy provides the opportunity to teach self-monitoring skills of internal cues in real time, taking breaks to recenter and group as necessary, and proceed at a pace that is controlled and consented to.

INTERNAL AND EXTERNAL RESOURCES FOR SAFETY

When people are sexually victimized, it is often in situations where they are powerless to protect themselves or stop what's happening. Sexual predators seek out these situations, because they want to be sure they can overpower the people they've targeted, whether by force, fear, confusion, or authority. Because our most intense experiences leave the deepest impressions, survivors of these abuses tend to go on seeing themselves as being as helpless and vulnerable as they were when their perpetrators abused them. They are left with painful memories, feeling unsafe, chronically stressed and easily triggered, reliving it repeatedly. We get stuck in those self-images even when they're no longer accurate, and our internal alarm system we needed to alert us is easily flipped on, and this can make us passive, fearful, and depressed. This activity will help you see whether you're stuck with a self-image you've outgrown or overcome, discover your real capacity to take care of yourself, and increase the things you do to make yourself safe and secure.

1. Please describe how you feel about your strengths and your physical, mental, emotional, and other abilities to prevent others from abusing you now and in the future.

    _____

    _____

2. Now talk to a friend or family member you trust, who knows you well, and ask that person to describe how they see you in the same areas. Summarize what that friend or relative tells you here.

    _____

    _____

3. Internal safety resources include mental and physical strengths, knowledge, and skills you can use to stay safe (ability to calm; confidence to manage triggers). These can include intelligence, situational alertness, being street-smart about how sexual predators operate, self-defense skills, and safe habits (e.g., looking inside cars before getting in). What internal safety resources do you have now that you didn't when your abuse happened?

    _____

    _____

4. What internal safety resources are you lacking that you want to have or improve upon? How will adding or improving them assist with feeling safe and help recovery efforts?

_____

_____

5. An external resource for safety is anything in your environment that helps ensure your safety. These might include having your own safe place to live, safe people to live with, good locks on your doors, having a dog and/or a security system, friendships with trustworthy neighbors, not being financially dependent on anyone untrustworthy, having reliable transportation, a safe workplace, always carrying a cell phone. What external safety resources do you have in your life now that you didn't have when your abuse happened?

_____

_____

6. What external safety resources are you lacking that you want to have or improve upon? How will adding and improving upon these help recovery efforts?

_____

_____

7. After reviewing these questions, do you feel differently about your strengths and your physical, mental, emotional, and other abilities to prevent others from abusing you? If so, how?

_____

_____

_____

8. What calming practice(s) do you have available to you to help you? What affirmations can you identify that are compassionate and nurturing to remind you of your strength, resilience, and resolve while you heal?

_____

_____

_____

Be sure to bring this handout back to your next therapy session and be prepared to talk about your thoughts and feelings about the exercise.

IS IT ROMANCE OR IS IT FEAR?

GOALS OF THE EXERCISE

1. Maintain a program of recovery that is free from addictive or high-risk behavior in relationships.
2. Identify and correct thoughts that trigger sexual promiscuity and learn to practice self-talk that promotes healthy sexual behavior and safe relationships.
3. Identify connections between childhood relationships with alcoholic, addicted, or otherwise dysfunctional parents and dysfunctional love relationships in adult life.
4. Achieve insight into the roots of dysfunctional relationships, both with alcoholic parents and adult partners, in feelings of responsibility for others' behavior.
5. Identify healthy nonromantic relationships to use as models for healthier love relationships.

ADDITIONAL PROBLEMS FOR WHICH THIS EXERCISE MAY BE USEFUL

- Adult-Child-of-an-Alcoholic (ACA) Traits
- Borderline Traits
- Dependent Traits
- Impulsivity
- Partner Relational Conflicts
- Sexual Abuse

SUGGESTIONS FOR PROCESSING THIS EXERCISE WITH THE CLIENT

The "Is It Romance or Is It Fear?" activity is for clients who have patterns of unhealthy relationship dynamics echoing childhood relationships with dysfunctional parents. This exercise is useful when clients present with dissatisfaction about dysfunctional relationships or loneliness and a desire to establish new relationships.

IS IT ROMANCE OR IS IT FEAR?

Do you repeatedly find yourself in romantic and/or sexual relationships with partners who are abusive, dishonest, neglectful, or otherwise bad for you—relationships that always seem to end in heartbreak, humiliation, fear, or abandonment—or become sexually intimate with someone with whom you have no meaningful emotional or lasting connection? Similar to substance-abusing behaviors, have you sought sexual relationships to cope or escape from stress or been sexually involved with others impulsively and later had regrets? Do you find that even knowing you'd be safer and happier with someone who was honest, considerate, and dependable, it's the "bad boys/bad girls" who excite you? This exercise will help you start addressing this painful pattern.

1. First, reflect on the relationship or relationships that stand out in your mind as having been hardest to cope with. The experiences that hurt most can include feeling used, ashamed by your behavior, or experiencing verbal and emotional abuse, physical abuse, dishonesty, abandonment, infidelity, neglect and emotional unavailability, addictive behaviors, and other irresponsible and self-destructive behavior by our partners. For each person that came to mind, think about what was most hurtful about the relationship, the other person's behavior, or what you most regretted.

    _____

    _____

2. If you thought about more than one relationship, do you see any trends or patterns? For example, some people repeatedly get into relationships with partners who are unfaithful. Others may be repeatedly drawn to partners with addictive behaviors. Please describe any patterns you see.

    _____

    _____

3. What insights do you have about what needs are satisfied by these relationships?

    _____

    _____

4. What are five consequences to your own recovery, your self-esteem, your satisfaction in relationships when you repeat this behavior or these relationships?

_____

_____

_____

_____

5. After being hurt, feeling used, emotionally devastated, or engaging in sexual behavior you later regretted, identify five thoughts you had about yourself or your behavior.

_____

_____

_____

_____

6. One of the most attractive qualities of dysfunctional partners is often the intensity and excitement we feel when we're with them. Another relationship marked by similar intensity and excitement is that of a person with an addiction and their drug or other addictive behavior. What other parallels do you see between a person with an addiction's relationship with a substance or a behavior and yours with your past partners?

_____

_____

7. What are three ways you could get the feelings you desire out of relationships in ways that are less damaging to you? If you struggle to come up with three, discuss in therapy or with your sponsor. How would the statements you make to yourself sound different if you weren't engaging in regretted behavior, feeling used, or emotionally devastated?

_____

_____

8. Think about your experience growing up in your family of origin. In many families where a caregiver had problems with addictions or mental illness, children can be emotionally neglected or abused; witness dysfunctional interactions or violence; survive divorces, abandonment, emotional unavailability, and instability, among other things. Look at the patterns you listed for your painful adult relationships and describe those that also describe your childhood experience with caregivers. What are your observations?

_____

_____

9. Think about your closest relationship today that is not a romantic one. This could be with a best friend or a family member. What qualities describe that person and your relationship with them (e.g., positive, dependable, sensitive, equal)? How do you feel when you are with them?

    _____

    _____

10. What would it be like to be in a romantic relationship with a person whose personality was like the person you thought about for question 8?

    _____

    _____

11. If you would rather be in such a relationship—less intense but more nurturing—how will it benefit you and your recovery?

    _____

    _____

Be sure to bring this handout back to your next therapy session and be prepared to talk about your thoughts and feelings about the exercise.

WORKING THROUGH SHAME

GOALS OF THE EXERCISE

1. Maintain a program of recovery that is free of sexual promiscuity and addictive behavior.
2. Recognize and understand issues of shame and negative self-image.
3. Understand connections between negative self-image and addictive behaviors.
4. Build a more positive self-image as part of a recovery program.

ADDITIONAL PROBLEMS FOR WHICH THIS EXERCISE MAY BE USEFUL

- Adult-Child-of-an-Alcoholic (ACA) Traits
- Borderline Traits
- Childhood Trauma
- Eating Disorders and Obesity
- Opioid Use Disorder
- Self-Harm

SUGGESTIONS FOR PROCESSING THIS EXERCISE WITH THE CLIENT

The "Working Through Shame" activity is intended to guide clients in correcting distorted perceptions and expectations that generate shame. Its approach is to guide the client in evaluating their own behaviors more objectively than in the past and to apply the same standards to themself as to others. Follow-up could include sharing responses and outcomes of the affirmation-style portion of the exercise with the therapist and treatment group, as well as Exercise 24.C, "Using Affirmations for Change," and bibliotherapy using the works of John Bradshaw, Janet Woititz, Claudia Black, and others who have written on this topic.

WORKING THROUGH SHAME

Shame results from thinking that you are bad, inadequate, defective, unworthy, or less than other people. It results in feeling hopeless, helpless, and unable to change or succeed. Shame frequently accompanies addictive behavior. There's a difference between guilt and shame. Guilt is feeling that an *action* is unacceptable, but shame is feeling that *we ourselves* are unacceptable. We can deal with guilt by correcting our actions, but shame is destructive, because we can't change who we are. If left unresolved, this puts us at high risk of returning to drinking, using, or other addictive and self-destructive behaviors. Shame convinces us that we can't get better and don't deserve to heal. This exercise will help you identify and correct shame in your beliefs about yourself.

1. In the first column, please list some mistakes you have made and things you have done wrong as a result of drinking, other drug use, or other addictive patterns. In the second column, list things you should have done but didn't because your addiction(s) interfered.

    Mistakes and Regrets   **Things Not Done**

    _____   _____

    _____   _____

    _____   _____

    _____   _____

2. What kinds of shaming things do you say to yourself about the things you listed? Describe any thoughts in which you call yourself bad, weak, stupid, lazy, evil, or other negative labels.

    _____

    _____

3. What positive messages and self-enhancing statements do you want to repeat to yourself about the things you listed in question 1, to replace these shaming messages (i.e., what might you say to a good friend who was in your situation)?

    _____

    _____

4. Making qualitative and sustained changes takes time. Making mistakes and having slips is part of the process. Do you continue to repeat any of these mistakes or regretted actions? When we struggle, we may tell ourselves that there is something wrong with us, particularly if we feel ashamed about our actions or it is discrepant with our values—for example: "I'm upset – I don't like this feeling – I want to avoid feeling this way – I shouldn't feel this way – What is wrong with me? – I'm worthless." This is where a self-compassionate action provides the opportunity to heal. Being kind and loving toward oneself during suffering and mistakes is when we need it most. If we can be more self-compassionate, we see that change is possible and we're worth it. What could you say to yourself that is kind, gentle, and nurturing?

   _____

   _____

5. List three ways being more compassionate toward yourself may be beneficial to you.

   _____

   _____

6. Each night for the next 2 weeks, please write your answer to the following questions, and talk with your therapist about what you write and any changes you see in your beliefs about yourself.

   "Of everything I did today, what do I feel the best about?"

   "I am responsible for caring for myself in the ways I care for others."

   After completing this exercise, write about the experience and any changes you notice in your thinking and feeling.

   _____

   _____

   _____

7. List some ways exploring spirituality and a higher power to turn the problem of shame and past behavior over to may be beneficial.

   _____

   _____

   Be sure to bring this handout back to your next therapy session and be prepared to talk about your thoughts and feelings about the exercise.

ASSESSING SLEEP PROBLEMS

GOALS OF THE EXERCISE

1. Restore a normal sleeping pattern.
2. Feel refreshed after sleeping.
3. Terminate fears of sleeping poorly.
4. Understand the effects of mood-altering chemicals and addictive lifestyle on sleep.

ADDITIONAL PROBLEMS FOR WHICH THIS EXERCISE MAY BE USEFUL

- Anxiety
- Chronic Pain
- Depression–Unipolar
- Eating Disorders and Obesity
- Grief/Loss Unresolved
- Medical Issues
- Posttraumatic Stress Disorder (PTSD)
- Relapse Proneness
- Self-Care Deficits—Primary
- Social Anxiety
- Substance Intoxication/Withdrawal

SUGGESTIONS FOR PROCESSING THIS EXERCISE WITH THE CLIENT

The "Assessing Sleep Problems" activity is designed to get clients to begin to pay attention to reasons for their poor sleep, link it to use of substances and other issues, and have them gather real-time data to help identify possible solutions. Follow-up to this exercise should include Exercise 42.B, "Improving Sleep Hygiene," in this manual, which is designed to assist the client in learning tools to begin to solve this complex problem. If behavioral and cognitive interventions do not resolve this issue completely, the client should be referred to a physician and/or sleep specialist prior to trying any medications, prescribed or over the counter. Any physician or specialist should be aware of the client's history/present addiction. Provide some psychoeducation about the body and the brain's need to heal; as recovery time increases for substance and mental health related concerns and the client engages in consistent self-care activities, sleep is likely to improve. The need to manage stress, anxiety, and worry will also be necessary.

ASSESSING SLEEP PROBLEMS

Getting adequate and restful sleep is vital to recovery and overall health. Many people in early sobriety/recovery from addictive behaviors struggle with sleep. Troubles with sleep are complex, because there may be physical, cognitive, and emotional components as well as behaviors that result in sleep issues. This exercise is designed for you to gather some information about your sleep issues, so you have the data to begin to plan steps to resolve the issue.

1. For 2 weeks, keep a sleep journal on the following things each night:
   a. The actual amount of time you sleep each night (excluding time in bed not sleeping)
   b. Any periods of insomnia (inability to sleep) and/or hypersomnia (sleeping too much)—when, how much, time frame
   c. The times you go to bed and the times you wake each day
   d. Level of fatigue you experience throughout the day
   e. Number of days experienced daytime sleepiness
   f. If you nap, when, where, and for how long
   g. Where you sleep (if you start out in one place and move to another)
   h. How much caffeine or other stimulants you use and when you use them
   i. Use of alcohol/other drugs/any over-the-counter medications, supplements either alone or as an attempt to induce sleep
   j. What happens when you sleep (wake often, interrupted, have nightmares)
   k. How long it takes you to fall asleep each night
   l. Number of times you wake at night and length of time it takes to get back to sleep
   m. Quality of the environment in which you're attempting to sleep (i.e., quiet, dark, significant outside noise/distraction, temperature, who sleeps in bed with you and the potential impact of this)
   n. When you eat and last meal/snack of the day
   o. How much you exercise each day and at what times
   p. How much nicotine you use and when you use it
   q. Medicines taken and times (talk to your doctor about any possible side effects that impact sleep in any ways)

    r. How you wake yourself each morning

    s. Any other notable things that affect your sleep:

    _____

2. What has been the relationship for you between your sleep and your substance use/ addictive behaviors (i.e., used substances to assist with sleep, substance withdrawal prohibits sleep)? Examples: poor sleep hygiene (stay up late/sleep late into the day); pull all-nighters; use substances to sleep and/or increase alertness during the day

    _____

    _____

3. What other issues impact sleep for you and how? Either too much or not enough.

    _____ Anxiety, worry

    _____ Nightmares

    _____ Other health issues (i.e., breathing, pain)

    _____ Depression

    _____ Chronic relapsing

    _____ Trauma response

    _____ Poor sleep habits

    _____ Variable work schedule

    _____ Child-rearing

    _____ Transition issues/stress

    _____ Sleepwalking

    _____ Other: _____

4. Describe the relationship of your current sleep issues on depression, anxiety, and relapse proneness.

    _____

    _____

5. Describe how much you worry about your sleep, and what do you tend to worry about? How does this affect sleep?

    _____

    _____

6. What ways have you attempted to correct your sleep issues? Comment on the results of each attempt.

    _____

    _____

7. What do you do if you are unable to fall asleep or if you wake often/early and cannot fall back to sleep?

    _____

    _____

Be sure to bring this handout back to your next session with your therapist and be prepared to talk about your thoughts and feelings about the exercise.

IMPROVING SLEEP HYGIENE

GOALS OF THE EXERCISE

1. Terminate fears of sleeping poorly.
2. Feel refreshed after sleeping.
3. Restore normal sleeping pattern.
4. Understand the effects of mood-altering chemicals on sleep.

ADDITIONAL PROBLEMS FOR WHICH THIS EXERCISE MAY BE USEFUL

- Anxiety
- Chronic Pain
- Depression–Unipolar
- Eating Disorders and Obesity
- Grief/Loss Unresolved
- Medical Issues
- Posttraumatic Stress Disorder (PTSD)
- Relapse Proneness
- Self-Care Deficits—Primary
- Social Anxiety
- Substance Intoxication/Withdrawal

SUGGESTIONS FOR PROCESSING THIS EXERCISE WITH THE CLIENT

The "Improving Sleep Hygiene" activity is intended for clients who struggle with irregular sleep patterns that interfere with their quality of life and/or make it difficult to carry out day-to-day activities in any domain of their lives. It builds on the previous exercise "Assessing Sleep Patterns" (42.A) to identify and change any chronic cognitive patterns related to sleep problems that then also interfere with sleep, creating a vicious cycle. Follow-up could include reviewing a sleep journal and brainstorming with the therapist or group about behavioral changes to improve sleep, then reporting back on the outcomes. If there is excessive daytime sleepiness (different from feelings of fatigue), encourage a discussion with a health care provider to rule out medical concerns.

IMPROVING SLEEP HYGIENE

Once medical issues are ruled out as causing issues with sleep, some basic strategies can help people in getting to sleep and getting adequate and restful sleep. Some of these strategies are contrary to the way many of us live our lives during our active addiction. Correcting sleep issues takes time and patience because we are changing behavioral and cognitive habits and/or waiting for our bodies to heal physically after use or abuse of alcohol/drugs or prescribed or over-the-counter medications and making significant life-style changes.

1. When you find you are unable to sleep, what thoughts run through your mind (i.e., fears, worries of sleeplessness, self-defeating statements)?

   _____

   _____

2. What alternate thoughts could you use to replace those you listed that would keep your anxiety, anger, and frustration from escalating? You may consider brainstorming these in individual or group sessions.

   _____

   _____

3. What habits will you need to alter in order to set yourself up to be ready to go to bed and ultimately to sleep (e.g., caffeine intake, same time to bed, develop sleep ritual, building sleep drive throughout the day with being active, etc.)?

   _____

   _____

4. How long do you lie in bed awake thinking/worrying about not sleeping? Identify what thoughts/worries you have. What can you do to reduce worries?

   _____

   _____

5. There is a strong connection between sleep issues and relapse. While you resolve this issue, what will you do to take extra care in this area?

    _____

    _____

6. Review your sleep journal from Exercise 42.A, "Assessing Sleep Problems" in this manual and create a sleep hygiene plan that addresses each of the difficulties you identified. Continue to journal so that you can continue to modify your plan to get the quality of sleep you need for sustained sobriety and recovery.

    _____

    _____

Be sure to bring this handout back to your next session with your therapist and be prepared to talk about your thoughts and feelings about the exercise. If changing behaviors, cognitions, and rituals do not help after concerted effort, please talk with a health care provider about additional behavioral interventions to address sleep problems or if additional medical intervention is warranted.

UNDERSTANDING THOUGHTS, WORRIES, AND FEARS

GOALS OF THE EXERCISE

1. Develop the social skills that are necessary to reduce excessive anxiety in social situations and terminate reliance on addiction as a coping mechanism.
2. Maintain a program of recovery that is free from excessive social anxiety and addiction.
3. Decrease thoughts that trigger anxiety, and increase positive, self-enhancing self-talk.
4. Learn the relationship between anxiety and addiction.
5. Identify how social anxiety impacts willingness and ability to access and develop recovery support.
6. Form relationships that will enhance a recovery support system.

ADDITIONAL PROBLEMS FOR WHICH THIS EXERCISE MAY BE USEFUL

- Anxiety
- Borderline Traits
- Dependent Traits
- Obsessive-Compulsive Disorder (OCD)
- Posttraumatic Stress Disorder (PTSD)
- Relapse Proneness
- Sexual Promiscuity

SUGGESTIONS FOR PROCESSING THIS EXERCISE WITH THE CLIENT

The "Understanding Thoughts, Worries, and Fears" worksheet is for clients who experience social anxiety and addiction. This exercise is intended to increase the client's awareness of how their social anxiety and addictive behavior are related. It first asks the client to complete a cost/benefit analysis to begin assessing readiness and motivation to address these problems effectively. It then asks the client to complete a self-monitoring exercise in order to gather real-time data rather than base actions on perceptions, fears, and beliefs.

This will get the client ready to use the data to create an action plan. Follow-up could include assigning Exercise 43.B, "Action Plan to Address Social Anxiety," which will guide the client through skill building in this area. Increasing practice and exposure in social situations is key; use group to practice. Additionally, providing skills training for calming oneself or use of relaxation or mindfulness skills concurrently is beneficial.

UNDERSTANDING THOUGHTS, WORRIES, AND FEARS

Anxiety and addiction are related in several ways. People who are socially anxious may have come to rely on substances to help them feel brave, reduce social fears, quiet internal self-criticism, and calm their bodies when interacting with others. However, at the same time, substance use erodes their confidence and ability to master necessary skills to interact with others. The excessive fear and worry in social situations do not generally have any factual basis, but it feels so real that it results in avoidance or an inability to fully engage with others. So, at times not only is it challenging to initiate social connections but there is also a struggle to grow or maintain them.

1. List five ways your social anxiety kept you using or relying on your addictive behavior(s) in social situations.

   _____

   _____

   _____

   _____

2. What negative consequences have you experienced because of your social anxiety?

   _____

   _____

3. How has social anxiety kept you from using available supports that could help you with both the problem of anxiety and the problem of addiction?

   _____

   _____

4. To get a better understanding of what maintains these issues and what may motivate you to take on these problems, complete the following cost/benefit analysis:

   _____

   _____

Benefits of Status Quo	Costs of No Change (Status Quo)
_____	_____
_____	_____
Benefits of Working Through Feared/Uncomfortable Situations	**Costs of Working Through Feared/ Uncomfortable Situations**
_____	_____
_____	_____

After completing the analysis, what conclusions can you draw? What are the benefits of tackling these issues of social anxiety?

_____

_____

5. Self-monitoring activity: Rank social situations (where, who's present, your participation/role) (in which you find yourself for the next 2 weeks that cause you to feel anxious, and give each an anxiety intensity ranking (0 = not at all to 10 = extreme anxiety)

   a. Situation: _____ Ranking: _____

   b. Situation: _____ Ranking: _____

   c. Situation: _____ Ranking: _____

   d. Situation: _____ Ranking: _____

   e. Situation: _____ Ranking: _____

   Continue with this format on a separate sheet. Include as many social situations as you find yourself in, so you have plenty of data to review.

6. In which of these situations did you have thoughts about use of substances or some other avoidance strategy? What thoughts did you find yourself thinking (at least two for each situation)?

   _____

   _____

7. For each situation, identify at least one fear, one doubt, and one criticism that accompanied each.

   _____

   _____

8. Of these situations, starting with those that had the lowest anxiety ranking and moving to those with the highest, what insight can you obtain about what makes the low-anxiety ones different from those that cause you higher anxiety?

_____

_____

9. Note any situations you did not avoid/escape; describe them and what you believe was different about these.

_____

_____

Be sure to bring this handout back to your next session with your therapist and be prepared to talk about your thoughts and feelings about the exercise.

ACTION PLAN TO ADDRESS SOCIAL ANXIETY

GOALS OF THE EXERCISE

1. Develop the social skills needed to reduce excessive anxiety in social situations and terminate reliance on addiction as a coping mechanism.
2. Maintain a program of recovery that is free from excessive social anxiety and addiction.
3. Decrease thoughts that trigger anxiety and increase positive, self-enhancing self-talk.
4. Learn the relationship between anxiety and addiction.
5. Form relationships that will enhance a recovery support system.

ADDITIONAL PROBLEMS FOR WHICH THIS EXERCISE MAY BE USEFUL

- Anger
- Anxiety
- Eating Disorders and Obesity
- Grief/Loss Unresolved
- Posttraumatic Stress Disorder (PTSD)
- Sexual Promiscuity
- Substance Use Disorders

SUGGESTIONS FOR PROCESSING THIS EXERCISE WITH THE CLIENT

The "Action Plan to Address Social Anxiety" is an activity designed for the client who is motivated to address social fears, self-critical thoughts, and self-doubt and recognizes the benefit of doing so but has been unable to do this work on their own. It is significant to note that many clients with social anxiety recognize the irrationality of their fears and may even know the solution(s), but they have been unable to effect change in their lives on their own. They often say, "Why can't I just . . .?" As a result, they have found ineffective and destructive ways to cope, have avoided many things along the way, including help, and their self-confidence has eroded.

They will be asked to work through both cognitive and behavioral strategies for seeking and using help and challenging all perceived barriers or those they have put in their own way. Follow-up and ongoing assignments should be running the behavioral experiments outlined in this activity. It is helpful when starting out to reward every honest attempt to help build confidence and motivation to continue.

Provide psychoeducation on the impact of avoidance. Encourage facing fears and discomfort so they learn that their worst fears won't come true, and they can feel more in control of anxiety.

ACTION PLAN TO ADDRESS SOCIAL ANXIETY

Many people with social anxiety recognize that their fears aren't realistic and may even know the solution but find they have been unable to make these changes in their lives on their own. They often say, "Why can't I just . . .?" As a result, they may have used destructive ways to cope and/or avoided many things along the way. They may even have avoided getting the help they needed. This exercise will help address cognitive (correcting distorted thoughts) and behavioral strategies for seeking and using help and challenging the perceived barriers we put in our own way.

1. List five worries and fears you have regarding social situations or interactions.

_____

_____

_____

_____

2. What experiences are related to these worries and fears (e.g., past rejections, harsh criticism, trauma, etc.)?

_____

_____

3. What negative consequences have resulted due to the fear and anxiety?

_____

_____

4. What thoughts accompany the five worries and fears you listed (e.g., you will be publicly ridiculed, will be humiliated, will offend others, or be rejected, etc.)?

_____

_____

_____

5. For each of the thoughts you identified in question 4, what reality-based cognitive messages (they have to be believable at a 4 or higher on a 10-point scale; 0 = not at all believable and 10 = very believable) can you think of to replace them? Use your group or therapy session if you have difficulty generating these messages on your own.

    _____

    _____

    _____

    _____

6. What social situations do you do well in or experience lower levels of social anxiety you can tolerate? What is your explanation for this?

    _____

    _____

7. Social anxiety can interfere with engaging in meaningful relationships with others, including those relationships we need to foster to stay sober. This can be by way of avoiding meetings due to discomfort at being with unfamiliar people, sitting silently at meetings, not knowing how to participate or socialize in meeting, being unable to even get yourself to go to one for fear of what others will think about you when you walk in the door, etc. Write an action plan for increasing exposure to the following challenging situations that will push your recovery forward. Start with those that bring the least anxiety and work up to those that create the most.

    a. Going to a meeting
    b. Going to a variety of meetings
    c. Sharing at a meeting
    d. Introducing myself at a meeting
    e. Seeking someone out to be a sponsor
    f. Reaching out to someone when in crisis
    g. Admitting a relapse or thoughts of relapse
    h. Going to treatment groups
    i. Others: _____

8. What will you do to calm yourself? What affirmation can you tell yourself to encourage yourself to face some of your fears?

    _____

    _____

9. Avoidance will only make your anxiety worse and keep you from the things and people who can help you the most and, most important, in crisis. The other benefit is that with each successful attempt, your confidence will build. How can you reward each honest attempt you make instead of berating yourself if you don't accomplish the entire task?

    _____

    _____

    _____

10. Remember, we all need some encouragement to face our fears. Letting people help you is not a weakness or a flaw. Trying new things without the cover of substances is generally anxiety provoking. The more you do it, the easier it gets. Who can help you, coach you, and cheer you on, and how will you ask for their help?

    _____

    _____

11. It is helpful to develop positive self-talk statements that you can repeat to yourself when you feel anxious approaching a social situation. Create some self-statements that you can use as a mantra to coach and calm yourself (e.g., "Breathe," "I will feel better about myself for trying," "I'm learning to take this a day at a time").

    _____

    _____

    _____

    _____

Be sure to bring this handout back to your next session with your therapist and be prepared to talk about your thoughts and feelings about the exercise.

UNDERSTANDING SPIRITUALITY

GOALS OF THE EXERCISE

1. Broaden the client's understanding of spirituality and how it applies to overcoming addictions.
2. Learn the difference between religion and spirituality.
3. Overcome resistance to 12-step programs based on antipathy toward religion.
4. Develop a concept of a higher power that is loving and supportive to recovery.
5. Resolve spiritual conflicts, allowing for a meaningful relationship with a higher power.

ADDITIONAL PROBLEMS FOR WHICH THIS EXERCISE MAY BE USEFUL

*   Grief/Loss Unresolved
*   Posttraumatic Stress Disorder (PTSD)
*   Substance Use Disorders

SUGGESTIONS FOR PROCESSING THIS EXERCISE WITH THE CLIENT

The "Understanding Spirituality" activity is written for clients whose therapeutic progress is impeded by resistance to spirituality as a resource for recovery based on antipathy toward organized religion or perceived conflicts with personal values. Follow-up could include bibliotherapy, including books such as *Where in the World Is God?* by Robert Brizee.

UNDERSTANDING SPIRITUALITY

This assignment will help you work through an issue that troubles many people who are new to recovery programs. There's no way that one handout can cover it all, but it can help you get started.

Why work on spirituality? Because it can make the difference between success or failure in recovery, and therefore maybe the difference between life or death. Addictive behaviors and lifestyles tend to chip away at or strip our spiritual center; getting re-centered is a critical recovery task, It's the key to effective use of Alcoholics Anonymous (AA), Narcotics Anonymous (NA), and other 12-step programs. When people attend their first meetings of 12-step programs and find they dislike these programs, the most common reason is discomfort with all the talk about God. This may look like a barrier, making these programs useless to them, but it doesn't have to be.

Many people feel skeptical about religion. They may have had bad experiences with religious people or institutions. Perhaps they just feel that God has not been there in their lives. Hearing God or a higher power mentioned in 7 of the 12 steps may be an immediate turnoff. However, many people who don't believe in God, or who believe that no one can know whether God exists, find that they can use AA, NA, and other 12-step programs to make the changes they want to make in their lives. The key is understanding the difference between *spirituality* and *religion*.

1. Write down your description of *religion*. What do you think of when you hear the word?

    _____

    _____

2. Now think about the word *spirituality* and write your definition for this word.

    _____

    _____

3. Are there differences in the meanings of *religion* and *spirituality* for you? If so, what is the biggest difference you see?

    _____

    _____

    _____

We could say it this way: A religion is a system that people create to try to achieve spirituality. We could think of spirituality as like water and religion as like a bottle, a container to hold water—but other containers can hold water, and some bottles contain other things instead of water.

4. What other containers for spirituality can you think of (i.e., other ways to help yourself focus on what is right in life)?

    _____

    _____

5. At this point, you may be thinking that the definition of *religion* also describes a 12-step program. It involves certain practices and rituals, and it's practiced in a specific organization. If you think 12-step programs like AA and NA resemble religion, what similarities do you see?

    _____

    _____

6. What differences do you see?

    _____

    _____

    Here are three key differences between 12-step groups and religions:
    - *Specific definitions of God.* A religion offers specific ways to understand God and may insist that no other way is correct. A 12-step program asks you to think in terms of a power greater than yourself and leaves it to you to decide what that power is and how it works.
    - *Authority.* Whereas a religion almost always has a formal hierarchy and structure of people in charge, in a 12-step group nobody is in charge. There is no chain of command. Decisions are made by the group through a vote called a "group conscience."
    - *Membership requirements.* Religions may restrict their membership in many ways—by birth, heritage, or obedience to given rules. By contrast, in any 12-step program, the Third Tradition says that the only membership requirement is a desire to solve the problem that group exists to overcome.

7. Going back to our definition of *spirituality*, how do you think that paying attention to the moral aspects of life and what is right could help you solve the problems facing you with alcohol, drugs, or other addictive behaviors?

    _____

    _____

    If you see that a focus on these parts of your life could be useful, that's all it takes to begin including spirituality in your recovery work.

8. List three ways a new understanding and acceptance of a higher power could help you in overcoming addiction.

_____

_____

9. If you were a faithful/spiritual person before, what is one step you can take to reconnect to this resource?

_____

_____

Be sure to bring this handout back to your next therapy session and be prepared to talk about your thoughts and feelings about the exercise.

FINDING A HIGHER POWER THAT MAKES SENSE

GOALS OF THE EXERCISE

1. Maintain a program of recovery free of addiction and spiritual confusion.
2. Resolve spiritual conflicts to allow for a meaningful relationship with a higher power.
3. Develop a concept of a higher power that is loving and supportive to recovery.
4. Identify ways a higher power can help to overcome addiction to achieve and maintain recovery.
5. Create a plan to make life more consistent with professed values and ideals.

ADDITIONAL PROBLEMS FOR WHICH THIS EXERCISE MAY BE USEFUL

- Adult-Child-of-an-Alcoholic (ACA) Traits
- Childhood Trauma
- Grief/Loss Unresolved
- Posttraumatic Stress Disorder (PTSD)
- Sexual Abuse
- Substance-Induced Disorders
- Suicidal Ideation

SUGGESTIONS FOR PROCESSING THIS EXERCISE WITH THE CLIENT

The "Finding a Higher Power That Makes Sense" activity is intended for the client who wants to achieve recovery but finds their skepticism and ambivalence regarding religion and spirituality an obstacle to participation in a 12-step or other spiritually based recovery program. Follow-up could include reading and journaling about the book *Where in the World Is God?* by Robert Brizee, as well as keeping a journal and reporting back to the therapist and treatment group on thoughts and observations based on this exercise. It is important for the therapist to assess cultural and religious history to cultivate an understanding of when connections were lost and the potential benefit of connecting with a particular faith or spiritual tradition.

FINDING A HIGHER POWER THAT MAKES SENSE

You may have had an experience that is very common among people attending their first meetings of Alcoholics Anonymous, Narcotics Anonymous, or other 12-step programs. The first reaction on meeting people and hearing them talk about their lives can be a feeling of elation. After years, maybe a lifetime, of feeling that no one really understands our lives and how we feel, suddenly we find a group where some of the people seem a lot like us! For many of us just entering recovery, it is the first experience in our lives of feeling that we fit in. More than that, they seem happy with their lives. They've found something we've been looking for, and it fills us with hope.

Then these people start talking a lot about God and/or their higher power. This may not be a problem for you if you are already content with your spiritual life, but for anyone who has become disillusioned and felt rejected, judged, or betrayed by religion and religious people, it can feel as if a wonderful gift has been offered and then snatched out of our grasp. That can lead to despair or an unwillingness to use a proven resource to help those with addiction live lives free of their addiction. Fortunately, it doesn't have to be that way. This activity is designed to help you overcome that dilemma.

1. First, it's important to acknowledge that a lot of the language in some 12-step program literature not only sounds religious, but it sounds specifically Christian. Furthermore, a lot of the people in the meetings may make it clear that their Higher Power is a Christian God. However, the key phrase in steps 3 and 11 is "God *as we understood Him*" (or "God *as we understood God,*" depending on which program you're visiting). This is one of the main differences between 12-step programs and religions or religious programs. When you first heard or read that phrase, what thoughts came to mind for you?

   _____

   _____

2. The first step in putting this concept to work is to set aside anything you've been told about God or a higher power that seems wrong to you—wrong either because it doesn't fit your experience of the real world or because it conflicts with your values and sense of what a loving higher power should be like. Figure out what kind of God

or higher power *would* make sense to you. Depending on your values and life experience, that may be the life force or spirit of the world or the universe, the essence of a perfect parent, a system of spiritual practices and values that lacks a specified god, or any other concept that really feels right to you.

How would you describe the God or higher power that would (a) fit the facts of the world as you've experienced it, (b) be *right* for you, and (c) be able to help you in your recovery from addiction?

_____

_____

3. What evidence would you be able to see in the world if your idea of a higher power really exists? This can be external (things you see happen outside of yourself) or internal (things happening with your own thoughts and feelings). If your conception of a higher power is a nonpersonalized value system, then this might mean asking yourself what you see happening in the lives of people living by that value system. For whatever your Higher Power would be if it exists, what external and internal evidence would you expect to observe/experience?

    _____

    _____

4. The final part is the simplest. Whatever kinds of evidence you decide would show you that there is a higher power around who can help you with recovery, watch for it; simply spend a few weeks in wait-and-see mode. Try to write for a few minutes each day about your experience in this activity. You may not see any evidence, in which case your next course would be to seek out others in recovery who have faced the same dilemma and ask what they've done, or to pursue a path such as Rational Recovery that doesn't involve spirituality. But if your experience is like that of a lot of other people, you may find that your higher power has been there all along, and you just didn't realize it because the signs didn't fit what you'd been taught about faith. Sometimes in the act of changing one's mindset from skepticism to being more open to possibilities, curiosity can help in this process.

    _____

    _____

5. How has the absence of or confusion regarding spirituality contributed to your addiction or negative attitude about recovery?

    _____

    _____

6. Identify five benefits there would be for you in acceptance of a higher power in your recovery efforts.

_____

_____

_____

_____

Be sure to bring this handout back to your next therapy session and be prepared to talk about your thoughts and feelings about the exercise.

USING MY SUPPORT NETWORK

GOALS OF THE EXERCISE

1. Learn the importance of beginning and maintaining a program of recovery from addiction and substance-induced disorder.
2. Identify the ways a support network can assist in the early stages of sobriety.
3. Learn to work on recovery with others rather than alone.
4. Form relationships that will enhance a recovery support system.

ADDITIONAL PROBLEMS FOR WHICH THIS EXERCISE MAY BE USEFUL

*   Adult-Child-of-an-Alcoholic (ACA) Traits
*   Chronic Pain
*   Dependent Traits
*   Peer Group Negativity
*   Posttraumatic Stress Disorder (PTSD)
*   Readiness to Change
*   Relapse Proneness
*   Self-Care Deficits—Primary
*   Self-Care Deficits—Secondary
*   Sexual Promiscuity
*   Substance Intoxication/Withdrawal
*   Substance Use Disorders

SUGGESTIONS FOR PROCESSING THIS EXERCISE WITH THE CLIENT

The "Using My Support Network" activity is for clients who have difficulty seeking and accepting support from others for therapeutic goals. Its approach is to guide the client in identifying potential sources of support from treatment, people in their lives, and the recovery community. Additionally, it asks clients to complete a cost/benefit analysis of identifying and using a support team versus not doing so. Initially, medical stabilization and improved mood and cognitive function may be necessary.

Follow-up could include homework assignments to talk with the people identified in this exercise and ask for their support, then report back to the therapist and group on the outcomes. For those clients who are more ambivalent/reluctant toward sobriety and/or help (possibly those who are mandated to treatment), spending more time processing the exact reasons they resist could be a precursor to this assignment.

USING MY SUPPORT NETWORK

It is common for people dealing with substance abuse or other addictive patterns to isolate themselves and to feel embarrassed or ashamed about their histories. Also, some people feel that because they got themselves into the messes they are in alone, they need to solve their problems alone. However, people embarking on this journey benefit when they seek help from others who care about them, or who are succeeding at the same goals. This exercise will get you started using the support of helpful people to increase your chances of success in making lifestyle changes related to addictive behavior.

1. What brought you to treatment? For those who are returning, what is the motivation this time? Your mood, thoughts, memory, sleep, and physical body may not have returned to normal yet. With ongoing sobriety, this will come. What are the benefits to you of staying in treatment?

    _____

    _____

2. What are the risks if you reject the help being offered or return to drinking, other drug use, or other addictive behavior patterns?

    _____

    _____

3. As you stabilize your physical, psychological, and emotional health, it is important to have people to help you. What supportive people can you ask to help you stay abstinent in the early stages of sobriety from your addiction? Identify one specific way each could be helpful to you.

    Family: _____

    Companions/partners: _____

    Friends: _____

    Work/School: _____

    Church/spiritual community: _____

    Others (e.g., coach, mentor): _____

4. In addition to the treatment staff and the people who support and know you, a recovery community is available to assist you. What are three potential benefits of using a 12-step recovery program in addition to treatment in the very early stages of establishing your sobriety?

   _____

   _____

   For those of you returning to a recovery program, recall how this helped last time and ways to avail yourself to it differently this time.

   _____

   _____

5. The biggest obstacle or barriers for me in asking for assistance and accepting it now is:

   _____

   _____

6. Reliance on others can be a challenge for several reasons; what are you most reluctant, fearful, skeptical about?

   _____

   _____

7. What will I tell these people about how I would like them to help me? List three things each can do to assist you in your efforts at stabilizing and staying sober.

   _____

   _____

   _____

   _____

   _____

8. You may have heard the common saying in many 12-step programs that the best way for one recovering person to stay clean and sober is to help someone else with their recovery. How do you think you might be helping others to maintain their sobriety by asking them to help you with your own? Identify one way you can positively contribute to another in sobriety/recovery.

   _____

   _____

Be sure to bring this handout back to your next therapy session and be prepared to talk about your thoughts and feelings about the exercise.

EXPLORING TREATMENT AND RECOVERY OPTIONS

GOALS OF THE EXERCISE

1. Restore normal sleep patterns; improve long- and short-term memory; develop more realistic perceptions, coherent communication, and focused attention; and maintain abstinence from addiction.
2. Learn the importance of working a 12-step program and maintain a program of recovery from addiction and substance-induced disorders.
3. Resolve psychiatric signs and symptoms secondary to substance abuse.
4. Effectively use available resources in personal and family recovery.
5. Reduce emotional and social isolation for self and family.
6. Augment treatment and after-care with resources that can be used indefinitely without cost.

ADDITIONAL PROBLEMS FOR WHICH THIS EXERCISE MAY BE USEFUL

*   Grief/Loss Unresolved
*   Legal Problems
*   Living Environment Deficiency
*   Medical Issues
*   Posttraumatic Stress Disorder (PTSD)
*   Self-Care Deficits—Primary
*   Self-Care Deficits—Secondary

SUGGESTIONS FOR PROCESSING THIS EXERCISE WITH THE CLIENT

The "Exploring Treatment and Recovery Options" activity is for clients who are not accustomed to asking for help or who may not know of available resources. Follow-up can include reporting on outcomes and referrals to specific community resources.

EXPLORING TREATMENT AND RECOVERY OPTIONS

Recovering from the effects of recent substance use takes time. It may be difficult to think about anything other than how you currently feel physically and mentally. Additionally, for those who have relapsed, they may feel disappointed, ashamed, and hopeless. Even at the very early stages of sobering up, it is important to assess what you need to do about your current situation and to look at the potential benefits of treatment and working toward longer-term recovery.

1. What current experiences are you having, if any, from the following list? Rate each of them in severity from 0 to 10 (0 = absent to 10 = extreme) and place an "X" next to those that are related to your use of substances/withdrawal/postacute withdrawal.

   a. Memory impairment   Rating ____ Related to substances _____

   b. Inability to focus   Rating ____ Related to substances _____

   c. Language or perceptual disturbances   Rating ____ Related to substances _____

   d. Hallucinations/delusions   Rating ____ Related to substances _____

   e. Depressed mood or euphoric mood   Rating ____ Related to substances _____

   f. Agitation, panic, obsessive thoughts   Rating ____ Related to substances _____

   g. Sleep disturbance   Rating ____ Related to substances _____

   h. Sexual dysfunction   Rating ____ Related to substances _____

   i. Other: _____

2. Look at those rated highest; outside of treatment these might result in a quick return to use. What medical, psychological, recovery strategies are in place to address them? What else do you need?

_____

_____

3. Some symptoms may improve over time but are stressful and uncomfortable. What is one thing you can do for each of the following areas: (a) increase motivation to persist, (b) increase optimism and hope that you can endure, (c) calm, soothe the stress of the discomfort, and (d) switch your focus from how you feel to how you are committed to surviving.

_____

_____

4. How could the following help you in resolving your current symptoms?

   a. Doctor, psychiatrist

   _____

   b. Partner, family

   _____

   c. Your faith

   _____

   d. Treatment/12-step support

   _____

5. If you feel like using substances or other addictive behaviors (your drug of choice or something else) to reduce the symptoms, what could you do instead?

_____

_____

6. Reevaluate symptoms daily and strategies you have in place. What is happening that is positive? Are there any areas you feel need additional attention or evaluation by a health care provider?

_____

_____

7. A variety of things work to help reduce symptoms of substance abuse, but getting through each day sober is the strongest step toward recovery you can take that day. What three things can you do today to help you stay sober and persist through the effects of a recent use?

_____

_____

Be sure to bring this handout back to your next therapy session and be prepared to talk about your thoughts and feelings about the exercise.

COPING WITH POSTACUTE WITHDRAWAL (PAW)

GOALS OF THE EXERCISE

1. Recover from substance intoxication/withdrawal and participate in a substance use disorder assessment.
2. Learn about a common syndrome in recovery from a substance use disorder, which might otherwise lead to demoralization, anxiety, and relapse.
3. Become empowered to cope with postacute withdrawal (PAW) and learn about resources and supports available for assistance.
4. Stabilize the client's condition medically, behaviorally, emotionally, and cognitively and begin to return to functioning within normal parameters.
5. Keep health care providers informed of withdrawal symptoms.
6. Comply with instructions of health care providers in coping with PAW.

ADDITIONAL PROBLEMS FOR WHICH THIS EXERCISE MAY BE USEFUL

- Depression–Unipolar
- Medical Issues
- Opioid Use Disorder
- Relapse Proneness
- Sleep Disturbance
- Substance-Induced Disorders
- Suicidal Ideation

SUGGESTIONS FOR PROCESSING THIS EXERCISE WITH THE CLIENT

The "Coping With Postacute Withdrawal" activity is intended primarily for clients who are in early recovery after long-term or heavy abuse of alcohol or barbiturates, but some of the features of PAW may be seen in users of other categories of substances as well, including opioids and stimulants. The exercise normalizes the experience of otherwise alarming persistent symptoms and relieves clients' fears that those symptoms are permanent, increasing their motivation to remain abstinent. Follow-up for this activity may include discussion of symptoms with the therapist, group, a physician, and a program sponsor; keeping a log of gradual improvement; and planning of coping strategies.

COPING WITH POSTACUTE WITHDRAWAL (PAW)

Heavy and long-term substance abuse upsets the balance in a person's body, especially in the brain. Although it may only take days or weeks for alcohol or other drugs to leave the system, this chemical balance can take months to get back to normal. This is called postacute withdrawal, or PAW. While this happens, a recovering person may continue to experience physical, mental, and emotional problems that are uncomfortable. It is important to know that although these PAW symptoms may hang on for months, they *will* keep gradually getting better if you stay clean and sober! This exercise will help you understand PAW and teach you how to get through these problems without a lapse or relapsing.

1. Some symptoms of PAW are as follows:

   _____ Difficulty thinking clearly

   _____ Problems with memory, especially short-term memory

   _____ Increased feelings of anxiety, depression, and/or irritability

   _____ Rapid mood swings that seem to happen for little or no reason (e.g., low frustration tolerance)

   _____ Emotional overreactivity or numbness

   _____ Sleep disturbances

   _____ General feelings of fatigue

   _____ Problems with physical coordination

   Have you repeatedly experienced any of these problems since you stopped using alcohol or other drugs? If so, please *check* the ones you've experienced.

2. What methods have you tried to cope with these symptoms?

   _____

   _____

3. What methods have worked best for you?

   _____

   _____

4. Your assignment is to talk with other people in recovery and ask how they have coped with PAW without returning to using/drinking. Who will you ask, and how will you ask them for this information?

_____

_____

5. Answer this question after talking with some other people about their experiences with PAW. Based on what you have found works for you and on the experiences of other people, please list five things you can do to cope with PAW if you experience the symptoms listed earlier.

   a. _____
   b. _____
   c. _____
   d. _____
   e. _____

Think about ways that address the physical experience of them, the emotional experience and the thinking troubles. Generally, it is wise to think about strategies (and use them) that you are able to do alone and those that rely on others. Consider both active strategies (physical activity if approved) and passive activity (meditation/prayer). If thoughts of return to use are present, what will you do to address them early?

Be sure to bring this handout back to your next therapy session and be prepared to talk about your thoughts and feelings about the exercise.

USING BOOKS AND OTHER MEDIA RESOURCES

GOALS OF THE EXERCISE

1. Find and effectively use media resources to help in personal and family recovery from substance dependence, abuse, and related problems.
2. Reduce shame and emotional isolation by learning that addictive issues affect many other people.
3. Increase the effectiveness of treatment and aftercare by augmenting them with resources that can be used outside of the treatment environment.

ADDITIONAL PROBLEMS FOR WHICH THIS EXERCISE MAY BE USEFUL

- Adult-Child-of-an-Alcoholic (ACA) Traits
- Anxiety
- Borderline Traits
- Childhood Trauma
- Depression—Unipolar
- Grief/Loss Unresolved
- Posttraumatic Stress Disorder (PTSD)
- Relapse Proneness
- Spiritual Confusion

SUGGESTIONS FOR PROCESSING THIS EXERCISE WITH THE CLIENT

The "Using Books and Other Media Resources" activity introduces the client to the use of media to explore personal issues. It invites the client to examine their reactions to books, movies, or songs that trigger strong feelings or seem relevant to their life issues. Follow-up may include discussion of these reactions and what insights they offer the client.

Note: It is important to co-create a safety plan with the client, teach him or her self-soothing techniques, and give them guidance on crisis coping resources and strategies to use in the event that any media resource triggers an abreaction intense enough to create the risk of relapse or self-harm. Refer to Appendix B in this manual for suggested bibliotherapy resources.

USING BOOKS AND OTHER MEDIA RESOURCES

Because they affect so many people and are important parts of every culture, the issues you are working on in treatment have inspired films, plays, TV shows, books, art, and music. In this day and age, there is social media content that is both helpful and upsetting, and we all have easy and immediate access to it, so we need to be responsible consumers. These materials can often give us useful information or inspiration, or they can move us emotionally in a powerful way that can help treatment. This exercise will help you think about how you can use some of this material to help you achieve your own goals.

1. Have you seen movies, plays, or TV series, read books, seen art, or listened to music/podcasts that dealt with issues of substance abuse, other addictive problems, or other life situations with which you identified? What was the content and what was your reaction to it?

    _____

    _____

2. How do you feel these works could help you or others overcome the problems that brought you into treatment? What content should you avoid, as it could be triggering or harmful to you at this time?

    _____

    _____

3. A basic way these materials, especially books, can be useful is by providing practical information about how your problems may have developed, obstacles and pitfalls that can endanger your recovery, guidance on actions you can take to get better, and stories of others who have succeeded to inspire you and provide examples. It is important to consider what you go looking for and what shows up without searching. Please describe any help of this kind that you've found.

    _____

    _____

4. There are a number of addiction recovery apps to support a recovery lifestyle. Some are free, others have a nominal fee. It is recommended to research them and choose ones that fit your daily recovery practice. Because most of us take our phones with us wherever we go, technology can assist in easily doing something recovery focused every day. By doing so, you will be better prepared to address triggers, cravings, PAW as they arise and stay actively focused on recovery. Many of the recovery apps have motivational content, sober tracking, inspirational quotes, daily readings; others have support group meeting features and chat functions; others have accountability checklists of activities dedicated to recovery, goal setting activities, and podcast links.

_____

Additionally, 12-step material is easily available online, and finding a meeting near your location is just clicks away.

With the help of your therapist, vet some of these resources and see which may align with your recovery and relapse prevention plan.

_____

_____

5. Talk with your therapist, and choose the first video, TV program, book, podcast, social media content, webcast, or piece of music you will use as part of your therapy. *Important note: Especially if you are in the early stages of your recovery, or if your experiences have been very painful and trigger intense emotions, don't do this without your therapist's guidance! You could expose yourself to overwhelming feelings that would put you at higher risk for relapse.* Once you and your therapist have talked it over and agreed on a plan, please watch, read, view, or listen to the creative work you've chosen, then write here about whatever emotions, thoughts, and new realizations you have.

_____

_____

Be sure to bring this handout back to your next therapy session and be prepared to talk about your thoughts and feelings about the exercise.

CONSEQUENCES OF CONTINUING ADDICTIVE LIFESTYLES

GOALS OF THE EXERCISE

1. Accept powerlessness over addictive behaviors and the accompanying unmanageability of life and participate in a recovery-based program.
2. Establish and maintain total abstinence from addictive behaviors while increasing knowledge of addiction and the process of recovery.
3. Clarify how destructive the negative consequences of substance abuse or other addictive behavior will have to get before they become too bad to tolerate without quitting.
4. Focus attention on the negative consequences of addictive behaviors for self and others.

ADDITIONAL PROBLEMS FOR WHICH THIS EXERCISE MAY BE USEFUL

- Eating Disorders and Obesity
- Gambling
- Legal Problems
- Nicotine Use/Dependence
- Occupational Problems
- Peer Group Negativity
- Readiness to Change
- Relapse Proneness
- Sexual Promiscuity

SUGGESTIONS FOR PROCESSING THIS EXERCISE WITH CLIENT

The "Consequences of Continuing Addictive Lifestyles" activity is for clients who are in denial or ambivalent about their addictive behavior(s). It aims to break down cognitive distortion. Follow-up can include bibliotherapy with personal stories from the book *Alcoholics Anonymous* or a book from another recovery program.

CONSEQUENCES OF CONTINUING ADDICTIVE LIFESTYLES

This assignment will help you see more clearly what your limits are with negative consequences of substance abuse or other addictive behaviors. Once you've finished this worksheet, it will be helpful to talk about it with your therapist, group, and/or your program sponsor and continue to reflect.

1. Identify the reason(s) you are in treatment and write about how you feel about it.

   _____

   _____

2. A *yet list* is a list of negative consequences of addiction that we know could happen, but we have not experienced *yet*. How could a yet list help you?

   _____

   _____

3. Create a yet list for drinking, using other drugs, or practicing other addictive behaviors that you can think of, which you have never experienced and would never want to. If you have a group to work with, you can have everyone brainstorm and make a shared list.

   _____

   _____

4. Now look at the list. If there are experiences you've simply escaped for reasons outside your control (e.g., not being caught when driving while impaired), what are they?

   _____

   _____

5. What experiences have you never risked when actively engaged in addictive behaviors? (e.g., if you never drive while impaired, you've never been in danger of arrest for DWI)

   _____

   _____

6. Which experiences from your list that haven't happened yet would be evidence that your behavior was unsafe or out of control?

    _____

    _____

7. The experiences you listed for question 6 are your yet list. They've happened to others but haven't happened to you yet. Since you've decided these events would mean your behavior was out of control, what will you do if one of them happens?

    _____

    _____

8. If you truly feel that the items on your yet list are unacceptable and would mean you had to quit drinking, using, gambling, or practicing some other compulsive behaviors, how do you plan to quit if one of these things happens?

    _____

    _____

9. Is there a reason to act now? How can you get started and how can others help you?

    _____

    _____

10. The fear of experiencing negatives can be motivating to want to change our using behaviors. Alternatively, thinking about the potential benefits that would result from changing our behavior tends to help us sustain motivation longer, persisting when it gets difficult. Describe the potential benefits of addressing behavior to prevent those negatives from happening.

    _____

    _____

11. Who can help you with this? It is a good idea to talk to them ahead of time, while you're calm and rational. We suggest specifically asking them how they would feel if you came to them for help. Use this space to record who you will ask for this help, when, how, and what you'll ask of them.

    _____

    _____

12. What are three things that matter most to you now? Describe how acting now to prevent likely harms would be consistent or help support them.

    _____

    _____

Be sure to bring this handout back to your next therapy session and be prepared to talk about your thoughts and feelings about the exercise.

ALTERNATIVES TO ADDICTIVE BEHAVIOR

GOALS OF THE EXERCISE

1. Establish and maintain abstinence from addictive behaviors, while increasing knowledge of the disease of addiction and the process of recovery.
2. Establish a sustained recovery, free from the abuse of mood-altering substances or other addictive behaviors.
3. Improve quality of life by participating in enjoyable activities as constructive and healthy alternatives to addictive behaviors.

ADDITIONAL PROBLEMS FOR WHICH THIS EXERCISE MAY BE USEFUL

- Chronic Pain
- Eating Disorders and Obesity
- Gambling
- Nicotine Use/Dependence
- Opioid Use Disorder
- Readiness to Change
- Self-Harm
- Substance-Induced Disorders

SUGGESTIONS FOR PROCESSING THIS EXERCISE WITH THE CLIENT

The "Alternatives to Addictive Behavior" activity is useful for clients who have a generalized pattern of avoiding or numbing, uncomfortable feelings in favor of activities that offer instant gratification or mood alteration, who are at risk for switching from one addictive behavior to another and may benefit from insight into their self-medication and awareness of more benign options. The exercise includes a cost/benefit analysis of addictive behavior, examination of underlying needs, and brainstorming other ways to meet those needs. It is important to convey that engaging in addictive behaviors was a best attempt to cope, particularly with those with significant trauma. Follow-up may include assignments to investigate groups dedicated to alternative activities (e.g., a hiking club) and a report to the therapist and/or treatment group on positive experiences.

ALTERNATIVES TO ADDICTIVE BEHAVIOR

For many people with addictive behaviors, most things they do for fun or relaxation involve drinking, using other drugs, or other addictive behaviors, with destructive consequences. Fun is a vital and necessary part of life. Nobody started engaging in addictive behaviors with an intent to develop problems with them. Learning to have a good time once sober and meeting needs in nonaddictive ways is a key part of recovery and is largely a matter of relearning. This exercise will help you identify positive ways to meet your needs and find enjoyment.

1. List the major benefits you got from drinking, other drug use, or other addictive behaviors.

   Physical   **Social**   **Mental or Emotional**

   _____   _____   _____

   _____   _____   _____

   _____   _____   _____

2. List the main drawbacks connected with these behaviors.

   Physical   **Social**   **Mental or Emotional**

   _____   _____   _____

   _____   _____   _____

   _____   _____   _____

3. List the benefits you can think of connected with abstinence from addictive behaviors.

   Physical   **Social**   **Mental or Emotional**

   _____   _____   _____

   _____   _____   _____

   _____   _____   _____

4. List any drawbacks you see connected with abstinence from these behavior patterns.

   Physical   **Social**   **Mental or Emotional**

   _____   _____   _____

   _____   _____   _____

   _____   _____   _____

5. List as many alternative ways as you can think of to get the benefits you listed for drinking, other drug use, or other addictive behaviors, but without such negative consequences.

    Physical   **Social**   **Mental or Emotional**

    _____   _____   _____

    _____   _____   _____

    _____   _____   _____

6. How will you respond to yearnings for the thrill or rush that you got from substance use or other addictive behaviors?

    _____

    _____

7. List three nondrinking/using/addictive behavior-related activities that:

    a. You enjoy:

        _____

    b. You might enjoy, but haven't tried:

        _____

    c. You've heard others talk about and are interested in:

        _____

    d. You could enjoy doing alone:

        _____

    e. You could enjoy doing with others:

        _____

8. What alternatives are available for nondrinking/using/addictive behavior-related recreation and connection with others through the 12-step program you are involved in?

    _____

    _____

9. What are the thoughts, beliefs, and perceptions you will have to challenge to try or get started trying new, or returning to previously enjoyed sober activities?

    _____

    _____

Be sure to bring this handout back to your next session with your therapist and be prepared to talk about your thoughts and feelings about the exercise.

PERSONAL RECOVERY PLANNING

GOALS OF THE EXERCISE

1. Establish sustained recovery, free from addictive behaviors, while increasing knowledge of addiction and the process of recovery.
2. Learn to think of recovery as something that involves every aspect of life and can be planned for and approached in a practical way.
3. Verbalize understanding of the need to maintain abstinence to remain free of negative legal and health consequences.
4. Create a recovery plan and a convenient list of people, groups, and techniques to lean on for support or information in times of distress.
5. Develop and articulate a concept of a higher power that is supportive to recovery.
6. Learn and demonstrate healthy social skills by developing a new peer group that is drug free and supportive of working a program of recovery.

ADDITIONAL PROBLEMS FOR WHICH THIS EXERCISE MAY BE USEFUL

- Adult-Child-of-an-Alcoholic (ACA) Traits
- Eating Disorders and Obesity
- Gambling
- Nicotine Use/Dependence
- Obsessive-Compulsive Disorder (OCD)
- Sexual Promiscuity

SUGGESTIONS FOR PROCESSING THIS EXERCISE WITH THE CLIENT

The "Personal Recovery Planning" activity is intended for clients who are at least somewhat motivated for recovery and need structure and direction. It guides clients in identifying their goals for recovery to frame planning and strengthen motivation, then walks them through several domains of life functioning and prompts them to identify supportive resources and relationships and commit to a plan to use them. Follow-up for this exercise can include Exercise 36.C, "Relapse Prevention Planning," and Exercise 24.C, "Use of Affirmations for Change"; keeping a journal; and reporting back to the therapist, treatment group, and sponsor on the outcomes of activities included in the personal recovery plan.

PERSONAL RECOVERY PLANNING

There are many ways to maintain a healthy lifestyle, free of self-defeating addictive behavior. Your recovery plan will be your creation, individualized and tailored to you, not exactly like anyone else's. It won't be a finished product when you're done, but it will give you a method to fall back on when things get difficult and confusing. You may have tried to cut back or quit addictive behavior and discovered that some methods work and some do not. Please draw on that experience as you work through this exercise. Your practice will evolve as you do.

1. When you think about recovery, what do you want to accomplish? Beyond abstinence, some goals may include self-respect and dignity, peace of mind, healthy relationships, improved health, career progress, and improved finances. Please list the three things that are most important to you, and for each, what successful result will show that you've achieved that desired outcome.

    a. _____

    b. _____

    c. _____

2. For each goal, how would a return to your addiction affect your chances of success?

    a. _____

    b. _____

    c. _____

3. For each goal, what specific warning signs will tell you if you're getting off track?

    a. _____

    b. _____

    c. _____

4. Success in recovery involves finding *things to do* that help you remain abstinent and knowing the *things not to do* because they may lead to relapse. Drawing on all you have learned and the experiences of others, please fill out the following.

    a. *Recovery activities*

        i.   What individual and/or group treatment sessions will I attend each week? When and where?

        _____

        ii. What goals will I address in treatment?

        _____

        iii. What support group meeting(s) will I attend during the week? When and where?

        _____

        iv. When, where, and for how long will I meet with my sponsor each week?

        _____

    b. *Creating a daily structure and routine*

        i.   What things will I do as part of my routine each day, and when will I do them?

        _____

        ii. Each week?

        _____

        iii. Each month?

        _____

    c. *Basic self-care.* Living compulsively, we often neglect the basics (e.g., proper nutrition, health care, adequate rest, and exercise). Building these into your life will help you cope with stress. What can you do in each of these areas to take care of yourself?

        i.   Proper nutrition:

        _____

        ii. Medical care:

        _____

        iii. Rest:

        _____

    iv. Exercise/physical activity:

_____

    v. Activities that bring joy, respite, calm:

_____

d. *Relationships and support systems.* Relationships with loved ones and friends can have a tremendous effect on recovery, either helping or hurting. You'll need to analyze past and current relationships and keep some, end some, and develop some new ones.

    i. *Old relationships.* What relationships are likely to support your recovery, and what will you do to strengthen them?

_____

    What relationships might undermine your efforts, and how will you end or distance them?

_____

    ii. *New relationships.* Where can you meet people to start some new, healthy, supportive relationships, and how will you go about finding them? What environments will give you a sense of belonging?

_____

    iii. *How you can get support from relationships.* Please list some people with whom you can talk when you feel troubled, confused, or discouraged, and write about how you will approach each of them to ask for this support.

Name	How I Will Ask for Support
_____	_____
_____	_____
_____	_____

e. *Spirituality.* Whether or not you're religious, recovery involves making changes in your values; people who include spiritual resources in recovery are usually more successful.

    i. How will I address this component of my recovery?

_____

    ii. What questions do I have about this, and whom can I ask for assistance?

_____

f. *Addressing emotional concerns.* Untreated or neglected emotional issues will likely result in relapse or return to other self-destructive behaviors. What am I doing to address these concerns?

_____

g. *Legal issues.* Dealing with the legal consequences of addictions is important to be a responsible person, to reduce long-term stress, and to gain self-respect. What am I doing to get any unfinished legal matters settled?

_____

h. *Finances.* This is another part of life with great impact on self-esteem and stress levels. Many newly recovering people are intimidated by financial problems when they get clean and sober, but with steady effort they can clear the difficulties up faster than expected.

    i. What financial problems do I have and what am I doing to resolve them?

    _____

    ii. What is my long-term plan for financial stability?

    _____

i. *Recreation.* Early recovery is a time to start having healthy fun, with activities you have enjoyed in the past or with new activities, to help you cope with stress and enjoy life.

    i. What old healthy recreational activities will I take up again?

    _____

    ii. What new activities will I try and/or am I interested in learning?

    _____

    iii. What steps will I take to incorporate this into my weekly schedule?

    _____

j. *Tests of personal control.* Offers from others, celebrations, attempts to "prove" you can handle substances and/or old hangouts challenge many people in early recovery. What is your plan to manage these tests if they present themselves?

_____

k. *Managing life stress and crisis management.* Your plan must include steps to handle crises. Please list things you'll do to handle an unexpected (or expected) crisis without relapsing into addictive behavior.

_____

5. Finally, list any high-risk situations you need to avoid because they may lead to relapse. This may mean not going to certain places, seeing some people, or engaging in particular work or recreational activities.

_____

_____

You've created a foundation on which to build and a reference that will come in handy when you're under stress and having trouble thinking clearly. By completing this exercise, you've done much of that thinking in advance. Review your motivation and hope for recovery each day. Affirm yourself daily (or more often as needed) that you deserve an improved life.

Be sure to bring this handout back to your next therapy session and be prepared to talk about your thoughts and feelings about the exercise and make modifications as needed.

TAKING DAILY INVENTORY

GOALS OF THE EXERCISE

1. Establish and maintain total abstinence from addictive behaviors, while increasing knowledge of addiction and the process of recovery.
2. Take responsibility for one's behavior and its consequences.
3. Identify patterns of thought, emotion, and behavior that pose a threat to sobriety and develop a plan of action for improvement.
4. Clarify the importance of taking inventory as part of preventing relapse.
5. Utilize behavioral and cognitive coping skills to help maintain sobriety.

ADDITIONAL PROBLEMS FOR WHICH THIS EXERCISE MAY BE USEFUL

- Antisocial Behavior
- Conduct Disorder/Delinquency
- Gambling
- Oppositional Defiant Behavior
- Readiness to Change
- Relapse Proneness
- Self-Harm

SUGGESTIONS FOR PROCESSING THIS EXERCISE WITH THE CLIENT

The "Taking Daily Inventory" activity is designed for clients who are not inclined toward introspection and need prompting to self-monitor for addictive patterns of thought, emotions, and behaviors. It highlights any drift toward addictive patterns before actual relapse occurs and is a good sequel to Exercise 36.A, "Early Warning Signs of Relapse." Additionally, self-monitoring is a useful activity. This worksheet could be assigned consistently between sessions to highlight positives and challenges in real time and brought back to sessions to process insights. Follow-up can include reporting to the therapist or treatment group about any trends that were noted by the client in daily inventories, feedback from the therapist or group about discrepancies between what the client reports and what they observe, and journaling assignments on any consistent challenges identified.

TAKING DAILY INVENTORY

Your daily emotions, attitudes, and actions move you either further into recovery or back toward addictive behavior. Checking your progress frequently is an important part of preventing relapse and staying sober. Early in sobriety, get in the habit of checking in regularly. It is strongly advised to be active in recovery efforts/practice/monitoring daily.

1. Using a scale in which 1 = low and 5 = high, score yourself daily on these items:

    Moving Further into Recovery

    Honest with self _____

    Honest with others _____

    Living for today _____

    Hopeful _____

    Active _____

    Prompt _____

    Relaxed _____

    Responsible _____

    Confident _____

    Realistic _____

    Reasonable _____

    Forgiving _____

    Trusting of others _____

    Content with self _____

    Helpful to others _____

    Active involvement in 12-step/
    faith-based/other recovery
    focused _____

    Moving Toward Relapse

    Dishonest _____

    Resentful _____

    Depressed _____

    Self-pitying _____

    Critical of self/others _____

    Procrastinating _____

    Impatient _____

    Angry _____

    Indifferent

    Guilty _____

    Anxious _____

    Ashamed _____

    Fearful _____

    Withdrawn _____

    Demanding _____

    Avoiding/minimizing12-step/
    faith-based/other recovery focused
    support _____

2. Thinking about your sobriety and recovery work yesterday, how did you improve today?

    _____

    _____

3. What roadblock(s) to recovery/progress did you identify today?

   _____

   _____

4. What, if anything, do you wish you had done differently today?

   _____

   _____

5. a. On a scale of 1 to 5, what is your level of commitment to recovery today?

   _____

   b. What can you do to reinforce your ongoing commitment to yourself today?

   _____

6. What did you learn about yourself today that you can use to assist continued progress forward?

   _____

   _____

7. If you began working on any new change today, what was that change?

   _____

   _____

8. Please look at your *Moving Toward Relapse* scores from question 1 and describe one concrete strategy to decrease your risk of relapse and increase your chances of staying in recovery.

   _____

   _____

Be sure to bring this handout back to your next session with your therapist and be prepared to talk about your thoughts and feelings about the exercise.

MAKING CHANGE HAPPEN

GOALS OF THE EXERCISE

1. Acquire the necessary skills to maintain long-term recovery from all addictive behaviors.
2. Strengthen motivation for change by identifying areas of life affected by drinking, other drug use, or other addictive behaviors, and identify alternatives available in recovery.

ADDITIONAL PROBLEMS FOR WHICH THIS EXERCISE MAY BE USEFUL

- Eating Disorders and Obesity
- Gambling
- Nicotine Use/Dependence
- Relapse Proneness
- Self-Harm
- Sexual Promiscuity

SUGGESTIONS FOR PROCESSING THIS EXERCISE WITH THE CLIENT

The "Making Change Happen" exercise can be used with a client who is entering treatment for the first or fifth time. It can be used with clients in any stage of recovery when motivation wanes, self-doubt increases, or relapse indicators surface. Before assigning this exercise, it is helpful to educate clients about the process of change and explain that the purpose of this activity is to help them see where they are in this process. Follow-up can include regular check-ins to track both progress and motivation and to continue educating the client about the process of change.

MAKING CHANGE HAPPEN

Substance use and other behaviors to which we can get addicted begin for one reason and continue for others. The same is true of other, more positive changes we decide to make in our lives—sometimes the reasons we decide to enter treatment will change along the way, and we continue in recovery for other reasons. People working to overcome addictions often go to professionals to find help and support for other changes too. This exercise will help you get a clear picture of where you've been, where you are, and where you want to go, as well as how to get there. After completing this exercise, you and your therapist may find it useful to go on to Exercises 47.C "Personal Recovery Planning," 36.C "Relapse Prevention Planning," and 24.C "Use of Affirmations for Change," which will help you continue defining how to get where you want to go and active engagement in behavior that furthers recovery.

1. Please identify the psychological factors that led you to use alcohol, other drugs, or other addictive behaviors (e.g., coping with physical or emotional pain, avoidance of problems, attempts to feel normal, pleasure-seeking).

    _____

    _____

2. Please list the social, cultural, and environmental reasons for your engaging in addictive behaviors (e.g., family norms, family history, availability of the drugs, activities, acceptability of use among people close to you, use among your peer group).

    _____

    _____

3. Please describe the progression of your addiction from experimentation to dependence. What did you notice along the way? Identify any breaks or attempts at sobriety? Losses? Other substance use or addictive behavior? Trauma?

    _____

    _____

4. If you've made attempts to quit, reduce, moderate, what were the reasons you went back to the addictive behavior(s)?

    _____

    _____

5. How have each of the following life areas been affected by your addictive behavior?

    a. Physical health: _____

    b. Emotional health: _____

    c. Social: _____

    d. Educational/career: _____

    e. Legal: _____

    f. Financial: _____

    g. Relationships/family: _____

    h. Spiritual: _____

    i. Self-image and self-esteem: _____

6. As you think over your history, what factors do you think helped maintain your addiction?

    _____

    _____

7. What is your motivation for seeking treatment now? What do you hope for this time around?

    _____

    _____

    a. What increases your motivation? _____

    b. What challenges it? _____

    c. What fears do you have right now about your treatment and recovery?

        _____

8. If you've tried to quit before either on your own or through treatment, what have you learned from those attempts that can help you in treatment this time?

    _____

    _____

    _____

9. How will the items in question 5 be addressed in this change plan?

    _____

    _____

10. What encouraging, compassionate words can you say to yourself to support motivation and commitment to change? With your therapist, please identify a primary area of your life where you will begin working for change, and plan what behavioral steps you will take to address that area. Be sure to write about what factors will help increase your motivation and what potential barriers could decrease it.

    _____

    _____

    As you begin and work through your change plan, there will be discoveries. Leave room for lessons of what to do more of and what to modify.

11. Regarding work, this may be easier than you think. Most people with addictions are excellent workers when they are clean and sober, and they often find they expect more of themselves than anyone else would ask of them. The chances are that your supervisor already knows about your problem, or at least knows you had some serious problem affecting your work. If you explain what you are doing now to overcome the problem, your supervisor may be supportive. And you might not have to push as hard as you think to regain your good standing on the job, if you follow through. List some people who can help you prepare to talk with your supervisor about your recovery and what you need to do to take care of yourself.

    _____

    _____

    Be sure to bring this handout back to your next therapy session and be prepared to talk about your thoughts and feelings about the exercise.

BALANCING RECOVERY, FAMILY, AND WORK

GOALS OF THE EXERCISE

1. Establish a sustained recovery, free of addictive behaviors.
2. Reduce potential family tension and conflicts in early recovery.
3. Avoid work-related difficulties undermining early sobriety.

ADDITIONAL PROBLEMS FOR WHICH THIS EXERCISE MAY BE USEFUL

- Adult-Child-of-an-Alcoholic (ACA) Traits
- Family Conflicts
- Occupational Problems
- Parent–Child Relational Problem
- Partner Relational Conflicts
- Relapse Proneness

SUGGESTIONS FOR PROCESSING THIS EXERCISE WITH THE CLIENT

The "Balancing Recovery, Family, and Work" activity is designed for clients who are experiencing stress or conflicts in their families, their work, or both due to the demands of early recovery. Its aim is (a) to normalize this experience and help clients see that this is not a failing on their part, (b) to identify and explore in therapy specific issues that often arise, and (c) to provide strategies for addressing these issues. Follow-up can include family therapy and keeping a journal.

BALANCING RECOVERY, FAMILY, AND WORK

An important part of recovery is balance in our lives. One key characteristic of an addictive lifestyle is lack of balance and a tendency to either go overboard or fail to do enough. Three important parts of our lives are (a) recovery activities, (b) family life, and (c) work life. At times, we may find them in conflict, and by trying to do all we feel we should in one area, we may neglect the others. This may make balance hard to achieve.

1. What are some ways in which you went overboard and did too much in your life before you began your recovery? What fueled this drive?

    _____

    _____

2. What are some aspects of your life that you neglected before recovery?

    _____

    _____

3. We often go to extremes in recovery programs too, especially in our early sobriety. If you have seen this in your life, what tells you you're going overboard?

    _____

    _____

4. Because we may have neglected our families, we may go overboard with them too. This can cause problems, because they may have gotten used to getting along without much help from us, and now we feel they're shutting us out. On the other hand, our families may feel we continue to neglect them to spend time with our newfound friends and activities in recovery. There may be some truth to this, as some of us get so absorbed in rebuilding our lives at work and in our recovery programs that we still have trouble finding time for our families. If things have gone either way with your family life, please describe how it's out of balance.

    _____

    _____

5. With work, too, it's easy to get carried away. It can be a major source of satisfaction and self-esteem. We want to repair our reputations or make up for lost time or don't yet know how to moderate; we may also fall into workaholism, a pattern in which we lose

ourselves in work the way we used to lose ourselves in drinking, drugging, or other addictions. If this happens, we may find we feel we need to put so much into work that we resent the demands of both our families and our recovery programs. If you see signs of workaholism in your life, what can you do to keep within healthy, moderate limits?

_____

_____

6. What will you do to deal with the stress related to work—the demands, setting limits, not overworking?

_____

_____

7. Our families are among those who know us best, but they may be too emotionally involved to see clearly how we are doing. The more they understand about what we are doing, the more helpful their feedback will be and the more likely they are to be supportive. What parts don't your loved ones understand? What do you need to communicate more clearly about your work life? What do you want them to understand?

_____

_____

8. We may see that our family members could also benefit from 12-step work, in a support group such as Al-Anon or Alateen. However, they might feel they've been doing a better job of dealing with life than we have and resent our seeming to tell them what they need to do. Often, our families stay angry or mistrustful of us for a long time after we begin recovery, and they may be skeptical about any aspect of that recovery, including 12-step groups. It's best not to be pushy. Here are ways many people have helped family and friends understand their recovery programs:

   a. Ask them to come to meetings with you and explain that you need their help to recover and want them involved as much as that is possible and helpful.

   b. Introduce them to friends from the program, especially your sponsor.

   c. Take them to program social functions.

   d. Share program literature.

   e. Tell them about meetings, specifically about how they helped.

   f. Introduce them to family members of other members of the program.

   If for a while they don't seem to understand, believe, or appreciate the change in you, be patient. List some people who might be able to help you in helping your family and friends to understand your 12-step program and the time and commitment you need to recover.

_____

_____

9.   Regarding work, this may be easier than you think. Most people with addictions are excellent workers when they are clean and sober, and they often find they expect more of themselves than anyone else would ask of them. The chances are that your supervisor already knows about your problem, or at least knows you had some serious problem affecting your work. If you explain what you are doing now to overcome the problem, your supervisor may be supportive. And you might not have to push as hard as you think to regain your good standing on the job, if you follow through. List some people who can help you prepare to talk with your supervisor about your recovery and what you need to do to take care of yourself.

_____

_____

Be sure to bring this handout back to your next therapy session and be prepared to talk about your thoughts and feelings about the exercise.

PROBLEM SOLVING AND SAFETY PLANNING

GOALS OF THE EXERCISE

1. Understand the relationship between suicidal ideation and addiction.
2. Identify the impact of substance abuse or other addictions on life goals.
3. Terminate all suicidal urges, express hope for the future, and remain abstinent from all nonprescribed mood-altering substances.
4. Identify strategies to get them through a suicidal crisis without acting in self-destructive ways.
5. Develop a sense of one's worth to other addicts and family members.

ADDITIONAL PROBLEMS FOR WHICH THIS EXERCISE MAY BE USEFUL

- Adult-Child-of-an-Alcoholic (ACA) Traits
- Borderline Traits
- Depression–Unipolar
- Relapse Proneness
- Sexual Abuse

SUGGESTIONS FOR PROCESSING THIS EXERCISE WITH THE CLIENT

The "Problem Solving and Safety Planning" activity is intended to strengthen the client's motivation for treatment, decrease suicidal risk, increase hope, and instill a sense that the problems they perceive as unsolvable actually have solutions. This assignment should be assigned only after the client's suicide risk and potential need for hospitalization have been thoroughly assessed. This assignment begins with increasing the client's recognition of ways they have successfully managed problems and then identifies additional alternatives. It asks clients to identify ways they may reinforce hopelessness themselves and asks them to identify alternatives to break that cycle. Lastly, it asks clients to identify support people and three reasons to persist. Any identified suicidal ideation warrants assessment, safety planning, and ongoing monitoring. Loss, hopelessness, co-occurring mental health disorders, return to use, impulsivity in both adolescents and adults is critical to include in safety planning.

PROBLEM SOLVING AND SAFETY PLANNING

Substance abuse, chronic relapse, depression, anxiety/agitation, unresolved grief, and other significant concerns can result in our feeling worthless and hopeless. We may convince ourselves that our lives don't matter or that our problems will never be resolved and that there is no point in living. Sometimes discomfort is overwhelming. Sudden stress often triggers thoughts about suicide, but other times it can be a gradual accumulation of stressors. Both situations can lead people to view their death as the only solution. This exercise will walk you through alternate ways to cope, as well as using coping strategies you've used before. Additionally, the exercise will ask you to create some safety measures, so if you need them, you've already thought them through.

1. We all grew up learning ways to solve problems from role models and experience. Using addictive behaviors, self-harm, or contemplating suicide may have been ways we learned to react to stress. There are other more constructive methods. Please list three situations in which you solved challenging problems in a healthy way and achieved your goals:

    _____

    _____

2. From this list of skills and traits, *check* the ones you used in those situations:

    _____ Asked for help

    _____ Attended to details

    _____ Decisiveness

    _____ Exercised persistence and patience

    _____ Brainstormed—generated lots of ideas and then picked out the best ones

    _____ Broke a big problem down into small steps

    _____ Explained and taught things to others

    _____ Flexibility

    _____ Humor

    _____ Learned by watching others

    _____ Listened carefully, took notes, and followed instructions

    _____ Negotiated

_____ Open-minded thinking

_____ Organized/worked with other people

_____ Planned use of time

_____ Practiced a difficult task until it became easy

_____ Practiced an easy task, then worked up to harder ones

_____ Recognized patterns

_____ Researched needed info (e.g., asking people, using books, the Internet)

_____ Trial and error

3. How can you use these skills when you feel discouraged, helpless, or as if there are no solutions to the difficulties with your mood and/or substance use?

_____

_____

Sometimes we can do nothing until the distress passes; how can I improve my ability to tolerate distress?

_____

_____

4. In addition to those skills and traits, you may have skills and strengths that can help you in recovery:
    -   *Communication skills*: Ask for help until you get what you need.
    -   *Determination*: Keep at it; don't give up.
    -   *Sense of humor*: Being able to laugh with others; playfulness; lightheartedness
    -   *Spirituality*: Stay clear on your values; use your faith; improve your relationship with your higher power; connect with someone who can help.
    -   *12-step support*: Read the Promises (on pages 83–84) in the Big Book.
    -   *Get out of yourself*: Help others because it changes our focus.
    -   *Rely on others*: Whatever problems you've faced or will face, someone else has faced them too; if they succeeded, so can you. Find out what they did.

    Think about something you worry a great deal about or the hardest part of staying sober. Plan how you could use these methods and qualities to tackle it.

_____

_____

5. Monitor your thoughts. What negative messages do you think to yourself that reinforce your self-doubt, your feelings of worthlessness, hopelessness, helplessness, and your suicidal thoughts?

_____

_____

6. Write a positive replacement thought for each negative in question 5 that is more supportive of recovery, your ability to persevere, your worthiness, etc. If you need assistance, ask your therapist or the group to help you.

   _____

   _____

7. Identify three people you can ask for help and one way each can help you. Share it with them and commit to seeking them out if you need them.

   _____

   _____

8. State three reasons for living your life in recovery.

   _____

   _____

9. What affirmation can you utilize to encourage, be gentle, remember who relies on you, the reasons you're working so hard, why your life matters?

   _____

   _____

   Be sure to bring this handout back to your next therapy session and be prepared to talk about your thoughts and feelings about the exercise.

WHY DO I MATTER AND WHO CARES?

GOALS OF THE EXERCISE

1. Accurately assess one's importance in other people's lives.
2. Examine evidence in others' behavior to identify caring and concern.
3. Create a plan to identify concerned others and reach out for their emotional support.
4. Resolve preoccupation with death, find new hope, and eliminate addictive or suicidal thought/behaviors.
5. Develop a sense of worth to other addicts and family members.

ADDITIONAL PROBLEMS FOR WHICH THIS EXERCISE MAY BE USEFUL

- Borderline Traits
- Depression–Unipolar
- Posttraumatic Stress Disorder (PTSD)
- Relapse Proneness
- Self-Harm
- Sexual Abuse

SUGGESTIONS FOR PROCESSING THIS EXERCISE WITH THE CLIENT

The "Why Do I Matter and Who Cares?" activity is aimed at clients who are at risk for suicidal gestures or attempts and at others who are suffering from interpersonal isolation and feelings of worthlessness. It leads clients to correct distorted perceptions of their worth by having them survey situations in which they are valued. It includes an assessment of actions by others indicating that they care about the client and creation of a safety plan the client will use to reach out for support. *Any expression of suicidal ideation should be thoroughly assessed; this is not a replacement for that assessment. Acute suicidality is an emergency.* This exercise is suitable for individual or group use, in session, or as homework. Follow-up can include keeping a journal and reporting to the therapist and group on outcomes of plans developed in this exercise.

WHY DO I MATTER AND WHO CARES?

When we are experiencing depression, we often feel worthless. We may become convinced that our lives don't matter, that no one understands or cares how we feel, or that others would be better off without us. These feelings and perceptions are symptoms of depression, but they are distorted and can be dangerous. This exercise will help you get a true picture that your life matters and others truly care about you, and help you create a plan to form stronger connections with people to whom you are important and get their emotional support.

1. First, think of things that others have done for you that have been helpful and important in your life. These others may have been family members, friends, teachers, faith leaders, employers, team coaches, or anyone else who has really helped you along the way. Please give three examples, describing who they were, what they did for you, and why it mattered to you.

    _____

    _____

2. Now reflect on whether you've done similar things for others. Name three people whose lives you've touched in a good way and describe what you did.

    _____

    _____

3. What do you think these people would say if someone asked them whether your life is important to them?

    _____

    _____

4. Ask three other people (friends or family members) the following question, and record their responses here: "If I were going to do something to help other people, what are some abilities I have or things I could do that would be helpful, and who could I help?"

    _____

    _____

5. Please use this space to create a simple plan to start doing one thing for other people during the next 2 weeks, either based on a suggestion in response to question 4 or to another idea.

    _____

    _____

6. Who do you believe really understands you and cares about your feelings?

    _____

    _____

7. Please think of a wise and caring person. This may be someone you see in meetings, or in your faith community, or in another setting who seems to have a lot of similar life experiences. It's best to choose a person, like a program sponsor, for whom you feel respect but no romantic attraction. Your task during the next week is to approach this person and tell them that you would like to talk and get some feedback on issues you're working on. Set a time and place when you can talk for at least an hour without interruptions. When you talk, tell this person about what's happening in your life and how you feel about it, and ask whether they have ever felt the same way. Record the other person's responses and how you felt after the conversation here.

    _____

8. People in recovery can relate to feeling worthless, ashamed, helpless, hopeless at times in their lives. The last part of this assignment is to create a plan to reach out for emotional support when you need it, as we all do sometimes. Please list five people you can talk to if you are feeling troubled, confused, or discouraged, and write about how you will approach each of them, in advance, to ask for this support.

Name	How I Will Ask for Support
_____	_____
_____	_____
_____	_____
_____	_____
_____	_____

9. What ways could a higher power assist you in overcoming the problem of suicidal thinking, hopelessness, and feeling as if you do not matter to others? You may have heard others in 12-step meetings or your group treatment sessions talk about this. What have they said is one way you can challenge your own self-talk about not mattering?

    _____

    Be sure to bring this handout back to your next therapy session and be prepared to talk about your thoughts and feelings about the exercise.

APPENDIX A:
ALTERNATE ASSIGNMENTS FOR PRESENTING PROBLEMS

ADULT-CHILD-OF-AN-ALCOHOLIC (ACA) TRAITS

Borderline Traits	Forming Stable Relationships
Borderline Traits	Seeing That We're All Just Human
Childhood Trauma	Corresponding With My Childhood Self
Childhood Trauma	Setting and Maintaining Boundaries
Dependent Traits	Building My Support Network
Depression–Unipolar	Gratitude
Family Conflicts	Creating Positive Family Rituals
Family Conflicts	Identifying Conflict Themes
Grief/Loss Unresolved	What Would They Want for Me?
Living Environment Deficiency	Assessing My Environment
Nicotine Use/Dependence	Use of Affirmations for Change
Parent–Child Relational Problem	Am I Teaching My Child Addictive Patterns?
Parent–Child Relational Problem	What Do I Want for My Children?
Partner Relational Conflicts	Communication Skills
Partner Relational Conflicts	Relationship Assessment
Posttraumatic Stress Disorder (PTSD)	Coping with Addiction and PTSD
Self-Harm	Understanding Self-Harm and Addiction
Sexual Abuse	Internal and External Resources for Safety
Sexual Abuse	It Wasn't My Fault
Sexual Promiscuity	Is It Romance or Is It Fear?
Sexual Promiscuity	Working Through Shame
Spiritual Confusion	Finding a Higher Power That Makes Sense
Substance-Induced Disorders	Using My Support Network
Substance Intoxication/Withdrawal	Using Books and Other Media Resources
Substance Use Disorders	Balancing Recovery, Family, and Work
Substance Use Disorders	Personal Recovery Planning
Suicidal Ideation	Problem Solving and Safety Planning

ANGER

Attention-Deficit/Hyperactivity Disorder (ADHD)—Adult	Self-Soothing: Calm Down, Slow Down
Conduct Disorder/Delinquency	How Do You Do That?
Conduct Disorder/Delinquency	Trading Places
Dangerousness/Lethality	Anger as a Drug
Dangerousness/Lethality	Managing Risk
Depression–Unipolar	Correcting Distorted Thinking
Family Conflicts	Identifying Conflict Themes
Impulsivity	Learning to Think Things Through
Occupational Problems	Workplace Problems and Solutions
Oppositional Defiant Behavior	Analyzing Acting-Out Behavior
Parent–Child Relational Problem	What Do I Want for My Children?
Partner Relational Conflicts	Communication Skills
Posttraumatic Stress Disorder (PTSD)	Coping with Addiction and PTSD
Social Anxiety	Action Plan to Address Social Anxiety

ANTISOCIAL BEHAVIOR

Anger	Is My Anger Due to Unmet Expectations?
Conduct Disorder/Delinquency	How Do You Do That?
Conduct Disorder/Delinquency	Trading Places
Dangerousness/Lethality	Anger as a Drug
Dangerousness/Lethality	Managing Risk
Gambling	Consequences and Benefits
Legal Problems	Handling Tough Situations in a Healthy Way
Legal Problems	What's Addiction Got to Do with My Problems?
Narcissistic Traits	Being Genuinely Unselfish
Narcissistic Traits	Getting Out of Myself
Occupational Problems	Workplace Problems and Solutions
Oppositional Defiant Behavior	Analyzing Acting-Out Behavior
Substance Use Disorders	Taking Daily Inventory

ANXIETY

Attention-Deficit/Hyperactivity Disorder (ADHD)—Adult	Self-Soothing: Calm Down, Slow Down
Depression–Unipolar	Correcting Distorted Thinking
Depression–Unipolar	Gratitude
Obsessive-Compulsive Disorder (OCD)	Interrupting Compulsive Thoughts and Urges
Obsessive-Compulsive Disorder (OCD)	Reducing Compulsive Behaviors
Posttraumatic Stress Disorder (PTSD)	Coping with Addiction and PTSD
Posttraumatic Stress Disorder (PTSD)	Safe and Peaceful Place Meditation
Self-Harm	Self-Harm Risk Factors, Triggers, and Early Warning Signs
Self-Harm	Understanding Self-Harm and Addiction
Sleep Disturbance	Assessing Sleep Problems
Sleep Disturbance	Improving Sleep Hygiene
Social Anxiety	Action Plan to Address Social Anxiety
Social Anxiety	Understanding Thoughts, Worries, and Fears
Substance Intoxication/Withdrawal	Using Books and Other Media Resources

ATTENTION-DEFICIT/HYPERACTIVITY DISORDER (ADHD)—ADOLESCENT

Anger	Is My Anger Due to Unmet Expectations?
Antisocial Behavior	Benefits of Helping Others
Antisocial Behavior	Taking Inventory of Destructive Behaviors
Attention-Deficit/Hyperactivity Disorder (ADHD)—Adult	From Recklessness to Calculated Risks
Attention-Deficit/Hyperactivity Disorder (ADHD)—Adult	Getting Organized
Conduct Disorder/Delinquency	Trading Places
Impulsivity	Handling Crisis Without Impulsivity
Impulsivity	Learning to Think Things Through
Occupational Problems	Interest and Skill Self-Assessment
Oppositional Defiant Behavior	Analyzing Acting-Out Behavior
Oppositional Defiant Behavior	Learning to Ask Instead of Demand
Peer Group Negativity	Creating Recovery Peer Support
Peer Group Negativity	What Do I Need and How Do I Get It?
Posttraumatic Stress Disorder (PTSD)	Safe and Peaceful Place Meditation

ATTENTION-DEFICIT/HYPERACTIVITY DISORDER (ADHD)—ADULT

Anger	Is My Anger Due to Unmet Expectations?
Antisocial Behavior	Benefits of Helping Others
Antisocial Behavior	Taking Inventory of Destructive Behaviors
Attention-Deficit/Hyperactivity Disorder (ADHD)—Adolescent	Developing a Recovery Program
Attention-Deficit/Hyperactivity Disorder (ADHD)—Adolescent	Staying Attentive and Other Negotiating Skills
Conduct Disorder/Delinquency	How Do You Do That?
Conduct Disorder/Delinquency	Trading Places
Impulsivity	Handling Crisis Without Impulsivity
Impulsivity	Learning to Think Things Through
Occupational Problems	Interest and Skill Self-Assessment
Oppositional Defiant Behavior	Analyzing Acting-Out Behavior
Oppositional Defiant Behavior	Learning to Ask Instead of Demand
Peer Group Negativity	Creating Recovery Peer Support
Peer Group Negativity	What Do I Need and How Do I Get It?
Posttraumatic Stress Disorder (PTSD)	Safe and Peaceful Place Meditation
Self-Care Deficits—Secondary	Working Toward Interdependence

BIPOLAR DISORDER

Attention-Deficit/Hyperactivity Disorder (ADHD)—Adult	From Recklessness to Calculated Risks
Impulsivity	Handling Crisis Without Impulsivity
Living Environment Deficiency	Assessing My Environment
Obsessive-Compulsive Disorder (OCD)	Interrupting Compulsive Thoughts and Urges
Obsessive-Compulsive Disorder (OCD)	Reducing Compulsive Behaviors
Psychosis	Coping with Addiction and Schizophrenia Spectrum Disorders
Psychosis	Planning a Stable Life
Self-Care Deficits—Primary	Assessing Self-Care Deficits
Self-Care Deficits—Primary	Relating Self-Care Deficits to My Addiction

BORDERLINE TRAITS

Adult-Child-of-an-Alcoholic (ACA) Traits	Addressing ACA Traits in Recovery
Adult-Child-of-an-Alcoholic (ACA) Traits	Understanding Family History
Anger	Is My Anger Due to Unmet Expectations?
Attention-Deficit/Hyperactivity Disorder (ADHD)—Adult	Self-Soothing: Calm Down, Slow Down
Childhood Trauma	Setting and Maintaining Boundaries
Depression–Unipolar	Correcting Distorted Thinking
Eating Disorders and Obesity	Creating a Preliminary Eating and Health Plan
Eating Disorders and Obesity	Eating Patterns Self-Assessment
Grief/Loss Unresolved	Am I Having Difficulty Letting Go?
Grief/Loss Unresolved	What Would They Want for Me?
Impulsivity	Handling Crisis Without Impulsivity
Impulsivity	Learning to Think Things Through
Medical Issues	Physical and Emotional Self-Care
Nicotine Use/Dependence	Use of Affirmations for Change
Obsessive-Compulsive Disorder (OCD)	Interrupting Compulsive Thoughts and Urges
Obsessive-Compulsive Disorder (OCD)	Reducing Compulsive Behaviors
Occupational Problems	Workplace Problems and Solutions
Parent–Child Relational Problem	Am I Teaching My Child Addictive Patterns?
Parent–Child Relational Problem	What Do I Want for My Children?
Partner Relational Conflicts	Communication Skills
Partner Relational Conflicts	Relationship Assessment
Posttraumatic Stress Disorder (PTSD)	Coping with Addiction and PTSD
Posttraumatic Stress Disorder (PTSD)	Safe and Peaceful Place Meditation
Self-Harm	Self-Harm Risk Factors, Triggers, and Early Warning Signs
Self-Harm	Understanding Self-Harm and Addiction
Sexual Abuse	Internal and External Resources for Safety
Sexual Abuse	It Wasn't My Fault
Sexual Promiscuity	Is It Romance or Is It Fear?
Sexual Promiscuity	Working Through Shame
Social Anxiety	Understanding Thoughts, Worries, and Fears
Substance Intoxication/Withdrawal	Using Books and Other Media Resources
Suicidal Ideation	Problem Solving and Safety Planning
Suicidal Ideation	Why Do I Matter and Who Cares?

CHILDHOOD TRAUMA

Adult-Child-of-an-Alcoholic (ACA) Traits	Understanding Family History
Anxiety	Anxiety Triggers and Warning Signs
Anxiety	Coping with Stress
Family Conflicts	Creating Positive Family Rituals
Family Conflicts	Identifying Conflict Themes
Grief/Loss Unresolved	Am I Having Difficulty Letting Go?
Grief/Loss Unresolved	Moving on After Loss
Parent-Child Relational Problem	Am I Teaching My Child Addictive Patterns?
Parent-Child Relational Problem	What Do I Want for My Children?
Posttraumatic Stress Disorder (PTSD)	Coping With Addiction and PTSD
Posttraumatic Stress Disorder (PTSD)	Safe and Peaceful Place Meditation
Sexual Abuse	Internal and External Resources for Safety
Sexual Abuse	It Wasn't My Fault
Sexual Promiscuity	Working Through Shame
Spiritual Confusion	Finding a Higher Power That Makes Sense
Substance Intoxication/Withdrawal	Using Books and Other Media Resources

CHRONIC PAIN

Anxiety	Anxiety Triggers and Warning Signs
Anxiety	Coping with Stress
Attention-Deficit/Hyperactivity Disorder (ADHD)—Adult	Self-Soothing: Calm Down, Slow Down
Dependent Traits	Building My Support Network
Depression–Unipolar	Gratitude
Medical Issues	Coping with Addiction and Other Medical Problems
Medical Issues	Physical and Emotional Self-Care
Nicotine Use/Dependence	Use of Affirmations for Change
Posttraumatic Stress Disorder (PTSD)	Safe and Peaceful Place Meditation
Self-Care Deficits—Primary	Assessing Self-Care Deficits
Sleep Disturbance	Assessing Sleep Problems
Sleep Disturbance	Improving Sleep Hygiene
Substance-Induced Disorders	Using My Support Network
Substance Use Disorders	Alternatives to Addictive Behavior

CONDUCT DISORDER/DELINQUENCY

Anger	Is My Anger Due to Feeling Threatened?
Antisocial Behavior	Benefits of Helping Others
Antisocial Behavior	Taking Inventory of Destructive Behaviors
Attention-Deficit/Hyperactivity Disorder (ADHD)—Adolescent	Developing a Recovery Program
Attention-Deficit/Hyperactivity Disorder (ADHD)—Adult	From Recklessness to Calculated Risks
Dangerousness/Lethality	Anger as a Drug
Family Conflicts	Creating Positive Family Rituals
Impulsivity	Learning to Think Things Through
Legal Problems	Handling Tough Situations in a Healthy Way
Legal Problems	What's Addiction Got to Do with My Problems?
Narcissistic Traits	Being Genuinely Unselfish
Narcissistic Traits	Getting Out of Myself
Peer Group Negativity	Creating Recovery Peer Support
Peer Group Negativity	What Do I Need and How Do I Get It?
Substance Use Disorders	Taking Daily Inventory

DANGEROUSNESS/LETHALITY

Anger	Is My Anger Due to Feeling Threatened?
Anger	Is My Anger Due to Unmet Expectations?
Bipolar Disorder	Early Warning Signs of Mania/Hypomania
Childhood Trauma	Setting and Maintaining Boundaries
Conduct Disorder/Delinquency	How Do You Do That?
Conduct Disorder/Delinquency	Trading Places
Depression–Unipolar	Correcting Distorted Thinking
Family Conflicts	Identifying Conflict Themes
Impulsivity	Learning to Think Things Through
Oppositional Defiant Behavior	Analyzing Acting-Out Behavior

DEPENDENT TRAITS

Adult-Child-of-an-Alcoholic (ACA) Traits	Addressing ACA Traits in Recovery
Borderline Traits	Forming Stable Relationships

Borderline Traits	Seeing That We're All Just Human
Childhood Trauma	Setting and Maintaining Boundaries
Depression–Unipolar	Correcting Distorted Thinking
Grief/Loss Unresolved	Am I Having Difficulty Letting Go?
Occupational Problems	Interest and Skill Self-Assessment
Parent–Child Relational Problem	Am I Teaching My Child Addictive Patterns?
Partner Relational Conflicts	Relationship Assessment
Peer Group Negativity	Creating Recovery Peer Support
Peer Group Negativity	What Do I Need and How Do I Get It?
Self-Care Deficits—Secondary	Working Toward Interdependence
Sexual Promiscuity	Is It Romance or Is It Fear?
Social Anxiety	Understanding Thoughts, Worries, and Fears
Substance-Induced Disorders	Using My Support Network

DEPRESSION–UNIPOLAR

Bipolar Disorder	Mania, Addiction, and Recovery
Dependent Traits	Building My Support Network
Grief/Loss Unresolved	Am I Having Difficulty Letting Go?
Grief/Loss Unresolved	Moving on After Loss
Living Environment Deficiency	Assessing My Environment
Living Environment Deficiency	What Would My Ideal Life Look Like?
Medical Issues	Physical and Emotional Self-Care
Narcissistic Traits	Getting Out of Myself
Nicotine Use/Dependence	Use of Affirmations for Change
Obsessive-Compulsive Disorder (OCD)	Interrupting Compulsive Thoughts and Urges
Obsessive-Compulsive Disorder (OCD)	Reducing Compulsive Behaviors
Occupational Problems	Interest and Skill Self-Assessment
Posttraumatic Stress Disorder (PTSD)	Coping with Addiction and PTSD
Psychosis	Coping with Addiction and Schizophrenia Spectrum Disorders
Psychosis	Planning a Stable Life
Self-Care Deficits—Primary	Assessing Self-Care Deficits
Self-Care Deficits—Primary	Relating Self-Care Deficits to My Addiction
Self-Harm	Self-Harm Risk Factors, Triggers, and Early Warning Signs

Self-Harm	Understanding Self-Harm and Addiction
Sleep Disturbance	Assessing Sleep Problems
Sleep Disturbance	Improving Sleep Hygiene
Substance Intoxication/Withdrawal	Coping with Postacute Withdrawal (PAW)
Substance Intoxication/Withdrawal	Using Books and Other Media Resources
Suicidal Ideation	Problem Solving and Safety Planning
Suicidal Ideation	Why Do I Matter and Who Cares?

EATING DISORDERS AND OBESITY

Anxiety	Anxiety Triggers and Warning Signs
Attention-Deficit/Hyperactivity Disorder (ADHD)—Adult	Self-Soothing: Calm Down, Slow Down
Childhood Trauma	Setting and Maintaining Boundaries
Medical Issues	Physical and Emotional Self-Care
Obsessive-Compulsive Disorder (OCD)	Interrupting Compulsive Thoughts and Urges
Obsessive-Compulsive Disorder (OCD)	Reducing Compulsive Behaviors
Readiness to Change	Addressing Readiness and Motivation
Relapse Proneness	Early Warning Signs of Relapse
Relapse Proneness	Identifying Relapse Triggers and Cues
Relapse Proneness	Relapse Prevention Planning
Sexual Abuse	Internal and External Resources for Safety
Sexual Abuse	It Wasn't My Fault
Sleep Disturbance	Assessing Sleep Problems
Sleep Disturbance	Improving Sleep Hygiene
Social Anxiety	Action Plan to Address Social Anxiety
Substance Use Disorders	Alternatives to Addictive Behavior
Substance Use Disorders	Consequences of Continuing Addictive Lifestyles
Substance Use Disorders	Making Change Happen
Substance Use Disorders	Personal Recovery Planning

FAMILY CONFLICTS

| Adult-Child-of-an-Alcoholic (ACA) Traits | Understanding Family History |
| Anger | Is My Anger Due to Unmet Expectations? |

Oppositional Defiant Behavior	Learning to Ask Instead of Demand
Parent–Child Relational Problem	Am I Teaching My Child Addictive Patterns?
Parent–Child Relational Problem	What Do I Want for My Children?
Partner Relational Conflicts	Communication Skills
Partner Relational Conflicts	Relationship Assessment
Sexual Abuse	Internal and External Resources for Safety
Sexual Abuse	It Wasn't My Fault
Substance Use Disorders	Balancing Recovery, Family, and Work

GAMBLING

Anxiety	Coping with Stress
Nicotine Use/Dependence	Use of Affirmations for Change
Obsessive-Compulsive Disorder (OCD)	Interrupting Compulsive Thoughts and Urges
Readiness to Change	Addressing Readiness and Motivation
Readiness to Change	Problem Identification: Is It Addiction?
Relapse Proneness	Early Warning Signs of Relapse
Relapse Proneness	Identifying Relapse Triggers and Cues
Relapse Proneness	Relapse Prevention Planning
Substance Use Disorders	Alternatives to Addictive Behavior
Substance Use Disorders	Consequences of Continuing Addictive Lifestyles
Substance Use Disorders	Making Change Happen
Substance Use Disorders	Personal Recovery Planning
Substance Use Disorders	Taking Daily Inventory

GRIEF/LOSS UNRESOLVED

Attention-Deficit/Hyperactivity Disorder (ADHD)—Adult	Self-Soothing: Calm Down, Slow Down
Bipolar Disorder	Mania, Addiction, and Recovery
Childhood Trauma	Corresponding with My Childhood Self
Dependent Traits	Building My Support Network
Depression–Unipolar	Gratitude
Posttraumatic Stress Disorder (PTSD)	Coping with Addiction and PTSD

Posttraumatic Stress Disorder (PTSD)	Safe and Peaceful Place Meditation
Sexual Abuse	Internal and External Resources for Safety
Sexual Abuse	It Wasn't My Fault
Sleep Disturbance	Assessing Sleep Problems
Sleep Disturbance	Improving Sleep Hygiene
Social Anxiety	Action Plan to Address Social Anxiety
Spiritual Confusion	Finding a Higher Power That Makes Sense
Spiritual Confusion	Understanding Spirituality
Substance-Induced Disorders	Exploring Treatment and Recovery Options
Substance Intoxication/Withdrawal	Using Books and Other Media Resources

IMPULSIVITY

Antisocial Behavior	Benefits of Helping Others
Antisocial Behavior	Taking Inventory of Destructive Behaviors
Attention-Deficit/Hyperactivity Disorder (ADHD)—Adolescent	Staying Attentive and Other Negotiating Skills
Attention-Deficit/Hyperactivity Disorder (ADHD)—Adult	From Recklessness to Calculated Risks
Bipolar Disorder	Early Warning Signs of Mania/Hypomania
Bipolar Disorder	Mania, Addiction, and Recovery
Conduct Disorder/Delinquency	How Do You Do That?
Conduct Disorder/Delinquency	Trading Places
Dangerousness/Lethality	Managing Risk
Obsessive-Compulsive Disorder (OCD)	Interrupting Compulsive Thoughts and Urges
Obsessive-Compulsive Disorder (OCD)	Reducing Compulsive Behaviors
Occupational Problems	Workplace Problems and Solutions
Oppositional Defiant Behavior	Analyzing Acting-Out Behavior
Parent–Child Relational Problem	What Do I Want for My Children?
Psychosis	Planning a Stable Life
Sexual Promiscuity	Is It Romance or Is It Fear?

LEGAL PROBLEMS

| Antisocial Behavior | Benefits of Helping Others |
| Antisocial Behavior | Taking Inventory of Destructive Behaviors |

Conduct Disorder/Delinquency	How Do You Do That?
Conduct Disorder/Delinquency	Trading Places
Occupational Problems	Workplace Problems and Solutions
Peer Group Negativity	Creating Recovery Peer Support
Peer Group Negativity	What Do I Need and How Do I Get It?
Substance-Induced Disorders	Exploring Treatment and Recovery Options
Substance Use Disorders	Consequences of Continuing Addictive Lifestyles

LIVING ENVIRONMENT DEFICIENCY

Attention-Deficit/Hyperactivity Disorder (ADHD)—Adult	Getting Organized
Dependent Traits	Building My Support Network
Dependent Traits	How Interdependent Am I?
Legal Problems	Handling Tough Situations in a Healthy Way
Legal Problems	What's Addiction Got to Do with My Problems?
Occupational Problems	Workplace Problems and Solutions
Peer Group Negativity	Creating Recovery Peer Support
Peer Group Negativity	What Do I Need and How Do I Get It?
Self-Care Deficits—Primary	Assessing Self-Care Deficits
Self-Care Deficits—Secondary	Filling in Self-Care Gaps
Substance-Induced Disorders	Exploring Treatment and Recovery Options

MEDICAL ISSUES

Anxiety	Coping With Stress
Attention-Deficit/Hyperactivity Disorder (ADHD)—Adult	Self-Soothing: Calm Down, Slow Down
Chronic Pain	Coping with Addiction and Chronic Pain
Chronic Pain	Managing Pain Without Addictive Drugs
Dependent Traits	Building My Support Network
Depression–Unipolar	Gratitude
Eating Disorders and Obesity	Creating a Preliminary Eating and Health Plan

Eating Disorders and Obesity	Eating Patterns Self-Assessment
Impulsivity	Handling Crisis Without Impulsivity
Living Environment Deficiency	Assessing My Environment
Posttraumatic Stress Disorder (PTSD)	Safe and Peaceful Place Meditation
Sleep Disturbance	Assessing Sleep Problems
Sleep Disturbance	Improving Sleep Hygiene
Substance-Induced Disorders	Exploring Treatment and Recovery Options
Substance Intoxication/Withdrawal	Coping with Postacute Withdrawal

NARCISSISTIC TRAITS

Antisocial Behavior	Benefits of Helping Others
Borderline Traits	Seeing That We're All Just Human
Conduct Disorder/Delinquency	Trading Places
Depression–Unipolar	Correcting Distorted Thinking
Depression–Unipolar	Gratitude
Occupational Problems	Workplace Problems and Solutions
Oppositional Defiant Behavior	Learning to Ask Instead of Demand
Partner Relational Conflicts	Communication Skills

NICOTINE USE/DEPENDENCE

Anxiety	Coping with Stress
Gambling	Consequences and Benefits
Obsessive-Compulsive Disorder (OCD)	Interrupting Compulsive Thoughts and Urges
Obsessive-Compulsive Disorder (OCD)	Reducing Compulsive Behaviors
Readiness to Change	Addressing Readiness and Motivation
Readiness to Change	Problem Identification: Is It Addiction?
Relapse Proneness	Early Warning Signs of Relapse
Relapse Proneness	Identifying Relapse Triggers and Cues
Relapse Proneness	Relapse Prevention Planning
Substance Use Disorders	Alternatives to Addictive Behavior
Substance Use Disorders	Consequences of Continuing Addictive Lifestyles
Substance Use Disorders	Making Change Happen
Substance Use Disorders	Personal Recovery Planning

OBSESSIVE-COMPULSIVE DISORDER (OCD)

Posttraumatic Stress Disorder (PTSD)   Safe and Peaceful Place Meditation
Social Anxiety   Understanding Thoughts, Worries, and Fears
Substance Use Disorders   Personal Recovery Planning

OCCUPATIONAL PROBLEMS

Attention-Deficit/Hyperactivity Disorder   Staying Attentive and Other Negoti-
   (ADHD)—Adolescent   ating Skills
Family Conflicts   Identifying Conflict Themes
Legal Problems   What's Addiction Got to Do with
                                              My Problems?
Partner Relational Conflicts   Communication Skills
Substance Use Disorders   Balancing Recovery, Family, and Work
Substance Use Disorders   Consequences of Continuing Addictive
                                              Lifestyles

OPIOID USE DISORDER

Relapse Proneness   Identifying Relapse Triggers and Cues
Relapse Proneness   Relapse Prevention Planning
Self-Care Deficits—Primary   Assessing Self-Care Deficits
Self-Care Deficits—Primary   Relating Self-Care Deficits to My Addiction
Self-Care Deficits—Secondary   Filling in Self-Care Gaps
Substance Intoxication/Withdrawal   Coping with Postacute Withdrawal
Substance Use Disorders   Alternatives to Addictive Behaviors

OPPOSITIONAL DEFIANT BEHAVIOR

Anger   Is My Anger Due to Feeling Threatened?
Anger   Is My Anger Due to Unmet Expectations?
Antisocial Behavior   Benefits of Helping Others
Antisocial Behavior   Taking Inventory of Destructive Behaviors
Attention-Deficit/Hyperactivity Disorder   From Recklessness to Calculated Risks
   (ADHD)—Adult
Conduct Disorder/Delinquency   How Do You Do That?
Conduct Disorder/Delinquency   Trading Places

Dangerousness/Lethality	Anger as a Drug
Dangerousness/Lethality	Managing Risk
Family Conflicts	Creating Positive Family Rituals
Family Conflicts	Identifying Conflict Themes
Impulsivity	Learning to Think Things Through
Legal Problems	Handling Tough Situations in a Healthy Way
Narcissistic Traits	Being Genuinely Unselfish
Narcissistic Traits	Getting Out of Myself
Partner Relational Conflicts	Communication Skills
Peer Group Negativity	Creating Recovery Peer Support
Peer Group Negativity	What Do I Need and How Do I Get It?
Substance Use Disorders	Taking Daily Inventory

PANIC DISORDER

Anxiety	Anxiety Triggers and Warning Signs
Posttraumatic Stress Disorder (PTSD)	Coping With Addiction and PTSD

PARENT–CHILD RELATIONAL PROBLEM

Adult-Child-of-an-Alcoholic (ACA) Traits	Understanding Family History
Anger	Is My Anger Due to Unmet Expectations?
Attention-Deficit/Hyperactivity Disorder (ADHD)—Adolescent	Staying Attentive and Other Negotiating Skills
Childhood Trauma	Corresponding with My Childhood Self
Childhood Trauma	Setting and Maintaining Boundaries
Family Conflicts	Creating Positive Family Rituals
Family Conflicts	Identifying Conflict Themes
Partner Relational Conflicts	Communication Skills
Partner Relational Conflicts	Relationship Assessment
Sexual Abuse	It Wasn't My Fault
Substance Use Disorders	Balancing Recovery, Family, and Work

PARTNER RELATIONAL CONFLICTS

Adult-Child-of-an-Alcoholic (ACA) Traits	Addressing ACA Traits in Recovery
Adult-Child-of-an-Alcoholic (ACA) Traits	Understanding Family History
Anger	Is My Anger Due to Unmet Expectations?
Attention-Deficit/Hyperactivity Disorder (ADHD)—Adolescent	Staying Attentive and Other Negotiating Skills
Borderline Traits	Forming Stable Relationships
Borderline Traits	Seeing That We're All Just Human
Childhood Trauma	Setting and Maintaining Boundaries
Dangerousness/Lethality	Managing Risk
Family Conflicts	Creating Positive Family Rituals
Family Conflicts	Identifying Conflict Themes
Narcissistic Traits	Being Genuinely Unselfish
Oppositional Defiant Behavior	Learning to Ask Instead of Demand
Parent–Child Relational Problem	Am I Teaching My Child Addictive Patterns?
Parent–Child Relational Problem	What Do I Want for My Children?
Self-Harm	Understanding Self-Harm and Addiction
Sexual Abuse	It Wasn't My Fault
Sexual Promiscuity	Is It Romance or Is It Fear?
Substance Use Disorders	Balancing Recovery, Family, and Work

PEER GROUP NEGATIVITY

Attention-Deficit/Hyperactivity Disorder (ADHD)—Adolescent	Developing a Recovery Program
Childhood Trauma	Setting and Maintaining Boundaries
Dependent Traits	Building My Support Network
Depression–Unipolar	Gratitude
Living Environment Deficiency	Assessing My Environment
Narcissistic Traits	Being Genuinely Unselfish
Oppositional Defiant Behavior	Analyzing Acting-Out Behavior
Relapse Proneness	Relapse Prevention Planning
Self-Care Deficits—Secondary	Working Toward Interdependence
Substance-Induced Disorders	Using My Support Network
Substance Use Disorders	Consequences of Continuing Addictive Lifestyles

POSTTRAUMATIC STRESS DISORDER (PTSD)

Anger	Is My Anger Due to Feeling Threatened?
Anxiety	Anxiety Triggers and Warning Signs
Attention-Deficit/Hyperactivity Disorder (ADHD)—Adult	Self-Soothing: Calm Down, Slow Down
Bipolar Disorder	Mania, Addiction, and Recovery
Childhood Trauma	Corresponding with My Childhood Self
Chronic Pain	Managing Pain Without Addictive Drugs
Dangerousness/Lethality	Managing Risk
Dependent Traits	Building My Support Network
Depression–Unipolar	Gratitude
Family Conflicts	Identifying Conflict Themes
Grief/Loss Unresolved	Am I Having Difficulty Letting Go?
Grief/Loss Unresolved	Moving on After Loss
Grief/Loss Unresolved	What Would They Want for Me?
Medical Issues	Physical and Emotional Self-Care
Nicotine Use/Dependence	Use of Affirmations for Change
Obsessive-Compulsive Disorder (OCD)	Interrupting Compulsive Thoughts and Urges
Obsessive-Compulsive Disorder (OCD)	Reducing Compulsive Behaviors
Psychosis	Planning a Stable Life
Relapse Proneness	Identifying Relapse Triggers and Cues
Sexual Abuse	Internal and External Resources for Safety
Sexual Abuse	It Wasn't My Fault
Sleep Disturbance	Assessing Sleep Problems
Sleep Disturbance	Improving Sleep Hygiene
Social Anxiety	Action Plan to Address Social Anxiety
Social Anxiety	Understanding Thoughts, Worries, and Fears
Spiritual Confusion	Finding a Higher Power that Makes Sense
Spiritual Confusion	Understanding Spirituality
Substance-Induced Disorders	Exploring Treatment and Recovery Options
Substance-Induced Disorders	Using My Support Network
Substance Intoxication/Withdrawal	Using Books and Other Media Resources
Suicidal Ideation	Why Do I Matter and Who Cares?

PSYCHOSIS

Attention-Deficit/Hyperactivity Disorder (ADHD)—Adult	Getting Organized
Bipolar Disorder	Mania, Addiction, and Recovery
Self-Care Deficits—Primary	Assessing Self-Care Deficits
Self-Care Deficits—Primary	Relating Self-Care Deficits to My Addiction
Self-Care Deficits—Secondary	Working Toward Interdependence

READINESS TO CHANGE

Attention-Deficit/Hyperactivity Disorder (ADHD)—Adolescent	Developing a Recovery Program
Bipolar Disorder	Mania, Addiction, and Recovery
Gambling	Consequences and Benefits
Gambling	Understanding Nonchemical Addictions
Legal Problems	What's Addiction Got to Do with My Problems?
Living Environment Deficiency	What Would My Ideal Life Look Like?
Nicotine Use/Dependence	Addressing Relapse Triggers
Nicotine Use/Dependence	Assessing Readiness and Preparing to Quit
Parent–Child Relational Problem	Am I Teaching My Child Addictive Patterns?
Relapse Proneness	Early Warning Signs of Relapse
Relapse Proneness	Identifying Relapse Triggers and Cues
Substance-Induced Disorders	Using My Support Network
Substance Use Disorders	Alternatives to Addictive Behavior
Substance Use Disorders	Consequences of Continuing Addictive Lifestyles
Substance Use Disorders	Taking Daily Inventory

RELAPSE PRONENESS

Anxiety	Anxiety Triggers and Warning Signs
Anxiety	Coping with Stress
Bipolar Disorder	Early Warning Signs of Mania/Hypomania
Chronic Pain	Coping with Addiction and Chronic Pain
Dependent Traits	Building My Support Network
Depression–Unipolar	Gratitude

Family Conflicts	Creating Positive Family Rituals
Gambling	Consequences and Benefits
Gambling	Understanding Nonchemical Addictions
Impulsivity	Handling Crisis Without Impulsivity
Living Environment Deficiency	What Would My Ideal Life Look Like?
Medical Issues	Coping with Addiction and Other Medical Problems
Medical Issues	Physical and Emotional Self-Care
Narcissistic Traits	Getting Out of Myself
Nicotine Use/Dependence	Addressing Relapse Triggers
Nicotine Use/Dependence	Assessing Readiness and Preparing to Quit
Nicotine Use/Dependence	Use of Affirmations for Change
Obsessive-Compulsive Disorder (OCD)	Interrupting Compulsive Thoughts and Urges
Obsessive-Compulsive Disorder (OCD)	Reducing Compulsive Behaviors
Peer Group Negativity	Creating Recovery Peer Support
Peer Group Negativity	What Do I Need and How Do I Get It?
Self-Harm	Self-Harm Risk Factors, Triggers, and Early Warning Signs
Sleep Disturbance	Assessing Sleep Problems
Sleep Disturbance	Improving Sleep Hygiene
Social Anxiety	Understanding Thoughts, Worries, and Fears
Substance-Induced Disorders	Using My Support Network
Substance Intoxication/Withdrawal	Coping with Postacute Withdrawal (PAW)
Substance Intoxication/Withdrawal	Using Books and Other Media Resources
Substance Use Disorders	Balancing Recovery, Family, and Work
Substance Use Disorders	Consequences of Continuing Addictive Lifestyles
Substance Use Disorders	Making Change Happen
Substance Use Disorders	Taking Daily Inventory
Suicidal Ideation	Problem Solving and Safety Planning

SELF-CARE DEFICITS—PRIMARY

Attention-Deficit/Hyperactivity Disorder (ADHD)—Adult	Getting Organized
Dependent Traits	Building My Support Network

Dependent Traits	How Interdependent Am I?
Eating Disorders and Obesity	Creating a Preliminary Eating and Health Plan
Eating Disorders and Obesity	Eating Patterns Self-Assessment
Living Environment Deficiency	Assessing My Environment
Medical Issues	Coping with Addiction and Other Medical Problems
Medical Issues	Physical and Emotional Self-Care
Psychosis	Coping with Addiction and Schizophrenia Spectrum Disorders
Self-Care Deficits—Secondary	Filling in Self-Care Gaps
Self-Care Deficits—Secondary	Working Toward Interdependence
Sleep Disturbance	Assessing Sleep Problems
Sleep Disturbance	Improving Sleep Hygiene
Substance-Induced Disorders	Exploring Treatment and Recovery Options
Substance-Induced Disorders	Using My Support Network

SELF-CARE DEFICITS—SECONDARY

Attention-Deficit/Hyperactivity Disorder (ADHD)—Adult	Getting Organized
Dependent Traits	Building My Support Network
Dependent Traits	How Interdependent Am I?
Eating Disorders and Obesity	Creating a Preliminary Eating and Health Plan
Eating Disorders and Obesity	Eating Patterns Self-Assessment
Legal Problems	Handling Tough Situations in a Healthy Way
Living Environment Deficiency	Assessing My Environment
Psychosis	Coping with Addiction and Schizophrenia Spectrum Disorders
Self-Care Deficits—Primary	Assessing Self-Care Deficits
Self-Care Deficits—Primary	Relating Self-Care Deficits to My Addiction
Substance-Induced Disorders	Exploring Treatment and Recovery Options
Substance-Induced Disorders	Using My Support Network

SELF-HARM

Attention-Deficit/Hyperactivity Disorder (ADHD)—Adult | From Recklessness to Calculated Risks

Borderline Traits | Seeing That We're All Just Human

Childhood Trauma | Corresponding with My Childhood Self

Chronic Pain | Managing Pain Without Addictive Drugs

Conduct Disorder/Delinquency | How Do You Do That?

Conduct Disorder/Delinquency | Trading Places

Depression–Unipolar | Gratitude

Eating Disorders and Obesity | Creating a Preliminary Eating and Health Plan

Eating Disorders and Obesity | Eating Patterns Self-Assessment

Grief/Loss Unresolved | What Would They Want for Me?

Impulsivity | Handling Crisis Without Impulsivity

Impulsivity | Learning to Think Things Through

Obsessive-Compulsive Disorder (OCD) | Interrupting Compulsive Thoughts and Urges

Obsessive-Compulsive Disorder (OCD) | Reducing Compulsive Behaviors

Posttraumatic Stress Disorder (PTSD) | Coping with Addiction and PTSD

Posttraumatic Stress Disorder (PTSD) | Safe and Peaceful Place Meditation

Relapse Proneness | Early Warning Signs of Relapse

Relapse Proneness | Relapse Prevention Planning

Sexual Abuse | It Wasn't My Fault

Sexual Promiscuity | Working Through Shame

Substance Use Disorders | Alternatives to Addictive Behavior

Substance Use Disorders | Making Change Happen

Substance Use Disorders | Taking Daily Inventory

Suicidal Ideation | Why Do I Matter and Who Cares?

SEXUAL ABUSE

Eating Disorders and Obesity | Creating a Preliminary Eating and Health Plan

Posttraumatic Stress Disorder (PTSD) | Coping with Addiction and PTSD

Posttraumatic Stress Disorder (PTSD) | Safe and Peaceful Place Meditation

Sexual Promiscuity | Is It Romance or Is It Fear?

Spiritual Confusion	Finding a Higher Power That Makes Sense
Suicidal Ideation	Problem Solving and Safety Planning
Suicidal Ideation	Why Do I Matter and Who Cares?

SEXUAL PROMISCUITY

Adult-Child-of-an-Alcoholic (ACA) Traits	Addressing ACA Traits in Recovery
Attention-Deficit/Hyperactivity Disorder (ADHD)—Adult	From Recklessness to Calculated Risks
Borderline Traits	Forming Stable Relationships
Childhood Trauma	Setting and Maintaining Boundaries
Gambling	Consequences and Benefits
Obsessive-Compulsive Disorder (OCD)	Interrupting Compulsive Thoughts and Urges
Obsessive-Compulsive Disorder (OCD)	Reducing Compulsive Behaviors
Oppositional Defiant Behavior	Analyzing Acting-Out Behavior
Readiness to Change	Addressing Readiness and Motivation
Relapse Proneness	Identifying Relapse Triggers and Cues
Relapse Proneness	Relapse Prevention Planning
Self-Harm	Understanding Self-Harm and Addiction
Social Anxiety	Action Plan to Address Social Anxiety
Social Anxiety	Understanding Thoughts, Worries, and Fears
Substance-Induced Disorders	Using My Support Network
Substance Use Disorders	Consequences of Continuing Addictive Lifestyles
Substance Use Disorders	Making Change Happen
Substance Use Disorders	Personal Recovery Planning

SLEEP DISTURBANCE

Anxiety	Anxiety Triggers and Warning Signs
Posttraumatic Stress Disorder (PTSD)	Safe and Peaceful Place Meditation
Substance Intoxication/Withdrawal	Coping with Postacute Withdrawal (PAW)

SOCIAL ANXIETY

Anxiety · Anxiety Triggers and Warning Signs

Anxiety · Coping with Stress

Attention-Deficit/Hyperactivity Disorder (ADHD)—Adult · Self-Soothing: Calm Down, Slow Down

Borderline Traits · Seeing That We're All Just Human

Childhood Trauma · Setting and Maintaining Boundaries

Dependent Traits · Building My Support Network

Depression–Unipolar · Correcting Distorted Thinking

Partner Relational Conflicts · Communication Skills

Sleep Disturbance · Assessing Sleep Problems

Sleep Disturbance · Improving Sleep Hygiene

SPIRITUAL CONFUSION

Depression–Unipolar · Gratitude

Grief/Loss Unresolved · Moving on After Loss

Grief/Loss Unresolved · What Would They Want for Me?

Occupational Problems · Interest and Skill Self-Assessment

Substance Intoxication/Withdrawal · Using Books and Other Media Resources

SUBSTANCE-INDUCED DISORDERS

Chronic Pain · Coping with Addiction and Chronic Pain

Medical Issues · Coping with Addiction and Other Medical Problems

Psychosis · Coping With Addiction and Schizophrenia Spectrum Disorders

Psychosis · Planning a Stable Life

Readiness to Change · Problem Identification: Is It Addiction?

Self-Care Deficits—Primary · Assessing Self-Care Deficits

Self-Care Deficits—Primary · Relating Self-Care Deficits to My Addiction

Spiritual Confusion · Finding a Higher Power That Makes Sense

Substance Intoxication/Withdrawal · Coping with Postacute Withdrawal (PAW)

Substance Use Disorders · Alternatives to Addictive Behavior

SUBSTANCE INTOXICATION/WITHDRAWAL

Chronic Pain	Managing Pain Without Addictive Drugs
Nicotine Use/Dependence	Use of Affirmations for Change
Posttraumatic Stress Disorder (PTSD)	Safe and Peaceful Place Meditation
Sleep Disturbance	Assessing Sleep Problems
Sleep Disturbance	Improving Sleep Hygiene
Substance-Induced Disorders	Using My Support Network

SUBSTANCE USE DISORDERS

Bipolar Disorder	Mania, Addiction, and Recovery
Borderline Traits	Forming Stable Relationships
Borderline Traits	Seeing That We're All Just Human
Chronic Pain	Coping with Addiction and Chronic Pain
Chronic Pain	Managing Pain Without Addictive Drugs
Dependent Traits	Building My Support Network
Family Conflicts	Creating Positive Family Rituals
Gambling	Consequences and Benefits
Gambling	Understanding Nonchemical Addictions
Legal Problems	What's Addiction Got to Do with My Problems?
Living Environment Deficiency	What Would My Ideal Life Look Like?
Medical Issues	Coping with Addiction and Other Medical Problems
Nicotine Use/Dependence	Addressing Relapse Triggers
Nicotine Use/Dependence	Use of Affirmations for Change
Obsessive-Compulsive Disorder (OCD)	Interrupting Compulsive Thoughts and Urges
Obsessive-Compulsive Disorder (OCD)	Reducing Compulsive Behaviors
Parent–Child Relational Problem	What Do I Want for My Children?
Psychosis	Coping with Addiction and Schizophrenia Spectrum Disorders
Readiness to Change	Addressing Readiness and Motivation
Readiness to Change	Problem Identification: Is It Addiction?
Relapse Proneness	Early Warning Signs of Relapse
Relapse Proneness	Identifying Relapse Triggers and Cues

Relapse Proneness	Relapse Prevention Planning
Social Anxiety	Action Plan to Address Social Anxiety
Spiritual Confusion	Understanding Spirituality
Substance-Induced Disorders	Using My Support Network

SUICIDAL IDEATION

Attention-Deficit/Hyperactivity Disorder (ADHD)—Adult	Self-Soothing: Calm Down, Slow Down
Bipolar Disorder	Mania, Addiction, and Recovery
Dependent Traits	Building My Support Network
Depression–Unipolar	Correcting Distorted Thinking
Depression–Unipolar	Gratitude
Grief/Loss Unresolved	Am I Having Difficulty Letting Go?
Grief/Loss Unresolved	Moving on After Loss
Grief/Loss Unresolved	What Would They Want for Me?
Impulsivity	Handling Crisis Without Impulsivity
Impulsivity	Learning to Think Things Through
Living Environment Deficiency	What Would My Ideal Life Look Like?
Narcissistic Traits	Getting Out of Myself
Partner Relational Conflicts	Relationship Assessment
Posttraumatic Stress Disorder (PTSD)	Coping with Addiction and PTSD
Relapse Proneness	Early Warning Signs of Relapse
Spiritual Confusion	Finding a Higher Power That Makes Sense
Substance Intoxication/Withdrawal	Coping with Postacute Withdrawal (PAW)

APPENDIX B:
SUGGESTED REFERENCES BY SELECT CHAPTERS/
AREAS OF CLINICAL FOCUS

The following references can be assigned to clients as bibliotherapy when appropriate and indicated and/or are suggested resources for clinicians.

ADULT-CHILD-OF-AN-ALCOHOLIC (ACA) TRAITS

ACA World Services Office. (2007). *Twelve steps of adult children steps workbook*. Author.

ACA World Services Office. (2017). *Adult children of alcoholics: Alcoholic/dysfunctional families*. Author.

Adult Children of Alcoholics/Dysfunctional Families Fellowship.. (2013). *Strengthening my recovery meditations for adult children of alcoholics/dysfunctional families*. Author.

Al-Anon Family Groups. (2008). *How Al-Anon works for families & friends of alcoholics*. Author.

Beattie, M. (1986). *Codependent no more*. Hazelden.

Black, C. (2020). *It will never happen to me: Growing up with addiction as youngsters, adolescents, adults* (3rd ed.). Hazelden.

CoDA. (2013). *Co-dependents anonymous* (3rd ed.). CoDA Resource Publishing.

Hesley, J. W., & Hesley, J. G. (2001). *Rent two films and let's talk in the morning: Using popular movies in psychotherapy* (2nd ed.). Wiley.

Napier, N. J. (1994). *Getting through the day: Strategies for adults hurt as children*. W.W. Norton & Co.

Ruiz, D. M. (1997). *The four agreements: A practical guide to personal freedom*. Amber Allen Publishing, Inc.

Woititz, J. G. (1990). *Adult children of alcoholics*. Health Communications, Inc.

ANGER

Deffenbacher, J. L., & McKay, M. (2000). *Overcoming situational and general anger: Therapist protocol (Best practices for therapy)*. New Harbinger.

Meichenbaum, D. (2001). *Treatment of individuals with anger control problems and aggressive behaviors: A clinical handbook*. Institute Press.

Rosellini, G., & Worden, M. (1997). *Of course you're angry: A guide to dealing with the emotions of substance abuse* (2nd ed.). Hazelden.

ANXIETY

Bernstein, D. A., Borkovec, T. D., & Hazlett-Stevens, H. (2000). *New directions in progressive muscle relaxation: A guidebook for helping professionals*. Praeger.

Clark, D. A., & Beck, A. T. (2010). *Cognitive therapy of anxiety disorders: Science and practice*. Guilford Press.

Eifert, G. H., Forsuth, J. P., & Hayes. S. C. (2005). *Acceptance and commitment therapy for anxiety disorders: A practitioner's treatment guide to using mindfulness, acceptance, and values-based behavior change strategies*. New Harbinger.

Hayes, S. C. (2005). *Get out of your mind and into your life: The new acceptance and commitment therapy*. New Harbinger Publications, Inc.

ATTENTION-DEFICIT/HYPERACTIVITY DISORDER (ADHD)

Barkley, R. A. (2015). *Attention-deficit hyperactivity disorder: A handbook for diagnosis and treatment* (4th ed.). Guilford Press.

Becker, S. P. (2020). *ADHD in adolescents: Development, assessment, and treatment*. Guilford Press.

Hallowell, E., & Ratey, J. J. (1995). *Driven to distraction: Recognizing and coping with add from childhood to adulthood*. Touchstone Books.

Kelly, K., & Ramundo, P. (2006). *You mean I'm not lazy, stupid or crazy?! The classic self-help book for adults with attention deficit disorder*. Scribner.

Solanto, M. V. (2011). *Cognitive-behavioral therapy for adult ADHD: Targeting executive dysfunction*. Guilford Press.

BIPOLAR DISORDER

Burgess, W. (2006). *The bipolar handbook: Real-life questions with up-to-date answers*. Avery/Penguin.

Colom, F., & Vieta, E. (2006). *Psychoeducation manual for bipolar disorder*. Cambridge University Press.

Frank, E. (2005). *Treating bipolar disorder: A clinician's guide to interpersonal and social rhythm therapy*. Guilford Press.

Holmes, E. A., Hales, S. A., Young, K., & Di Simplicio, M. (2019). *Imagery-based cognitive therapy for bipolar disorder and mood instability*. Guilford Press.

Miklowitz, D. J., & Goldstein, M. J. (2008). *Bipolar disorder: A family-focused treatment approach* (2nd ed.). Guilford Press.

BORDERLINE TRAITS

Dimeff, L. A., & Koerner, K. (Eds.). (2007). *Dialectical behavior therapy in clinical practice: Applications across disorders and settings*. Guilford Press.

Kreisman, J. J., & Straus, J. (2021). *I hate you—Don't leave me: Understanding borderline personality*. Tarcher Perigree.

Linehan, M. M. (1993). *Cognitive-behavioral treatment of borderline personality disorder*. Guilford Press.

Linehan, M. M. (2015). *DBT skills training manual* (2nd ed.). Guilford Press.

Linehan, M. M. (2015). *DBT skills training handouts and worksheets* (2nd ed.). Guilford Press.

Rizvi, S. L. (2019). *Chain analysis in dialectical behavior therapy*. Guilford Press.

CHILDHOOD TRAUMA

Remen, R. N. (2006). *Kitchen table wisdom: Stories that heal*. Riverhead Trade.

CHRONIC PAIN

Dahl, J., Wilson, K. G., Luciano, C., & Hayes, S. C. (2005). *Acceptance and commitment therapy for chronic pain*. Context Press.

Kabat-Zinn, J. (1990). *Full catastrophic living: How to cope with stress, pain and illness using mindfulness and meditation*. Bantam Books.

McCracken, L. M. (2005). *Contextual cognitive-behavioral therapy for chronic pain*. International Association for the Study of Chronic Pain.

Thorn, B. E. (2017). *Cognitive therapy for chronic pain: A step-by-step guide*. Guilford Press.

Turk, D. C., & Gatchel, R. J. (Eds.). (2018). *Psychological approaches to pain management: A practitioner's handbook* (3rd ed.). Guilford Press.

CONDUCT DISORDER/DELINQUENCY

Barkley, R. A. (2013). *Defiant children: A clinician's manual for assessment and parent training* (3rd ed.). Guilford Press.

Barkley, R. A., & Robin, A. L. (2014). *Defiant teens: A clinician's manual for assessment and family intervention*. Guilford Press.

Kazdin, A. E. (2005). *Parent management training: Treatment for oppositional, aggressive, and antisocial behavior in children and adolescents*. Oxford University Press.

McMahon, R. J., & Forehand, R. (2003). *Helping the noncompliant child: Family-based treatment for oppositional behavior* (2nd ed.). Guilford Press.

McNeil, C. B., & Hembree-Kigin, T. L. (2011). *Parent-child interaction therapy* (2nd ed.). Springer.

Sukhodolsky, D. G., & Scahill, L. (2012). *Cognitive-behavioral therapy for anger and aggression in children*. Guilford Press.

DEPRESSION–UNIPOLAR

Copeland, M. E., & McKay, M. (2002). *The depression workbook: A guide to living with depression and manic depression* (2nd ed.). New Harbinger Publications.

Kanter, J. W., Busch, A. M., & Rusch, L. C. (2009). *Behavioral activation*. Routledge.

Martell, C. R., Dimidjian, S., & Herman-Dunn, R. (2010). *Behavioral activation: A clinician's guide*. Guilford Press.

Real, T. (1998). *I don't want to talk about it: Overcoming the secret legacy of male depression*. Scribner.

Rosellini, G., & Worden, M. (1987). *Here comes the sun: Dealing with depression*. Hazelden.

Segal, Z. V., Williams, J. M. G., & Teasdale, J. D. (2013). *Mindfulness-based cognitive therapy for depression* (2nd ed.). Guilford Press.

Thompson, T. (2019). *The beast: A journey through depression*. Plume.

Weissman, M. M., Markowitz, J. C., & Klerman, G. L. (2007). *Clinician's guide to inter personal psychotherapy*. Oxford University Press.

Zettle, R. D. (2007). *ACT for depression: A clinician's guide to using acceptance and commitment therapy in treating depression*. New Harbinger.

EATING DISORDERS AND OBESITY

Agras, W. S., & Apple, R. F. (2007). *Overcoming eating disorders: A cognitive-behavioral therapy approach for bulimia nervosa and binge-eating disorder. Therapist guide* (2nd ed.). Oxford University Press.

Fairburn, C. G. (2008). *Cognitive behavior therapy and eating disorders*. Guilford Press.

LeGrange, D., & Lock, J. (2007). *Treating bulimia in adolescents: A family-based approach*. Guilford Press.

LeGrange, D., & Lock, J. (2011). *Eating disorders in children and adolescents: A clinical handbook*. Guilford Press.

Lock, J., LeGrange, D., Agras, W. S., & Dare, C. (2013). *Treatment manual for anorexia nervosa: A family-based approach* (2nd ed.). Guilford Press.

Mehler, P. S., & Andersen, A. A. (2022). *Eating disorders: A comprehensive guide to medical care and complications* (4th ed.). John Hopkins University Press.

Overeaters Anonymous. (2001). *Overeaters Anonymous* (2nd ed.). Author.

Zweig, R. D., & Leahy, R. L. (2012). *Treatment plans and interventions for bulimia and binge-eating disorder*. Guilford Press.

FAMILY CONFLICTS

Alberti, R. E., & Emmons, M. L. (2017). *Your perfect right: Assertiveness and equality in your life and relationships* (10th ed.). New Harbinger.

GAMBLING

Gamblers Anonymous. (2007). *Gamblers Anonymous: A new beginning* (5th ed.). Gamblers Anonymous Publishing.

Gamblers Anonymous. (2007). *Sharing recovery through Gamblers Anonymous*. Author.

Ladouceur, R., & Lachance, S. (2007). *Overcoming pathological gambling: Therapist guide*. Oxford University Press.

McIntosh, C., & O'Neill, K. (2017). *Evidence-based treatments for problem gambling.* Spring.

GRIEF/LOSS UNRESOLVED

James, J. W., & Friedman, R. (2017). *The grief recovery handbook: The action program for moving beyond death, divorce, and other losses including health, career and faith.* Harper-Collins.

MEDICAL ISSUES

Miller, W. R., & Rollnick, S. (2013). *Motivational interviewing: Helping people change* (3rd ed.). Guilford Press.

Remen, R. N. (2021). *Kitchen table wisdom* (10th anniversary ed.). Bluebird.

Safren, S., Gonzalez, J., & Soroudi, N. (2007). *Coping with chronic illness: A cognitive-behavioral approach for adherence and depression: Therapist's guide.* Oxford University Press.

NARCISSISTIC TRAITS

Hesley, J. W., & Hesley, J. G. (2001). *Rent two films and let's talk in the morning: Using popular movies in psychotherapy* (2nd ed.). Wiley.

NICOTINE USE/DEPENDENCE

Abrams, D. B., Niaura, R., Brown, R. A., Emmons, K. M., Goldstein, M. G., & Monti, P. M. (2003). *The tobacco dependence treatment handbook: A guide to best practices.* Guilford Press.

Perkins, K. A., Conklin, C. A., & Levine, M. D. (2008). *Cognitive-behavioral therapy for smoking cessation: A practical guidebook to the most effective treatments.* Routledge.

OBSESSIVE-COMPULSIVE DISORDER (OCD)

Abramowitz, J. S. (2006). *Understanding and treating obsessive-compulsive disorder: A cognitive-behavioral approach.* Routledge.

Abramowitz, J. S., Deacon, B. J., & Whiteside, S. P. H. (2019). *Exposure therapy for anxiety: Principles and practices* (2nd ed.). Guilford Press.

Foa, E. B., Yadin, E., & Lichner, T. K. (2012). *Exposure and response (ritual) prevention for obsessive-compulsive disorder: Therapist guide* (2nd ed.). Oxford University Press.

OCCUPATIONAL PROBLEMS

Bolles, R. N., & Brooks, K. (2021). *What color is your parachute: Your guide to a lifetime of meaningful work & career success.* Ten Speed Press.

Tieger, P. D., Barron-Tieger, B., & Tieger, K. (2021). *Do what you are: Discover the perfect career for you through the secrets of personality type* (6th ed.). Little, Brown & Co.

OPIOID USE DISORDER

Connors, G., Donovan, D., & DiClemente, C. C. (2001). *Substance use treatment and the stages of change: Selecting and planning interventions.* Guilford Press.

DiClemente, C. C. (2018). *Addition and change: How addictions develop and addicted people recover.* (2nd ed.). Guilford Press.

Higgins, S. T., Silverman, K., & Heil, S. H. (Eds.). (2007). *Contingency management in substance abuse treatment.* Guilford Press.

Marlatt, G. A., & Donovan, D. M. (Eds.). (2005). *Relapse prevention: Maintenance strategies in the treatment of addictive behaviors.*(2nd ed.). Guilford Press.

Marlatt, G. A., Larimer, M. E., & Witkiewitz, K. (2012). *Harm reduction: Pragmatic strategies for managing high-risk behaviors* (2nd ed.). Guilford Press.

Petry, N. M. (2011). *Contingency management for substance abuse treatment: A guide to implementing this evidence-based practice.* Routledge.

Turner, N., Welches, P., & Conti, S. (2014). *Mindfulness-based sobriety: A clinician's treatment guide for addiction recovery using relapse prevention therapy, acceptance and commitment therapy, and motivational interviewing.* New Harbinger.

OPPOSITIONAL DEFIANT BEHAVIOR

See Conduct Disorder/Delinquency section for recommended resources.

PANIC DISORDER

Eifert, G. H., Forsyth, J. P., & Hayes, S. C. (2005). *Acceptance and commitment therapy for anxiety disorders: A practitioner's treatment guide to using mindfulness, acceptance, and values-based behavior change strategies.* New Harbinger.

PARENT–CHILD RELATIONAL PROBLEM

Grizzard, L. (2012). *My daddy was a pistol and I'm a son of a gun.* Dell.

Hesley, J. W., & Hesley, J. G. (2001). *Rent two films and let's talk in the morning: Using popular movies in psychotherapy* (2nd ed.). Wiley.

Johnson, S. M. (2019). *Attachment theory in practice: Emotionally focused therapy (EFT) with individuals, couples, and families.* Guilford Press.

PARTNER RELATIONAL CONFLICTS

Fals-Stewart, W., O'Farrell, T., Birchler, G., & Gorman, C. (2006). *Behavioral couples therapy for drug abuse and alcoholism: A 12-session manual.* Addiction and Family Research Group.

Jacobson, N. S., & Christensen, A. (1996). *Integrative couple therapy: Promoting acceptance and change*. Norton.

Jacobson, N. S., & Christensen, A. (1998). *Acceptance and change in couple therapy: A therapist's guide to transforming relationships*. Norton.

Johnson, S. M. (2019). *Attachment theory in practice: Emotionally focused therapy (EFT) with individuals, couples, and families*. Guilford Press.

Woititz, J. G. (1993). *The intimacy struggle: Revised and expanded for all adults*. Health Communications, Inc.

POSTTRAUMATIC STRESS DISORDER (PTSD)

Foa, E., Hembree, E., Rothbaum, B., & Rauch, S. A. M. (2019). *Prolonged exposure therapy for PTSD: Emotional processing of traumatic experience—therapist guide* (2nd ed.). Oxford University Press.

Meichenbaum, D. A. (1995). *Clinical handbook—practical therapist manual for assessing and treating adults with posttraumatic stress disorder (PTSD)*. Institute Press.

Menakem, R. (2017). *My grandmother's hands: Racialized trauma and the pathway to mending our hearts and bodies*. Central Recovery Press.

Najavits, L. M. (2002). *Seeking safety: A treatment manual for PTSD and substance abuse*. Guilford Press.

Porges, S. W. (2017). *The polyvagal theory: The transformative power of feeling safe*. W. W. Norton & Company, Inc.

Resick, P. A., Monson, C. M., & Chard, K. M. (2017). *Cognitive processing therapy for PTSD: A comprehensive manual*. Guilford Press.

Schauer, M., Neuner, R., & Elbert, T. (2011). *Narrative exposure therapy: A short-term treatment for traumatic stress disorder* (2nd ed.). Hogrefe.

Shay, J. (1995). *Achilles in Vietnam: Combat trauma and the undoing of character*. Simon & Schuster.

Shay, J. (2003). *Odysseus in America: Combat trauma and the trials of homecoming*. Scribner.

Taylor, S. (2017). *Clinician's guide to treating PTSD: A cognitive-behavioral approach* (2nd ed.). Guilford Press.

VanderKolk, B. (2015). *The body keeps score: Brain, mind & body in the healing of trauma*. Penguin Publishing Group.

PSYCHOSIS

Bellack, A. S., Mueser, K. T., Gingerich, S., & Agresta, J. (2004). *Social skills training for schizophrenia: A step-by-step guide* (2nd ed.). Guilford Press.

Hagen, R., Turkington, D., Berge, T., & Grawe, R. W. (2011). *CBT for psychosis: A symptom-based approach*. Routledge.

McFarlane, W. R. (2002). *Multifamily groups in the treatment of severe psychiatric disorders*. Guilford Press.

READINESS TO CHANGE

Brown, B. (2020). *The gift of imperfection*. Hazelden Publishing.

DiClemente, C. C. (2018). *Addiction and change: How addictions develop and addicted people recover* (2nd ed.). Guilford Press.

Miller, W. R., Forcehimes, A. A., & Zweben, A. (2019). *Treating addiction: A guide for professionals* (2nd ed.). Guilford Press.

Miller, W. R., & Rollnick, S. (2012). *Motivational interviewing: Helping people change* (3rd ed.). Guilford Press.

Wilson, K. G., & DuFrene, T. (2012). *The wisdom to know the difference: An acceptance and commitment therapy workbook for overcoming substance abuse*. New Harbinger Publications, Inc.

Rosengren, D. B. (2018). *Building motivational interviewing skills: A practitioner workbook* (2nd ed.). Guilford Press.

Z., P. (1990). *A skeptic's guide to the twelve steps*. Hazelden.

RELAPSE PRONENESS

Copeland, M. E. (2011). *Wellness Recovery Action Plan (WRAP)*. Peach Press.

Marlatt, G. A., & Donovan, D. M. (Eds.). (2005). *Relapse prevention: Maintenance strategies in the treatment of addictive behaviors* (2nd ed.). Guilford Press.

SELF-HARM

Levenkron, S. (1999). *Cutting: Understanding and overcoming self-mutilation*. Norton.

Linehan, M. M. (2015). *DBT skills training manual* (2nd ed.). Guilford Press.

Strong, M. (1998). *A bright red scream: Self-mutilation and the language of pain*. Penguin.

Turner, V. J. (2002). *Secret scars: Uncovering and understanding the addiction of self-injury*. Hazelden.

Walsh, B. (2012). *Treating self-injury: A practical guide* (2nd ed.). Guilford Press.

SLEEP DISTURBANCE

Edinger, J. D., & Carney, C. E. (2014). *Overcoming insomnia: A cognitive behavioral therapy approach workbook (treatments that work)* (2nd ed.). Oxford Press.

Perlis, M. L., Aloia, M., & Kuhn, B. (Eds.). (2011). *Behavioral treatments for sleep disorders: A comprehensive primer of behavioral sleep medicine interventions*. Academic Press.

Perlis, M. L., Jungquist, C., Smith, M. T., & Posner, D. (2008). *CBT of insomnia: A session-by-session guide*. Springer.

SOCIAL ANXIETY

Bernstein, D. A., Borkovec, T. D., & Hazlett-Stevens, H. (2000). *New directions in progressive muscle relaxation: A guidebook for helping professionals*. Praeger.

Eifert, G. H., Forsyth, J. P., & Hayes, S. C. (2005). *Acceptance and commitment therapy for anxiety disorders: A practitioner's treatment guide to using mindfulness, acceptance, and values-based behavior change strategies*. New Harbinger.

Harris, R. (2009). *ACT made simple: An easy to read primer on acceptance and commitment therapy* (2nd ed.). New Harbinger.

Heimberg, R. G., & Becker, R. E. (2002). *Cognitive-behavioral group therapy for social phobia: Basic mechanisms and clinical strategies*. Guilford Press.

Hofmann, S. G., & Otto, M. W. (2008). *Cognitive behavioral therapy for social anxiety disorder: Evidence-based and disorder specific treatment techniques*. Routledge.

Neff, K., & Gerner, C. (2018). *The mindful self-compassion workbook: A proven way to accept yourself, build inner strength and thrive*. Guilford Press.

SPIRITUAL CONFUSION

Brizee, R. (1987). *Where in the world is God?* The Upper Room.

Peck, M. S. (2003). *The road less traveled: A new psychology of love, traditional values, and spiritual growth*. Touchstone.

SUBSTANCE USE DISORDERS

Alcoholics Anonymous. (2002). *Alcoholics Anonymous: The big book* (4th ed.). AA World Services Office, Inc.

Alcoholics Anonymous. (2019). *Twelve steps and twelve traditions*. AA World Services Offices, Inc.

Bruce, T. J., & Jongsma, A. E. (2012). *Evidence-based treatment planning for substance use disorders*. John Wiley & Sons, Inc.

Connors, G., Donovan, D., & DiClemente, C. C. (2001). *Substance abuse treatment and the stages of change: Selecting and planning interventions*. Guilford Press.

Daley, D. C., & Marlatt, G. A. (2006). *Overcoming your alcohol or drug problem: Effective recovery strategies—therapist guide*. Oxford University Press.

DiClemente, C. C. (2018). *Addiction and change: How addictions develop and addicted people recover* (2nd ed.). Guilford Press.

Marlatt, G. A., & Donovan, D. M. (Eds.). (2005). *Relapse prevention: Maintenance strategies in the treatment of addictive behaviors* (2nd ed.). Guilford Press.

Miller, S. C., Fiellin, D. A., Rosenthal, R. N., & Saitz, R. (2018). *The ASAM principles of addiction medicine* (6th ed.). LWW.

Miller, W. R., Forcehimes, A. A., & Zweben, A. (2019). *Treating addiction: A guide for professionals* (2nd ed.). Guilford Press.

Miller, W. R., Zweben, A., DiClemente, C. C., & Rychtarik, R. G. (1992). *Motivational Enhancement Therapy manual: A clinical research guide for therapists treating individuals with alcohol abuse and dependence* (Vol. 2, Project MATCH Monograph Series). NIAAA.

Narcotics Anonymous. (2000). *It works: How and why: The twelve steps and twelve traditions of Narcotics Anonymous*. NA World Services, Inc.

Narcotics Anonymous. (2008). *Narcotics Anonymous* (6th ed.). NA World Services, Inc.

Trimpey, J. (1996). *Rational recovery: The new cure for substance addiction*. Gallery Books.

SUICIDAL IDEATION

Bryan, C. J. (2015). *Cognitive behavioral therapy for preventing suicide attempts: A guide to brief treatments across clinical settings*. Routledge.

Jamison, K. R. (2000). *Night falls fast: Understanding suicide*. Vintage.

Jobes, D. (2016). *Managing suicidal risk: A collaborative approach* (2nd ed.). Guilford Press.

Joiner, T. (2007). *Why people die by suicide*. Harvard University Press.

APPENDIX C:
ALPHABETICAL INDEX OF EXERCISES